British History in Perspective
General Editor: Jeremy Black

PUBLISHED TITLES

Rodney Barker *Politics, Peoples and Government*
C. J. Bartlett *British Foreign Policy in the Twentieth Century*
Eugenio Biagini *Gladstone*
Jeremy Black *Robert Walpole and the Nature of Politics in Early Eighteenth-Century Britain*
D. G. Boyce *The Irish Question and British Politics, 1868–1996 (2nd edn)*
Keith M. Brown *Kingdom or Province? Scotland and the Regal Union, 1603–1715*
A. D. Carr *Medieval Wales*
Anne Curry *The Hundred Years War*
John W. Derry *British Politics in the Age of Fox, Pitt and Liverpool*
Susan Doran *England and Europe in the Sixteenth Century*
Seán Duffy *Ireland in the Middle Ages*
William Gibson *Church, State and Society, 1760–1850*
David Gladstone *The Twentieth-Century Welfare State*
Brian Golding *Conquest and Colonisation: the Normans in Britain, 1066–1100*
Sean Greenwood *Britain and the Cold War, 1945–1991*
S. J. Gunn *Early Tudor Government, 1485–1558*
J. Gwynfor Jones *Early Modern Wales, c.1525–1640*
Richard Harding *The Evolution of the Sailing Navy, 1509–1815*
David Harkness *Ireland in the Twentieth Century: Divided Island*
Ann Hughes *The Causes of the English Civil War (2nd edn)*
Ronald Hutton *The British Republic, 1649–1660*
Kevin Jefferys *The Labour Party since 1945*
T. A. Jenkins *Disraeli and Victorian Conservatism*
T. A. Jenkins *Sir Robert Peel*
D. M. Loades *The Mid-Tudor Crisis, 1545–1565*
Diarmaid MacCulloch *The Later Reformation in England,1547–1603*
A. P. Martinich *Thomas Hobbes*
John F. McCaffrey *Scotland in the Nineteenth Century*
W. David McIntyre *British Decolonization, 1946–1997. When, Why and How did the British Empire Fall?*
Roger Middleton *The British Economy Since 1945*
W. M. Ormrod *Political Life in Medieval England, 1300–1450*
Richie Ovendale *Anglo-American Relations in the Twentieth Century*
Ian Packer *Lloyd George*
Keith Perry *British Politics and the American Revolution*
Murray G. H. Pittock *Jacobitism*
A. J. Pollard *The Wars of the Roses*
David Powell *British Politics and the Labour Question, 1868–1990*
David Powell *The Edwardian Crisis*
Richard Rex *Henry VIII and the English Reformation*
G. R. Searle *The Liberal Party: Triumph and Disintegration,1886–1929*
Paul Seaward *The Restoration, 1660–1668*

D0774043

John Stuart Shaw *The Political History of Eighteenth-Century Scotland*
W. M. Spellman *John Locke*
William Stafford *John Stuart Mill*
Robert Stewart *Party and Politics, 1830–1852*
Bruce Webster *Medieval Scotland*
Ann Williams *Kingship and Government in Pre-Conquest England*
John W. Young *Britain and European Unity, 1945–92*
Michael B. Young *Charles I*

Please note that a sister series, *Social History in Perspective*, is now available. It covers the key topics in social, cultural and religious history.

British History in Perspective
Series Standing Order
ISBN 0–333–71356–7 hardcover
ISBN 0–333–69331–0 paperback
(*outside North America only*)

You can receive future titles in this series as they are published by placing a standing order. Please contact your bookseller or, in case of difficulty, write to us at the address below with your name and address, the title of the series and one or both of the ISBNs quoted above.

Customer Services Department, Macmillan Distribution Ltd
Houndmills, Basingstoke, Hampshire RG21 6XS, England

THE BRITISH ECONOMY SINCE 1945

Engaging With The Debate

Roger Middleton

First published in Great Britain 2000 by
MACMILLAN PRESS LTD
Houndmills, Basingstoke, Hampshire RG21 6XS and London
Companies and representatives throughout the world

A catalogue record for this book is available from the British Library.

ISBN 0–333–68482–6 hardcover
ISBN 0–333–68483–4 paperback

First published in the United States of America 2000 by
ST. MARTIN'S PRESS, INC.,
Scholarly and Reference Division,
175 Fifth Avenue, New York, N.Y. 10010

ISBN 0–312–22862–7

Library of Congress Cataloging-in-Publication Data
Middleton, Roger,. 1955–
The British economy since 1945 : engaging with the debate / Roger Middleton.
p. cm. — (British history in perspective)
Includes bibliographical references and index.
ISBN 0–312–22862–7 (cloth)
1. Great Britain—Economic policy—1945–1964. 2. Great Britain—Economic
policy—1964–1979. 3. Great Britain—Economic policy—1979– 4. Great
Britain—Economic conditions—20th century. I. Title. II. Series.

HC256.5.M5   1999
338.941 21—dc21
                                                                99–043511

This book is printed on paper suitable for recycling and made from fully managed and
sustained forest sources.

10   9   8   7   6   5   4   3   2   1
09   08   07   06   05   04   03   02   01   00

Printed in Hong Kong

For Penny

CONTENTS

List of Figures	ix
List of Tables	xi
List of Conventions and Symbols	xiii
List of Abbreviations	xiv
Preface	xv
Acknowledgements	xix

1	**Introduction**	**1**
	1.1 Envisioning economic performance	3
	1.2 A basic toolkit for analysing economic policy and performance	10
	1.3 Why do economies grow?	15
	1.4 What can governments do to manage the economy?	18
	1.5 Summary and interim conclusions	21
2	**Economic Performance since 1945**	**25**
	2.1 Macroeconomic performance and growth accounting	26
	2.2 Economic trends	35
	2.3 Explaining economic underperformance: a British disease?	57
	2.4 Summary and interim conclusions	65
3	**Economic Policies since 1945**	**67**
	3.1 Politics and policy since 1945	68
	3.2 The public sector since 1945	74
	3.3 The institutions and practice of economic policy-making	82
	3.4 The phases of economic policy	85
	3.5 Summary and interim conclusions	98

Contents

4   Policy Effectiveness since 1945   100
   4.1   Macroeconomic policies   102
   4.2   Microeconomic policies   117
   4.3   Summary and interim conclusions   132

5   Conclusions   136

Appendices   139
   I   **Glossary**   139
   II   **Key Economic Statistics**   145
   III   **Using and Interpreting Economic Statistics** 153

Notes   171
Guide to Further Reading   189
Index   191

FIGURES

1.1   OECD-16: real GDP per worker-hour (1990 US$) in
        1870 (UK = 100) and annual average growth rates
        of real GDP per worker-hour, 1870–1992   7
1.2   UK, Germany, US and OECD-16 averages: real GDP
        per worker-hour, 1870, 1938 and 1992   8
1.3   The triangular policy space   9
2.1   Growth rate of real GDP and unemployment rate (%),
        1948–97   41
2.2   Current account balance of payments as a percentage
        of GDP, 1948–97   43
2.3   Administrative unemployment rates (%), 1881–1997   50
2.4   Annual change in RPI (%), 1915–97   51
2.5   Index (1914 = 100) of purchasing power of pound,
        1915–97   51
3.1   Okun discomfort index (%), 1945–97   68
3.2   Total public expenditure by economic classification as
        a percentage of GDP at current market prices, 1900–93   76
3.3   Total public sector receipts as a percentage of GDP
        at current market prices, 1900–93   78
3.4   Rates of income tax, financial years (%), 1900–97   79
3.5   Gross domestic fixed capital formation by sector as a
        percentage of total GDFCF, 1900–93   80
3.6   Public sector financial balances as a percentage of GDP
        at current market prices, current and capital
        accounts, 1900–93   80
4.1   Real GDP: actual, 1951–97, and 1951–73 and 1973–9
        trends extrapolated   133

Figures

III.1   Index (1951 = 100) of exports and GDP at
         current market prices, 1951–73   157
III.2   Retail price index (January 1974 = 100), 1948–97   158
III.3   Index (1990 = 100) of nominal and real GDP, 1948–97   160
III.4A   UK: employment in manufacturing industry as a per-
         centage of civilian employment, 1960–90 (full Y-axis)   163
III.4B   UK: employment in manufacturing industry as a
         percentage of civilian employment, 1960–90
         (truncated Y-axis)   164
III.5   Inflation and unemployment rates (%), 1951–73   165
III.6   Public sector employment as a percentage of total
         employment, selected years, 1950–92   166
III.7   Total employment by sector (%), 1992   166
III.8   OECD–16: real GDP per capita and general
         government expenditure as a percentage of GDP, 1979   168

TABLES

1.1   UK and comparators: economic growth performance,
1950–97   4

2.1   UK growth accounting and real GDP and components
by business-cycle phases, annual average percentage
growth rates, 1856–1997   28

2.2   Step-by-step example of UK growth accounting exercise,
annual average compound growth rates (%), 1950–73   30

2.3   UK, Germany, Japan and US: identifiable forces explaining GDP growth (step-by-step growth accounting), annual
average compound percentage points contributions to
GDP growth, 1950–92   31

2.4   UK and other G-7 states and EU, G-7 and OECD-17
averages: comparative macroeconomic performance,
1950–73 and 1973–97   34

2.5   Measures of competitiveness (%), selected years, 1950–97   36

2.6   UK and comparators: distribution of employment by sector
as a percentage of civilian employment, selected years,
1950–94   44

2.7   Area and commodity composition of British exports and
imports of goods (% of total), selected years, 1938–96   48

2.8   UK regional unemployment rates (%), selected years,
1948–97   54

2.9   UK manufacturing: value-added and labour productivity
(percentage rates of growth), 1970–92   56

2.10 Estimates for 1967/8 and 1972 of the potential benefits
had British manufacturing adopted best practice standards   62

3.1   British political facts, 1945–97   69

3.2   Total public expenditure as a percentage of GDP at current
market prices by functional classification, selected years,
1900–93   77

3.3 Macroeconomic indicators, annual averages by
government, 1945–97   86

4.1 Macroeconomic policy regimes, selected years, 1945–97   104

4.2 The timing of and signals for 'Stop-Go' policies using
then current macroeconomic indicators, 1951–79   105

4.3 MTFS: £M3 and PSBR targets and out-turns,
1978/9–83/4   115

4.4 Microeconomic policy regimes, selected years, 1945–97   117

4.5 Estimates of the NAIRU for males and decomposition
of the rise in unemployment, 1956–79   128

II.1 GDP by category of expenditure at market prices
(£ millions), 1948–97   146

II.2 Unemployment, unemployment rate and RPI, 1948–97   149

II.3 Balance of payments, current account (£ millions),
1948–97   150

CONVENTIONS AND SYMBOLS

1. **Dates:**
   / is used for financial years, e.g. 1975/6 for the financial
   year ended 31 March 1976.

   – is used for two or more calendar years, e.g. 1975–6 for the
   two calendar years 1975 and 1976.

   Roman numerals are used for quarters of the calendar year, e.g.
   1976.IV for the fourth quarter of 1976.

2. **Rounding:** In many of the tables estimates are given in such a
   way that components may not add exactly to totals.

3. **Negative numbers:** these are given in parentheses in tables.

4. **Symbols:**
   n.a. = not applicable
   .. = not available
   -     = nil
   — = less than half the smallest unit used in the table.

5. **Growth rates:** unless otherwise stated in the text, geometric means
   are used.

6. **Words emboldened in the text:** see Appendix I for a glossary.

ABBREVIATIONS

AES	Alternative economic strategy
CSO	Central Statistical Office
DEA	Department of Economic Affairs
EC	European Community
EEC	European Economic Community
ERM	Exchange Rate Mechanism
EU	European Union
G-7	Group of seven leading industrial economies
GATT	General agreement on tariffs and trade
GDFCF	Gross domestic fixed capital formation
GDP	Gross domestic product
GFCF	Gross fixed capital formation
MTFS	Medium-term financial strategy
NAIRU	Non-accelerating-inflation rate of unemployment
NEDC	National Economic Development Council
NEDO	National Economic Development Office
OECD	Organisation for Economic Co-operation and Development
ONS	Office for National Statistics
PACE	Public authorities' current expenditure on goods and services
PAYE	Pay-as-you-earn
PSBR	Public Sector Borrowing Requirement
RPI	Retail Price Index
£M3	Sterling M3 (broad money supply measure)
TFI	Total factor inputs
TFP	Total factor productivity
TPE	Total public expenditure

PREFACE

In a recent, major revisionist account of modern British history the observation is made that as the century draws to a close, all confidence has evaporated that in Britain's twentieth-century history there might be anything to celebrate and instead it 'threatens to become a history of decline, centred on the question: where did it go wrong?'[1] In this 'history as tragedy', *fin de siècle* concerns and post-modern angst are clearly detectable, but above all this pessimistic version of contemporary British history is dominated by the notion of long-term decline deriving from endemic and manifold economic weakness.

However, when this notion is made operational, and above all when quantitative assessment is attempted, decline is shown to be a deeply problematic narrative. Britain may well have lost an empire and experienced grave difficulties in adjusting its geopolitical aspirations to its more limited economic capability, but so-called decline also coincides with sufficient of an economic transformation to sustain Britain as a leading, advanced industrial economy. Indeed, the years since the Second World War are marked by the most pronounced rise in living standards ever experienced by the British people, such that in the half century after 1945 average **real** earnings (the usual measure of the standard of living which adjusts **nominal** incomes from employment for the effects of **inflation**)[2] rose over two and a half times, more than twice as fast on average as in the preceding century. We have, therefore, much to explain: in particular, why a historical record, which in almost all other countries would be represented as an economic triumph, has become codified as a disaster; and why the dominant approach of historians and many other commentators is to write postwar British history as a catalogue of missed opportunities? In short, why has postwar British economic history been largely written within the mould of what David Edgerton calls the modern English vice of 'inverted Whiggism'?[3]

To confront this declinism, the label historians now give to this obsession with national decline, requires that we court the disapproval of many contemporary historians who deny the possibility of any objective truth in history. Whilst mindful of how post-modernism has enriched many topics of historical enquiry, and our understanding of economic debates, I remain firmly of the view that objective historical truth is both desirable and attainable.[4] Indeed, the profoundly ideological nature of the debate about the British economy can be understood only after first establishing the 'facts', that is the economic record in historical and comparative (cross-country) perspective according to the 'best' estimates currently available. While an exploration of the dissonance between historical perception and reality underlies all books in the British History in Perspective series, the task is perhaps more difficult with our chosen topic. Not only are we entering the realm of contemporary history, with all of its attendant dangers of mistaking the ephemeral for the fundamental, but this is economic history, an area traditionally avoided like the plague by British history students and students of recent British history. Moreover, to gain the most from this book requires a willingness to think quantitatively, a preparedness to engage with the debate through use of numbers – another traditional aversion of British history students, *and* their teachers and lecturers.

Accordingly, while this book, like others in the series, seeks to cover the principal themes and competing interpretations of our topic, it also has a secondary aim: to widen the vocabulary of historians by encouraging engagement with economic arguments and quantitative analysis. Without such engagement only a limited part of the debate about Britain's economic performance can be understood. Moreover, there are three further arguments for studying economic history. The first, perhaps perversely, is that it is intellectually difficult, harder or whatever than some of the alternatives like diplomatic or – dare one say in these politically correct times – gender history. As a hybrid discipline economic history requires that its practitioners master the theoretical techniques of the economist whilst maintaining their analytical rigour and sensitivities as historians. This is no easy task, and whilst it is currently fashionable in education to shun the unfashionable and challenging, it is to be hoped that rigour will eventually regain its appeal in school and university history. This leads directly to our second justification: the student or their teacher, having discarded economic history as too boring or too difficult and having sought solace in their diplomatic or gender history, will without a firm understanding of the economic history of their period/country be quite unable to make real progress in their refuge. Without a firm understanding of how economic capability conditions possible foreign policy postures, or an appreciation of the workings of the labour market with respect to the economic circumstances of men and women, the student and their teacher have chosen to limit their intellectual progress. Their chosen refuges are thus less solace than an asylum for those unable to cope with the challenge of reconstructing history in its entirety.[5]

Finally, with the production of data of all sorts now ubiquitous, and with their use so pervasive a feature of contemporary life, the student and their teacher who does not move beyond the qualitative (the text) to the quantitative (merely, in reality, another form of text) is forever excluded from a deep understanding of what is to be studied, as well as being less equipped as a citizen to monitor the activities of those who make decisions on their behalf, be they politicians, bureaucrats or market agents. *The British Economy since 1945* is thus being offered as a means for the historian to overcome this aversion. However, to reassure the sceptical and/or the nervous that what we have in mind is merely quantification as more rigorous and formalised description, the lowest level of technique for specialist quantitative historians,[6] what follows is written for those without 'A' level mathematics or indeed any training in economics.[7]

A note is also appropriate here about the structure, sources, geographical coverage, comparators and initial and terminal dates for this study. First, this study is structured around economic concepts and problems and, for the most part, deliberately avoids a chronological progression through the post-1945 period so as to discourage conventional narrative history (none the less, those needing a chronology are directed to the guide to further reading, pp. 188–9).

Secondly, on sources, given the above forewarning, you will encounter numbers in abundance, but beyond this there is a rich literature on both economic performance and policy.[8] With respect to the latter set of themes, however, the operation of the '30 year rule' for British official papers results in our having a much fuller historiography based on primary sources for the years before the 1964 general election than for subsequent years. This is, of course, part of the problem – and the challenge – of contemporary history. Accordingly, as we progress with the narrative we are inevitably working with a raw material of political memoirs, et cetera, which are frequently deeply compromised by the self-serving objectives of their authors.[9]

Thirdly, readers should note that this is a study of Britain, not the United Kingdom (UK). The exclusion of Northern Ireland is defensible on many grounds, not least that there is almost no published economic history of its postwar development.[10] None the less, given the 'troubles', and the contribution of economic underperformance and perceived inequalities to that conflict, Ulster's situation is an important input into British economic policy and performance, and does feature in our account in so far as the UK is the preferred national statistical identity.

This leads us to the question of comparators, by which is meant the groups of countries with which Britain's economic record must be compared. Just as Britain's post-1945 economic performance must be judged in relation to previous epochs, so must it be compared with that of other economies of comparable maturity and/or membership of regional/international organisations. The three comparator groups to which reference is made are as follows: the European Union (EU) states, including a subset of them, the original six member states (Belgium, France, Germany, Italy, Luxembourg and the Netherlands) which will be referred to as EC-6; the G-7, the group of seven largest industrial economies (Canada, France, Germany, Italy, Japan, UK and US); and the Organisation for Economic Co-operation and Development (OECD), which currently has 29 members and embracing all those of the EU, some aspirant EU members, the non-European members of the G-7, together with Australia, Korea, Mexico and New Zealand. Here reference will typically be made to two other subsets, the OECD-16/OECD-17, the 16/17 most significant of these economies and the ones for which an important historical dataset of national accounts has been developed.[11]

Finally, a note on the period covered is appropriate. Whilst contemporary historians and political scientists are now debating whether the 'postwar period' (meaning post-Second World War) is a useful organising and temporal demarcation,[12] we have less inhibitions here because so much of the debate about economic decline does use the years since 1945 as the survey period (or, for various reasons to do with data availability and comparability, 1948). Our chosen terminal date should also not be contentious: 1997, the year in which after a long period of Conservative governments, New Labour secured power and embarked upon a further phase in the modernisation of the British economy, polity and society.

ACKNOWLEDGEMENTS

A number of people have helped me in the production of this study. I thank first the hundreds of (perhaps now over a thousand) students from Durham and Bristol Universities over the last 20 years who have taken my degree-level and continuing education classes on the modern British economy. From them I think I have learnt at least how not to construct the story here told, what concepts, problems and policy episodes can be used to good effect and, hopefully, how to mix the quantitative and the qualitative to produce a more or less workable and intellectually engaging account of recent British economic history. In particular, I would like to thank Matthew O'Leary and Ruth Bransom from this year's group who read this study in draft and made many useful suggestions, as did my colleague Kirsty Reid who bravely volunteered as a self-professed non-numerate, non-economic (but gender) historian to market test the chapters. I thank also my colleague Mark Wickham-Jones for help with references and a Labour Party news release. My next debt is to the staff of my university library who have, as ever, provided an excellent service in increasingly difficult circumstances, and I thank them, as I do also acknowledge financial assistance from the University of Bristol Research Fund. I thank also Jeremy Black as general editor of the British History in Perspective series for his faith that I might be the right person for this particular job (the series's first, but hopefully not last, foray into economic history). Finally, I thank Penny Starns for her special combination of candid critical spirit and warm heart.

1

INTRODUCTION

Our starting point is with the dissonance we have just identified, between unparalleled affluence and the contemporary preoccupation with decline, for this not only embraces the central question of postwar British economic history, but it introduces at an early point the vital distinction between absolute and relative change. With this established, we can then proceed to examine the basics of how and why economies grow, and from this assign some benchmarks for assessing British economic performance and the effectiveness of government policies.

This chapter is organised as follows. In Section 1.1 we introduce the three standard measures whereby national economic performance is conventionally assessed:

- the headline growth rate (real **GDP**, that is money GDP adjusted for inflation);
- a quantitative measure of the standard of living (real GDP per capita); and
- an aggregate **labour productivity** measure (real GDP per worker-hour), the foundation upon which the headline growth rate and thus living standards must ultimately depend.

In the process we make clear that when examining an economy, the observer must bear in mind that the historical forces underlying the growth of an economic variable such as GDP, and the absolute level it has attained by any particular year, may be an exceptional historical performance but none the less deficient relative to:

- the rate of change and final level attained by comparable countries; and/or
- the feasible growth rate were the economy more efficient.

With this distinction established it then becomes much easier to understand fully why living standards are now lower in Britain than the average for the OECD countries, for the question that needs to be asked is not so much why productivity is lower in Britain but why it grew more slowly, that is what constrained the growth rate and thus prevented the absolute level of productivity from converging on that of the leading economies.

In Section 1.2 we then introduce certain key concepts from the economist's toolkit which are necessary to analyse economic policy and performance. The reader's exposure to economics is kept to the minimum necessary, but that minimum is necessary if the richness of the historical literature is to be appreciated. Moreover, the minimum really is very manageable, with economics thought of, in the words of its most famous twentieth-century British practitioner, not as 'a body of settled conclusions immediately applicable to policy [but as] a doctrine, an apparatus of the mind, a technique of thinking, which helps its possessor to draw correct conclusions.'[1] With economic theory thus established as an engine of analysis, as a set of tools to be employed rather than as a body of theorems to be learnt, we progress to Section 1.3 where we examine what is known in theory about why economies grow, how that theory has evolved over the postwar period and what we can then identify as potentially important in practice for understanding the British case. We are then in a position in Section 1.4 to discuss what governments can, in theory, do to manage the economy in the broader sense, leaving the extent to which they have actually practised economic management, and the consequences of their policies for economic performance, for later chapters.

Finally, given the reliance we are about to place on the use and interpretation of economic statistics, you are *strongly advised* to read Appendix III (pp. 153–70) now, before proceeding further with this introductory chapter. You should also not be inhibited about returning to this Appendix on a second or subsequent occasion as its content is not just to be read, but to be understood and then related to the chapters of this book which make use of the concepts and techniques therein explained. Your attention is also drawn to the Glossary (pp.

139–43) which explains all of the major technical terms you will encounter in this and later chapters.

1.1 Envisioning economic performance

Consider Table 1.1, which in panel A gives estimates of the national incomes (expressed in constant 1990 US dollars) of the UK and comparator economies (G-7 countries and EU and OECD-17 averages) for 1950, 1973 and 1997, together with associated growth rates. The initial year is that routinely taken by economic historians as the first normal peacetime year, the beginning of the long boom known as the golden age which ends with our intermediate year, 1973. Our terminal year is determined by data availability, being 1997 for panels A and B, where we can augment the Maddison historical dataset with the latest estimates issued by the OECD, but 1992 for panel C where it has not been possible to update Maddison's estimates.[2] We stress that Table 1.1 reports highly processed cross-country data obtained by adjusting each country's GDP at current prices and exchange rates for the effects of inflation between the initial and terminal years, for the differing purchasing power of each country's national currency and for any territorial changes (important in the case of Germany which was reunified in 1990). The derivation of these statistics poses a number of significant problems, but we leave these aside for the moment and instead focus on what these numbers might tell us about Britain in comparative perspective.

Taking absolute magnitudes first, it is clear that in 1950 the UK economy, if not the workshop of the world, was still the second largest of the advanced capitalist economies (behind the US), whereas by 1997 it had slipped to fifth place (now also behind France, Germany and Japan, and only just ahead of Italy). The size of a country's national income is, of course, partly a function of the size of its population, and when this is factored in (as in panel B where population is the **denominator** in the calculation) a somewhat different picture emerges, with the UK slipping from sixth place in 1950 to fourteenth by 1997. Moreover, since this measure is the economists' favoured indicator of the standard of living, it is clear that the relative decline of the British economy was even more pronounced. Thus, by this measure, the standard of living rose on average by 2.1 per cent

Table 1.1 UK and comparators: economic growth performance, 1950–97

	1950	1973	1997[b]	Annual average % change: 1950–73	1973–97[b]	1950–97[b]	OECD-17 ranking:[a, c] 1950	1973	1997[b]	1950–97[b] growth rate
A. Real GDP (1990 US$m.)										
G-7 countries:										
Canada	96,800	301,880	590,361	5.1	2.8	3.9	7	7	7	4
France	218,409	674,404	1,109,403	5.0	2.1	3.5	3	4	4	9
Germany	213,976	815,138	1,343,236	6.0	2.1	4.0	4	3	3	2
Italy	161,351	570,200	997,932	5.6	2.4	4.0	5	6	6	3
Japan	156,546	1,197,152	2,593,122	9.3	3.3	6.2	6	2	2	1
UK	344,859	674,061	1,051,149	3.0	1.9	2.4	2	5	5	17
US	1,457,624	3,519,224	6,350,209	3.9	2.5	3.2	1	1	1	11
Arithmetic averages:										
EU	116,219	333,450	548,162	4.7	2.1	3.4	n.a.	n.a.	n.a.	n.a.
G-7	378,509	1,107,437	2,005,059	4.8	2.5	3.6	n.a.	n.a.	n.a.	n.a.
OECD-17	176,858	512,639	921,043	4.7	2.5	3.6	n.a.	n.a.	n.a.	n.a.
B. Real GDP per capita (1990 US$m.)										
G-7 countries:										
Canada	7,047	13,644	19,654	2.9	1.5	2.2	5	3	9	12
France	5,221	12,940	18,959	4.0	1.6	2.8	11	7	12	8
Germany	4,281	13,152	20,346	5.0	1.8	3.4	13	6	5	4
Italy	3,425	10,409	17,376	5.0	2.2	3.5	16	16	15	3
Japan	1,873	11,017	20,591	8.0	2.6	5.2	17	14	4	1
UK	6,847	11,992	18,013	2.5	1.7	2.1	6	11	14	14
US	9,573	16,607	23,566	2.4	1.5	1.9	1	2	2	16

Arithmetic averages:

EU	5,225	12,215	18,437	3.8	1.7	2.7	n.a.	n.a.	n.a.	n.a.
G-7	5,467	12,823	19,786	3.8	1.8	2.8	n.a.	n.a.	n.a.	n.a.
OECD-17	5,904	12,745	19,694	3.4	1.8	2.6	n.a.	n.a.	n.a.	n.a.

C. Real GDP per worker-hour (1990 dollars)

G-7 countries:

Canada	9.78	19.09	25.32	3.0	1.5	2.3	2	2	8	1
France	5.65	17.77	29.62	5.1	2.7	4.0	10	6	1	5
Germany	4.37	16.64	27.55	6.0	2.7	4.5	12	8	5	2
Italy	4.28	15.58	24.59	5.8	2.4	4.3	13	12	9	4
Japan	2.03	11.15	20.02	7.7	3.1	5.6	16	16	16	1
UK	7.86	15.92	23.98	3.1	2.2	2.7	5	11	11	12
US	12.66	23.45	29.10	2.7	1.1	2.0	1	1	2	16

Arithmetic averages:

EU	5.57	16.41	25.27	4.8	2.3	3.7	n.a.	n.a.	n.a.	n.a.
G-7	6.66	17.09	25.74	4.2	2.2	3.3	n.a.	n.a.	n.a.	n.a.
OECD-16	6.44	16.69	25.04	4.2	2.2	3.3	n.a.	n.a.	n.a.	n.a.

Notes:

a. OECD-17 comprises G-7 plus Australia, Austria*, Belgium*, Denmark*, Finland*, Netherlands*, New Zealand, Norway, Sweden* and Switzerland (* indicates an EU member state).
b. In panel C, terminal year is 1992.   c. In panel C, OECD-16 ranking.
Sources: Derived from Maddison, *Monitoring the World Economy*, tables C16, D1, J5; OECD, *Economic Outlook*, 63 (June 1998), annex table 1; and IMF, *World Economic Outlook*, May 1998, table A4.

per annum between 1950 and 1997 in the UK (equivalent to a doubling of the standard of living every 33.4 years) as against 5.2 per cent in Japan (equivalent to a doubling every 13.7 years), the fastest growing of the OECD economies. Sustained over the postwar period this allowed the Japanese economy to catch up from a position of having a real GDP per capita of just 27 per cent of the British level in 1950 (a level equivalent to the British figure of the 1820s) to being over 14 per cent *above* the British figure by 1997.

We can see, therefore, from panel B that whilst in absolute terms the British people by the 1990s were enjoying a standard of living which was more than double that attained at the end of the Second World War, in relative terms over the preceding half century almost all other OECD economies had grown more affluent at a faster rate than had Britain and had reached a higher level by the 1990s. The principal exception, when viewed at the relative level, is of course the US, the leading economy by size and in terms of GDP per capita. We have, therefore, the situation that the two slowest growing OECD economies since the Second World War have been the nineteenth-century workshop of the world (Britain) and the twentieth-century industrial leader (US). In explaining this finding we begin by invoking the hypothesis of catch-up and convergence, one which is now used routinely to examine the economic growth of all economies, developed and less developed.

The concept of catch-up and convergence is relatively new, but derives from a long-standing observation by economic historians that latecomers to industrialisation grew faster than the early-starters and that the forces underlying that late industrialisation might be substantially different, in particular that the role of the state might be enhanced relative to the *laissez-faire* stance of the nineteenth-century British and American governments.[3] Catch-up can be conceived as a process whereby latecomers use new technology and best organisational practices to move towards comparable absolute levels of productivity to those now enjoyed by the early-starters, with convergence the tendency for all countries, subject to differing natural resource endowments and certain other conditioning factors, to eventually attain more or less comparable absolute productivity levels. We envision the process of catch-up in Figure 1.1, where we chart on the Y axis the absolute level of aggregate labour productivity attained in 1870, the (approximate) high point of British industrial hegemony, with the

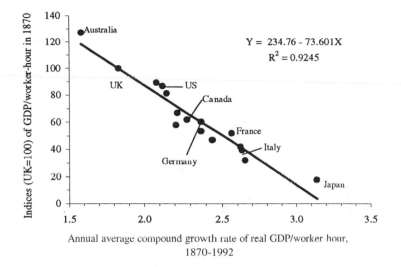

Figure 1.1 OECD-16: real GDP per worker-hour (1990 US$) in 1870 (UK = 100) and annual average growth rates of real GDP per worker-hour, 1870–1992
Source: Derived from Maddison, *Monitoring the World Economy*, Table J-5.

subsequent growth rate in aggregate labour productivity over the period 1870–1992. For catch-up to be present we would expect an inverse relationship between the two series, and we do indeed observe that from the fitted trend line. We should also notice the high value for the R^2 statistic, indicating a small difference between the Y values as represented on the trend line and the Y values existing as data points • (see p. 169 for an explanation of the R^2 statistic). At this stage, therefore, we can have some confidence in the catch-up hypothesis.

Clearly, however, the achievement of the potential catch-up bonus (the gap between a country's actual absolute level of productivity and the level attained by the leading economies) is not automatic. Were it so there would be no less-developed economies: no countries like Nepal with levels of GDP per capita (1995 figures) of US$200, only those like the Netherlands with US$24,000 or even Switzerland, the country with the world's highest standard of living, with US$40,630.[4] Thus catch-up is neither automatic, nor is it necessarily complete. Indeed, econometric research suggests that the growth paths and

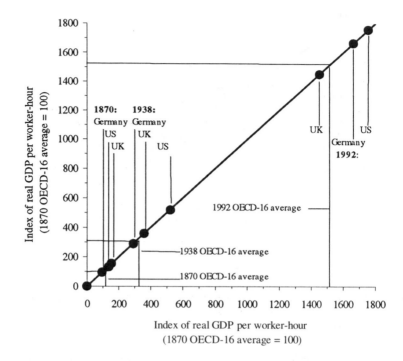

Index of real GDP per worker-hour
(1870 OECD-16 average = 100)

Figure 1.2 UK, Germany, US and OECD-16 averages: real GDP per worker-hour, 1870, 1938 and 1992
Source: Derived from Maddison, *Monitoring the World Economy*, Table J-5.

characteristics of the leading economies are not consistent with the view that absolute productivity levels tend towards equalisation and that countries differ in their productivity levels by more than would be expected from their levels of investment in physical capital (i.e. machinery) and **human capital** (i.e. education and vocational training), the two principal vehicles whereby new technologies and production practices are translated into higher output.

This leads to an important conclusion: if differences in the scope for catch-up are a conditioning rather than a determining factor in economic growth, we have room once more to investigate why some economies succeed and some fail. This is obviously of some importance for the British case. We envision this process of conditional catch-up in Figure 1.2 which compares the aggregate productivity experience of Britain, Germany, the US and the OECD-16 averages for 1870, 1938 (representing the position on the eve of the Second World War) and 1992. Clearly, all economies have advanced absolutely since 1870, but it is also clear initially that Britain's relative decline was very much more marked with respect to the US and much less with respect to the principal European economy or, indeed, the OECD average. It is thus only since the Second World War that there emerges scope for a generalised failure of the British economy, and even this must be qualified by the finding that by 1992, by this measure, Britain was only 4 per cent behind the OECD average.

We will explore in Section 1.3 what is known about why economies grow. At this outline stage, where our interest is on why some economies are able, and some not, to realise the potential catch-up bonus, it is sufficient to introduce one further component of the catch-up and convergence literature: that of social capability, here defined as a complex of economic, social, attitudinal and other factors, such as investment in education and vocational training, which bear upon a country's capacity to acquire and use advanced technology. This further concept is of assistance because it leads on to the distinction between failures that might be ascribed to the workings of the market and those resulting primarily from the activities of government. We thus arrive at the heart of the debate about Britain's economic performance: if the charge of failure be proven, which agents, operating through which mechanisms, were responsible?

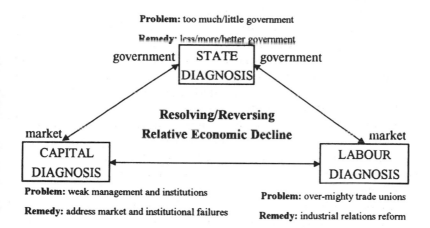

Figure 1.3 The triangular policy space

One way of conceptualising this is provided by Figure 1.3 which identifies three distinct diagnoses of economic failure (government, capital and labour) together with their supposed appropriate remedies. Before we explore these themes further, we need first to introduce some additional terms and organising concepts which will assist us with this later analysis.

1.2 A basic toolkit for analysing economic policy and performance

In this section we equip you with some basic concepts drawn from the corpus of economic theory which you will encounter in your reading and which, once mastered, will encourage you from their simplicity and capacity for universal application that economic history is actually less daunting and more rewarding than initially supposed. In this raid upon the economist's toolbox we first highlight the standard distinction in economics between **macroeconomics** and **microeconomics**. The former refers generally to aggregate behaviour and aggregate economic variables, such as GDP, while the latter focuses on the behaviour and characteristics of a particular group or representative individual. Thus, for example, in macroeconomics we might examine the course and determinants of the national unemployment rate, whereas in microeconomics our focus might be to explain the fortunes of a particular industry and why unemployment was rising/falling in that industry.

This leads to our second set of tools, ones central to both macro- and microeconomics and, indeed, arguably the bedrock of economic analysis: **supply** and **demand**. Supply and demand analysis relates prices to quantities demanded (from the buyers in a market) and supplied (from the sellers in a market). In microeconomics the quantity of a good/service demanded is generally inversely related to the price, while the supply of goods/services offered is generally positively related to price. Not surprisingly, given economics' reputation as an arcane science, there are exceptions to this formulation and, of course, many additions: for example, demand also depends upon income and the price of other goods which are complements or substitutes, while supply will also depend on the extent to which markets are competitive or prone to imperfect competition of various degrees. At the macroeconomic level, you will also encounter the terms demand-side and supply-side when reading about policy. The former can be thought of as the constituent parts of GDP, that is aggregate demand (figures in parenthesis are the percentage shares of GDP for 1997 – see Appendix II, Table 1):

- consumers' expenditure (64.7%);
- general government final expenditure (18.4%);
- capital investment (16.7%);
- stocks (0.4%); and
- the foreign balance, that is exports of goods/services less imports of goods/services (-0.1%).[5]

Demand-side policies relate to the factors promoting or retarding the growth of these components of GDP, while by contrast, supply-side policies relate more to the factors that affect the motivation, behaviour and thus ultimately the cost of the **factors of production**: capital, labour and land. A typical demand-side policy would be a cut in income tax to stimulate consumers' expenditure and thus aggregate demand and hence employment. However, such a policy change could also be represented as a supply-side policy because, by increasing net of tax incomes, it might increase the incentives to work and thus the potential labour supply available for production.

Economics is often defined as the discipline which studies human behaviour as a relationship between ends and scarce means which have alternative uses. It is thus a study of social choice, with the understanding of how scarce resources should be allocated amongst these competing ends typically formulated in terms of rational, self-serving behaviours by representative agents.[6] Such a definition of the discipline, and the extent to which the rational calculus can actually be applied to *observed* human behaviour, are acutely controversial, but what such a conception of the discipline does provide for our purpose is a benchmark against which to assess actual behaviours in the context of Britain's **managed-mixed economy** and the bridge to a number of terms routinely used in the topics we shall cover.

Starting with rationality, and adopting some simplifications which allow us to cut through a huge swath of complications and refinements in the economics literature, we can say that at the aggregate level, the claim that markets are a superior allocation system to alternatives such as command planning (e.g. as existed in the former Soviet Union) rests upon a number of assumptions relating to rationality and the informational role of markets which imbue economic agents with strong pecuniary incentives (profits) for firms to achieve best-practice combinations of inputs and outputs because if they fail to do so, they face the penalty of inferior profits and vulnerability to bankruptcy/ takeover. Incentives and penalties also operate at a less aggregate, microeconomic level, affecting single firms, households and individuals in terms of incomes, trading and employment. What binds all these factors together is the proposition that through rational deliberation and responses to the **invisible hand** of the market, there exists some **optimum** in which it becomes impossible to consume/ produce more of one good/service without consuming/producing less of another good/service.

This leads directly to the concept of economic efficiency, which necessarily underlies the growth of productivity, and which economists use in three distinct senses:[7]

- allocative (or static) efficiency: the general case whereby free, competitive markets generate the optimal allocation of resources as between competing ends;
- dynamic (or innovative) efficiency: whereby, relative to other allocative systems, free markets promote cost-reducing technologies, new markets and higher product quality; and
- X-efficiency: the capability of free markets to lower costs and raise the factor productivity of any given technology by stimulating organisational improvements. It thus differs from allocative efficiency, which concerns the correctness or not of the distribution of resources to produce particular goods/services, by focusing on the efficiency of resource use once that allocation decision has been made.

We have then three benchmarks for markets which encompass the optimal allocation of resources between competing ends (how many cars, how many computers to be produced?); the ability to promote change (improved price-performance of both cars and computers); and the efficiency with which factors of production are applied (resulting in the lowest costs of production of cars and computers). But these are just benchmarks, and in the real world there are many forces which impede such productive efficiency. More generally, we will also detect a dissonance between what theory suggests as rational and what we observe on the ground in the historical record: what economists call market failure. Much of this concept is straightforward common sense. For example, economists speak of decisions as bounded rationality, by which they mean because agents lack full information, they cannot necessarily evaluate all possibilities and thus cannot arrive at the same view as if all relevant information was fully available. This has an obvious application when considering investment projects where, to justify the outlay, a view has to be taken about an unknowable future and how this conditions prospective rates of return.

Other examples of market failure include:[8]

- market power, where there occurs a concentration of production (e.g. monopoly) which undermines the market incentives/penalties that maximise productive efficiency;
- **externalities** and **public goods**: where there exists a dissonance between the costs-benefits borne/enjoyed by private economic agents and by society (e.g. pollution generated by a private company, the costs of which are borne by neighbouring people) the resulting allocation of resources will not be optimal; and
- general equilibrium problems: a highly technical set of issues which relate to the ability of economies to respond to shocks, and in particular whether economies tend towards full employment.

Market failure matters supremely because its existence is taken as the justification for government intervention. It also has a counterpart: government failure. Both concepts are discussed more fully in Sections 1.1 and 1.3 (pp. 20, 184 5), but here we argue that they are additionally important because if a dissonance is observed between what appears rational and what actually occurred, the economic historian is uniquely equipped to make sense of this phenomenon. For example, many debates in economic history concern the rationality of technological choice, and in particular why some firms forego the latest technology and organisational practices. Without a sensitivity to the real world operation of institutions and individuals such choices are liable to be dismissed as irrational, whereas when the historian digs deeper and uses well-developed forensic skills, it becomes apparent that economic agents are making the best (or near to) second-best technological choices they can given prevailing market conditions, institutions, and the behaviours of other agents who generate externalities which limit the real choices available.

Here also is an appropriate point to introduce the concept of path-dependency, whereby a 'particular sequence of events in the past are capable of exerting persisting effects upon current conditions; of how adventitious, seemingly transient actions may become so magnified as to exercise a controlling (and sometimes pernicious) influence over matters of far greater economic and social significance.' The central element of this approach, which we will apply later to British economic policy, is that path-dependent processes are non-ergodic; that 'systems possessing this property cannot shake off the effects of past events' and this limits their future possibilities, unless the system is subject to severe shocks.[9]

As we shall see the past casts a shadow over the present with respect to both economic performance and policy, conditioning the (in)effectiveness of markets and government. In understanding the social choices that constitute economic behaviour the following additional concepts will also be helpful. We have, first, opportunity cost, the embodiment of economics as the relationship between scarcity and choice, whereby if all demands cannot be met because of scarcity, something (an alternative good/service or an opportunity) has to be foregone if a particular objective is to be attained. This leads naturally to what economists call trade-offs, that where there exists an inverse relationship between two economic variables, the pursuit of one of these may entail a cost in terms of the deterioration in the performance of the other (e.g. the Phillips curve which expresses the predicted cost in terms of inflation for attaining a set unemployment rate – see pp. 67–8, 103–5, 165).

Trade-offs matter for politicians hungry for votes, and interested only in economic outcomes in so far as they influence those votes. Three other trade-offs are relevant for our purposes:

- efficiency-equity: the presumption in mainstream economics that attempts to alter market-determined processes to improve equity will entail a cost in terms of lower efficiency;
- inter-temporal: the choice between present as against future consumption and production, of which the clearest example is the act of saving, which is equivalent to foregoing consumption today for some future date; and
- continuity-change: the system characteristics that deliver stability versus the flexibility needed to ensure that the economy can respond to shocks and opportunities.

1.3 Why do economies grow?

Since the rate of economic growth is the principal determinate of the long-term economic welfare of a nation, the question of why growth rates differ between nations is deservedly one of the most actively researched by economists and economic historians. In a recent book Barro, a major contributor to the growth literature, provides the following summary of what is now known:[10]

> The data now available for a broad panel of [over 100] countries over [the last] thirty years provide the information necessary to isolate determinants of economic growth. With respect to government policies, the evidence indicates that the growth rate of real per capita GDP is enhanced by better maintenance of the rule of law, smaller government consumption and lower inflation. Increases in political rights initially increase growth, but tend to retard growth once a moderate level of democracy has been attained. Growth is also stimulated by greater starting levels of life expectancy and of male secondary and higher schooling, lower fertility rates, and improvements in the **terms of trade**. For given values of these variables, growth is higher if a country begins with a lower starting level of real per capita GDP; that is, the data reveal a pattern of conditional convergence.

This is both immensely promising, but profoundly unhelpful for our purposes. Thus, whilst the latest survey evidence draws us to important questions concerning the role of government and confirms that convergence is indeed conditional, because the growth literature is generally very highly abstract it does not provide us with a menu from which we can choose so much A and so much B as promoting growth, and thus so much C and so much D as inhibiting growth. Moreover, the British case is one of many surveyed, with the results pooled to deliver general conclusions, while the **non-linear** relationship between democracy and economic growth that Barro and others identify poses considerable problems in interpreting what is realistic for the mature phase of the first industrial nation now enjoying a relatively high degree of democracy. Indeed, non-linearity is exhibited by many relationships between economic variables, with the consequence 'that small differences in policy regimes can easily mean the difference between growth and stagnation.'[11] Thus economic policies can matter supremely even in economies in which government appears to take little role.

To make sense of this literature, and indeed to understand what economists have been saying about economic growth since the 1950s when it first became an identifiable topic, it is helpful to distinguish between three different levels of explanations:

1. The *proximate* sources of growth: these identifiable as the growth of factor inputs and productivity, these in turn being determined by innovative activity, investment rates, education and vocational training which increases human capital formation, et cetera.
2. The *ultimate* sources of growth: the underlying explanations for the behaviour of factor inputs and productivity, these in turn being grounded in terms of actions by workers, managers, politicians, bureaucrats and other economic agents, and how these are affected by government policies and market institutions.
3. The *fundamentals* of growth: the base motives (incentives/avoidance of penalties) which drive economic agents in a capitalist democracy, typically votes for politicians, wages for workers and the lure of profits for businesses.

Our understanding of the broad determinants of economic growth has been transformed in the last 15 years or so. Indeed, economists now talk of a 'new' growth economics, one which locates productivity growth at the heart of the growth process and regards technological change, as against investment in ever more of the same capital goods, as the central element in sustaining long-run growth. This new thinking is often labelled post-neoclassical **endogenous** growth theory. While somewhat of a mouthful, and indeed when uttered by the then shadow Chancellor of the Exchequer Gordon Brown in September 1994, the cause of some hilarity by a press deeply sceptical of economics and economists,[12] this new theory does offer many insights of relevance to our purpose, not least in illuminating how far thinking about economic growth has progressed since the Second World War.

In decomposing this label we highlight the neoclassical and endogenous elements. Neoclassical refers to mainstream Western economic theory, that prevailing from the 1940s to the early 1980s which, when we cut through its many intricacies, emphasised the importance of capital investment and assumed that technological progress was **exogenous**. This latter term, the obverse of endogenous, is employed by economists to signify that a variable (in this case technological progress) is determined by factors outside of the model, with the internal (endogenous) factors being the starting point of an economy (whether scope for catch-up), the growth rate of population (determining the growth of the labour force) and the savings rate (determining the rate of capital accumulation). We have thus the situation that, for all of its sophistication and elegance, economists were trying to explain long-run growth without adequately accounting for new technologies, which are necessarily the vehicle whereby capital investment promotes economic growth by embodying more efficient production methods.

The new growth theory not only seeks to explain technological progress in a more satisfactory (endogenous) manner, by linking it to the profit motive, but also emphasises a new sort of capital: human or knowledge capital which can be accumulated either by learning-by-doing or by education and training. The role of policy, especially supply-side policies, is thus once more emphasised, with education having a strongly positive effect on an economy's ability to absorb new technologies[13] – what we earlier termed social capability – and with incentive structures central to explaining cost-reducing innovations which underpin productivity growth. Another way of understanding these changes in thinking is to say that over the postwar period economists and policy-makers, and even perhaps many managers of firms, have moved from a preoccupation with aggregates (increasing the size of the manufacturing sector) and quantities (maximising the volume of investment and the size of the labour force) to an appreciation that it is quality that matters: whether investment is allocatively efficient and cost-reducing (X-efficient) and whether the labour force is flexible and embodies the appropriate skills (human capital).

There is something of an irony that the old growth theory, which actually accorded little theoretical role to government, was dominant during the phase when many Western governments actively intervened to promote growth (1960s and 1970s), whereas the new growth theory, which sanctions a stronger role for governments, emerged in the 1980s whilst governments were trumpeting the virtues of the market and minimal government.

This new growth theory has been actively embraced by leading economic historians of the post-1945 period, and especially Nick Crafts whose voluminous writings now dominate the literature.[14] For Crafts, the existence of the catch-up bonus explains why the British economy was not amongst those with the highest growth rates;

however, it does not provide an exoneration. When account is taken of the catch-up issue, and when the feasible growth rate is taken as the appropriate standard, Crafts concludes that the British economy underperformed during the golden age (1950–73) by something between one half and a full percentage point on the annual growth rate, but that after 1979 the trend of relative economic decline was halted and, by some indicators, reversed as a consequence of the major shift in economic policy associated with the Thatcher years. Indeed, for Crafts and many others, the radical shift in policy regime that occurred gives to the years since 1979 the nature of a laboratory, in which to test all of the competing explanations for economic underperformance before 1979. In the next chapter we will agree generally with this verdict.

1.4 What can governments do to manage the economy?

The maximisation of economic welfare and the tasks now assumed as governmental responsibilities are, however, much wider than simply the promotion of economic growth.[15] Thus postwar governments have typically pursued economic policies which combine the following three additional macroeconomic objectives:

1. Full employment.
2. Price stability.
3. Equilibrium in the balance of payments.

To achieve these multiple objectives, governments have available to them, or acquire, policy instruments, a typical listing of which would be:

1. Fiscal powers: the getting of revenue through taxation and its spending as public expenditure. Each of these two sides of the budget can alter market-determined allocations of resources, the incentive structures underlying the market economy and, through the balance of the budget (revenue less expenditure), impact on aggregate demand and monetary policy.
2. Monetary powers: the government, as the monopoly supplier of legal tender, and working through its agent the Bank of England, can influence the quantity and/or the price of credit whilst, through

its management of the foreign exchange reserves, it can regulate foreign-exchange transactions and influence the exchange rate of sterling *vis-à-vis* other currencies.

3. Public ownership: the means for government to impact directly on the pricing, investment and employment policies of a significant part of an economy's productive activities, both goods and services.

4. Legal powers, typically assuming two forms: (a) the maintenance of a legal framework within which the private sector operates, such as competition policies which aim to counteract potential market failures such as monopoly, which **ceteris paribus** undermine individual markets as efficient allocative devices; and (b) direct controls, the regulation of specific activities such as consumer credit, wage and price legislation, et cetera which affect economic behaviours and will be reflected in relative prices.

The unifying characteristic of all of these policy objectives and instruments is that they entail the public authority (typically, but not exclusively, central government and its agents) altering the market-determined distribution of resources in pursuit of the public interest or some version of this adjusted for the political preferences (the need to maximise votes to ensure re-election) of the governing political party. We have then governmental economic policies, like the economic behaviour of an individual or household, progressing from the decision: what one wants to achieve (the objectives), to the process of selecting the means for its achievement (the instruments) and onward to the implementation of policy subject to certain constraints and trade-offs between policy objectives.

The constraints conditioning the potential choice and effectiveness of economic policies can be divided into three categories, deriving from:

• the economic market: how and with what effect will markets (especially the City of London) and key economic agents (notably trade unions and employers' associations) react to policies;

• the political market: actual or expected political reactions which condition the mix of policy objectives/instruments, their effectiveness and from this the probability that a government will secure sufficient popularity to be re-elected; and

- the internationalisation of both economic and political life: the
  trend towards **globalisation** of trade and capital, together with the
  growing political interconnectedness and mutual obligations of the
  advanced economies, acting to reduce the autonomy of any one
  national government to frame economic policies in isolation from
  those being pursued elsewhere.

Taken together these constraints determine the potential capability
of governments and their economic policies. As we shall see in
Chapters 3–4, such governmental capacity has eroded through time.
Thus in the immediate aftermath of the Second World War, there was
a near universal belief in the virtues of big government and in its
capacity to act decisively and in the public interest for it had appeared
to do so in its management of the war economy. This was the high-
water mark for the belief that markets were more prone to failure
than were governments. Thereafter, however, as normal peacetime
politics and economics were re-established, and as it became perceived
that the British economy was underperforming at least in part because
of poor economic policies, this consent for big, highly interventionist
government was eroded. This transition to the present day, to the
position where politicians of all political parties have succeeded in
downgrading public expectations of what governments can reasonably
deliver in their economic policies, can be understood in terms of two
processes:

1. The growing appreciation that, in practice, government policies
   often fail to achieve their stated objectives and may, in fact, reduce
   economic welfare.
2. The recognition that the trade-offs between policy instruments
   were deteriorating, such that both Labour and Conservative
   governments in the 1970s reached an impasse in their efforts to
   find new and effective policy instruments which would lessen these
   trade-offs.

Such is the significance of this reappraisal of government's economic
policy capability that to study postwar British economic policy is, in
effect, to examine these trade-offs: how they were calibrated, how they
varied over time and how governments have, largely unsuccessfully,
sought additional policy instruments to lessen individual trade-offs
and thereby increase what is known as the policy space. The policy

space is a useful concept designed to capture the interplay of past policies, choices and inherited institutional structures, and the way in which they influence the definition of current problems, the perception of the range and efficacy of potential policy instruments, and the resulting space for manoeuvre.[16] The preoccupation with trade-offs is well captured in the label 'Stop-Go', which is routinely applied as a description for British economic policy since the 1950s, by which is meant that the economy lurched from crisis to crisis (boom-bust) as successive governments sought to attain simultaneously the four policy objectives, but in practice were forced periodically to sacrifice high growth and low unemployment in order to attain price and balance of payments stability.[17] As we shall see, the British economy has been plagued with persistent balance of payments problems, but these were part cause and part consequence of the underlying relative economic decline and its manifestation as competitive weakness.

We thus return once more to the problem of how and why British productivity levels did not converge on the levels attained by the leading OECD countries. We will demonstrate that the reasons for this stem from a complex of failures originating in both the operation of the market and of the activities of government directed at remedying the defects of markets. Meanwhile, we conclude at this stage that current thinking amongst mainstream Western economists is that government does have a distinctive role to play in promoting performance at both the macro- and microeconomic levels, and that the debate of government *versus* the market might better be represented as government *and* the market, for the cross-country evidence suggests that the most successful economies are ones where government responds to market failures 'not by replacing markets but by working with them, complementing them, and even helping to create them'.[18]

1.5 Summary and interim conclusions

British economic history since the Second World War is often played out as the search for scapegoats: between, at one level, government and the market; at another, between different governments (Labour and Conservative); and, ultimately, as another manifestation of the class struggle between workers, managers and the owners of capital. The historiography is accordingly riven with disputes, set against a backcloth of an accumulating sense of economic underfulfilment, with policy initiative after initiative failing to resolve the economic problem, and with bad news always more interesting than good or no news.

This chapter, when read in conjunction with Appendix III, provides a basic set of conceptual and numerical tools with which to engage with this debate. In plotting a course through the literature, be conscious that there is typically much confusion and/or imprecision about the meaning of economic decline and also much rhetoric, in particular arguments that proceed from false analogies which liken economic development to wars and other sporting contests. As McCloskey rails, economies are not like football teams in which you have to be first, the leader, or you have in some absolute sense lost: 'The fixation of Number One ... forgets that in economic affairs being Number Two, or even Number Twelve, is very good indeed.' Thus: 'The prize for second in the race of economic growth was not poverty.' We will explore this metaphor of failure, what McCloskey calls the language of disease, defeat and decline, in more detail later.[19] For the present we note that for Britain, declinism has become something of an ideology.[20]

Within much of the declinist literature there is typically also an implicit blueprint for modernisation: some counterfactual postwar Britain which would have been very different if, at some strategic point (invariably 1945), an alternative set of policies and attitudes had prevailed.[21] Whether there existed real historical opportunities for the British people to exercise very different collective choices, and whether these would have made a substantive difference is, of course, acutely controversial. While we will never know the outcome of such counterfactuals in any epistemological sense, the question of whether the British people could have done better remains a very real one; the bread and butter of political competition as remedies for economic underperformance came to dominate the agenda.

Finally, you should be forewarned of a number of additional problems which you will encounter with the historiography of Britain's postwar economic policy and performance:

- The overriding insularity of the national debate which makes absolutely vital that wherever possible, Britain's position is placed in cross-country context with respect to both economic policy and performance.
- The preponderance of economists and economic historians with

ideological and other agendas. These have always been present, but particularly so since 1979 when many have felt the need to demonstrate that the Thatcher years were a testbed for all of the explanations previously advanced for economic decline, and that 'improved' performance since 1979 vindicates a particular pro-market view of the previous century of relative decline.

- This characteristic is often associated with the understandable, but none the less undesirable application of 20:20 hindsight to the economic policy choices confronting postwar economic agents. Thus you will often encounter claims for the efficacy of policy instruments and regimes which are anachronistic, and you should be conscious of Crafts's conclusion that postwar British experience is 'strongly suggestive of policies to avoid', but 'less good at identifying helpful interventions'.[22]

- The frequency with which conflicts become apparent between different types of evidence, especially between macroeconomic and microeconomic/industrial data. This counsels caution in drawing strong conclusions.

- The tyranny of aggregates: the preoccupation with national data hiding regional differences, differences between sectors (especially manufacturing vs. services) and differences within sectors (e.g. the declinist literature makes much of the troubles affecting the motor vehicle sector, but reports little on British success stories like pharmaceuticals).

- The need to be vigilant about the business cycle and its implications, especially for the measurement of economic growth which should be peak-to-peak and not, as is often the case in the hands of politicians and their advisers, trough-to-peak.

- The importance of not becoming too excited about small differences in growth rates, combined with a consciousness that when compounded over long periods, such differences will generate vast differences between countries' standards of living. Be conscious, therefore, of the quality of the data being invoked in arguments and try to look for datasets that are used by a number of authors who draw differing conclusions. This is one reason for favouring the Maddison and Feinstein datasets,[23] but even here you must be aware that pre-Second World War data is deemed far less reliable than more recent national income estimates. Thus, for example, in the Feinstein dataset, the GDP growth rates for the late-Victorian and Edwardian period – a very contentious era where many date the onset of economic decline – are subject to margins of error of 25–33 per cent. In addition, of course, and for all periods, cross-national comparisons are gravely handicapped by the problems created by exchange rates and shifts in territory.

• Finally, although the league table approach to national economic performance now dominates, this is very sensitive to the indicators chosen for enumeration. For example, from panel C of Table 1.1 we observe that, in terms of our preferred measure of whole economy labour productivity (GDP per worker-hour), the UK ranked eleventh in the OECD-17 and Japan ranked sixteenth in 1992. Had we instead used GDP per person employed, as many do, these rankings would have changed to thirteenth and ninth respectively.[24] Our preferred measure picks up the long working hours culture in Japan and, given that the opportunity cost of work is leisure foregone, it thus provides a more realistic measure not just of productivity, but of economic welfare. We should note, however, that in recent years a long hours culture has also taken root in Britain, evidence perhaps that workers and firms are trying to compensate for below OECD average wages and productivity through increasing the number of hours worked and thus remunerated.

2

ECONOMIC PERFORMANCE SINCE 1945

The record of British economic performance from the end of the Second World War until the present day has attracted, generally, such a bad press that we need to begin with a simple historical fact: that, notwithstanding all of the evidence of relative decline, and the higher unemployment and inflation rates after the first oil price shock in 1973 (OPEC I), the British economy has delivered unparalleled and sustained improvements in living standards and personal economic security for the majority of its people over the past half-century. Our backdrop is thus one of unparalleled historical success and of an economy transformed. Admittedly, in terms of all four of the macroeconomic objectives identified earlier (p. 18), the economic record was weaker after OPEC I than before, and spectacularly so in the case of unemployment, but the point must be pressed that for a quarter of a century or so after the Second World War the British people enjoyed full employment, no major recessions and the fastest rate of economic growth ever experienced on a sustained basis, as well as its most egalitarian distribution. That it might have been otherwise is a measure of the extent to which the Thatcherite message, of the pre-1979 years as ones of generalised failure, has been absorbed into the public consciousness and corrupted our historical reading of the years since 1945.

In surveying this economic record we come, first, across the problem of shifts in the perception of what the British economy ought to be able to deliver and, second, the issue of the most appropriate periodisation. Clearly, the challenges facing the British economy in 1945 were somewhat different from those of today. In 1945 the economic authorities sought a successful transition from a war to a peacetime economy which they conceived in terms of avoiding a postwar slump, encouraging private industry to be more efficient (in recognition of the substantial productivity gap that had now opened up between Britain and the US) and of recovering prewar living standards. There are some similarities with today's economy, most notably the preoccupation with unemployment and deficiencies in productivity performance, but also major differences forced by structural changes in both the domestic economy, with services replacing manufacturing as the dominant sector, and the international setting, most notably with globalisation and Britain's membership of the EU. Above all, however, in today's economy it is the objective of high and sustainable economic growth that dominates perceptions and aspirations. In terms of periodisation we adopt the following scheme. We accept that 1973 and the first oil price shock is the appropriate divide so far as economic performance is concerned, but since we take 1979 as the critical turning-point for economic policy we are left with something of a buffer zone or transitional period with the years 1973–9.

This chapter is arranged as follows. In Section 2.1 we discuss the proximate causes of growth. In Section 2.2 we introduce the important concept of competitiveness and then chart and explain the main economic trends. Section 2.3 then outlines the main classes of explanations for economic underperformance and explores whether there was, and perhaps still is, something distinctive about the British case. Some preliminary conclusions are then drawn in Section 2.4.

2.1 Macroeconomic performance and growth accounting

As Table 2.1 panel A shows, in historical perspective the British economy has never performed as well as during the golden age: an annual average growth rate of real GDP of 2.8 per cent for 1951–73 as against 2.2 per cent for the earlier and 2 per cent for the later standard peacetime business cycle phases, respectively 1924–37 and 1973–97. While the growth rate was slower after 1973, this was in fact characteristic of all OECD economies (see Table 1.1, pp. 4–5), and was at least comparable to that experienced during the peacetime phases stretching from the middle of the nineteenth century to the interwar years. Moreover, while the pace of relative economic decline was fastest during the golden age and abated thereafter, there is no paradox here: with compound interest a growth differential of 1 to 2 percentage points between the British and competitor growth rates is bound to deliver a final absolute gap of some significance after a quarter-century or so. This is not an attempt to explain away British economic underperformance, but simply to assert at an early point that our task is to explain both why growth was faster during the golden age for all OECD economies and what characteristics were special to the British case in both the golden age and thereafter. We should note also that the phases of growth reported in Table 2.1 are all business cycle peaks,[1] the correct method of calculating trend growth rates, but that there are problems with the growth accounting exercise after 1973 when the cyclical peaks were no longer ones of full employment.

Panel A of Table 2.1, which is based on the pioneering work of Matthews et al.,[2] provides also a means of exploring the proximate sources of growth through what is known as growth accounting, a procedure whereby GDP growth is decomposed into its constituent parts: that deriving from additions to the volume and quality of factors of production (Total Factor Inputs, TFI) and that originating from increases in the productivity of those factors of production (Total Factor Productivity, TFP).

There are two accounting identities underlying Table 2.1:

$$\Delta GDP = \Delta TFI + \Delta TFP$$
and
$$\Delta TFI = \Delta L_{QA} + \Delta K$$

where Δ is the notation for a first order difference (the change in the value of a variable, here measured in terms of percentage points contributions to GDP growth); real GDP growth (col. 5, ΔGDP) is equivalent to the sum of TFI (col. 3) and TFP (col. 4) growth; with column 3 (TFI) in turn the sum of columns 1 and 2, respectively the contributions of quality adjusted labour (L_{QA}) – that is labour supply augmented through greater education and training – and capital (K) to TFI.

Table 2.1 UK growth accounting and real GDP and components by business-cycle phases, annual average percentage growth rates, 1856–1997

| A. Standard phases: real output, inputs and total factor productivity | Total factor inputs: | | | Total factor productivity (TFP) | GDP (Y) |
	Quality adjusted labour (L_{QA})	Capital (K)	Total		
	(1)	(2)	(3)	(4)	(5)
1856–73	0.8	0.8	1.6	0.6	2.2
1873–1913	1.0	0.8	1.8	0.0	1.8
1913–24	(0.3)	0.4	0.1	(0.2)	(0.1)
1924–37	1.5	0.5	2.0	0.2	2.2
1937–51	0.7	0.4	1.1	0.7	1.8
1951–73	0.1	0.9	1.0	1.8	2.8
1973–97	..	..	..	..	2.0

B. Postwar business cycles, peak-to-peak: growth rates of GDP and components	Consumers' expenditure	General government current expenditure on goods and services	Gross domestic fixed capital formation	Exports of goods and services	Imports of goods and services	GDP
	(1)	(2)	(3)	(4)	(5)	(6)
1951–5	3.1	2.3	6.5	3.6	3.3	2.9
1955–60	2.7	(0.2)	5.3	2.8	4.4	2.5
1960–4	3.1	2.5	6.7	3.3	4.0	3.5
1964–8	2.1	3.0	5.6	5.6	4.5	2.7
1968–73	3.7	2.3	2.1	6.9	6.9	3.5
1973–9	1.3	1.9	0.2	4.3	2.4	1.5
1979–90	3.2	0.9	3.4	3.1	4.7	2.2
1990–7	2.0	1.0	1.2	6.0	4.8	2.0
Averages:						
1951–73	3.0	1.9	5.1	4.5	4.7	3.0
1973–97	2.3	1.2	1.5	4.3	4.1	2.0

Sources:
A: 1856–1973: Matthews et al., *British Economic Growth*, Table 16.2; 1973–97: ONS, *Economic Trends, Annual Supplement*, 1998 edn, Table 1.3.
B: ONS, *Economic Trends, Annual Supplement*, 1998 edn, Table 1.3.

Before examining what conclusions we may draw from these data we should note:

- TFP is not directly measured – it is a residual left over after direct measurement of TFI, and is meant to capture the effects of advances in knowledge and other miscellaneous determinants (es-

pecially the effects of technological progress) which are not included in L_{QA} and K;

- TFP is a measure of the productivity of all factors of production,
  capital as well as labour. It is thus a broader productivity measure
  than the one introduced in Chapter 1 (real GDP per worker-hour),
  and particularly appropriate for Britain where there have been
  significant differences between the productivity of labour and of
  capital (see Table 2.3, row 5); and

- the values of L_{QA} and K derive from coefficients which are calcu
  lated using procedures which rest upon some strong theoretical
  and empirical assumptions.

These problems notwithstanding, the growth accounting framework is
widely employed and does yield some striking conclusions about the
performance of the British and other OECD economies. First, we see how
exceptional the golden age was and how experience since 1973 has been
closer to the British long-term steady-state growth rate of between 2 and
2¼ per cent. Secondly, we observe that the proximate cause of this higher
golden age growth relative to interwar experience lies with enhanced TFP
growth. Thirdly, and again by contrast with the interwar period, when
decomposed, TFI growth is explained not by the traditional expansion of
the labour input (typically fuelled by population growth), but by the much
higher contribution of the capital input. Indeed, as we shall see in Section
2.2.4, two notable characteristics of the whole postwar era have been the
slow growth of the workforce and the contraction of the aggregate labour
input when measured in terms of total hours worked. This latter
phenomenon has complex causes: later entry into the labour force because
of extended education and earlier exit because of higher unemployment
(in the second half of our period) and other economic and social factors;
the growth of part-time employment, especially for women; and a shorter
working year through longer holidays and reductions in hours of the
normal working week.[3]

Clearly then TFP growth is critical to an understanding of postwar
growth. A richer perspective on the growth process is provided in the
more recent, more detailed and cross-country growth accounting exercises
undertaken by Maddison.[4] These are reported in Tables 2.2 and 2.3 as
two comparable, but slightly different step-by-step procedures which
begin with changes in the quantity and quality of the two main factors of
production and then augments these with additional significant
explanatory variables. It should be noted that for the golden age years,

Table 2.2 Step-by-step example of UK growth accounting exercise, annual average compound growth rates (%), 1950–73

	Category	Value
1	GDP	3.03
2	Labour input calculation	
2.1	Labour force	0.48
2.2	Employment	0.49
2.3	Labour hoarding	0.00
2.4	Hours per person	(0.64)
2.5	Quantity of labour (items 2.2+2.3+2.4)	(0.15)
2.6	Impact of education	0.29
2.7	Gender balance	(0.12)
2.8	Quality of labour (items 2.6+2.7)	0.17
2.9	Augmented labour input (items 2.5+2.8)	0.02
3	Capital input calculation	
3.1	Quantity of non-residential capital	5.11
3.2	Quality of non-residential capital	1.67
3.3	Augmented non-residential capital input	6.86
3.4	Residential capital	2.94
4	Augmented joint factor input calculation	
4.1	Weighted augmented labour input (from item 2.9, weighted 0.7)	0.01
4.2	Weighted augmented non-residential capital input (from item 3.3, weighted 0.23)	1.58
4.3	Weighted residential capital (from item 3.4, weighted 0.07)	0.21
4.4	Total augmented joint factor input (items 4.1+4.2+4.3)	1.76
5	Foreign trade effect	0.25
6	Structural effect	0.10
7	Technology diffusion	0.07
8	Scale	0.09
9	Energy effect	(0.01)
10	Natural resource windfall	0.00
11	Total explained (items 4.4+5+6+7+8+9+10)	2.28
12	Unexplained residual (item 1–11)	0.76

Source: Derived from Maddison, *Dynamic Forces in Capitalist Development*, Tables 5.3, 5.10 and 5.19.

Tables 2.2 and 2.3 report slightly different GDP growth rates (respectively 3.03 and 2.96 per cent), indicative of how such exercises always produce provisional results as the underlying data are subject to on-going refinement.

In Table 2.2 Maddison begins with the physical quantity of labour (item 2.2) and adjusts this, first, for the effects of labour hoarding (item 2.3) and the reduction in hours worked (item 2.4) and, second, for changes in the quality of labour arising from greater education (item 2.6) and changes in the gender balance (item 2.7) which act on the productivity of labour.[5] A similar exercise is then conducted for

Table 2.3 UK, Germany, Japan and US: identifiable forces explaining GDP growth (step-by-step growth accounting), annual average compound percentage points contributions to GDP growth, 1950–92

	Germany		Japan		UK		US	
	1950–73	1973–92	1950–73	1973–92	1950–73	1973–92	1950–73	1973–92
1. GDP	5.99	2.30	9.25	3.76	2.96	1.59	3.92	2.39
2. Total hours worked	0.00	(0.38)	1.44	0.61	(0.15)	(0.57)	1.15	1.27
3. Labour productivity (GDP per worker hour)	5.99	2.69	7.69	3.13	3.12	2.18	2.74	1.11
4. Total non-residential capital stock	5.93	3.37	9.18	6.81	5.17	3.32	3.27	3.13
5. Capital productivity (GDP per unit of non-residential capital)	0.05	(1.04)	0.06	(2.85)	(2.10)	(1.67)	0.63	(0.72)
6. Total factor productivity[a]	4.05	1.54	5.08	1.04	1.48	0.69	1.72	0.18
7. Foreign trade effect	0.48	0.15	0.53	0.09	0.32	0.15	0.11	0.05
8. Structural and labour (dis)hoarding effects	0.68	0.17	2.10	0.09	0.10	(0.09)	0.10	(0.17)
9. Scale effect	0.18	0.07	0.28	0.11	0.09	0.05	0.12	0.07
10. Unexplained residual	2.71	1.15	2.17	0.75	0.97	0.58	1.39	0.23

Note:
[a] Calculated as the ratio of GDP growth (line 1) to the weighted average of associated inputs (labour, human capital, non-residential gross fixed capital and land).
Source: Derived from Maddison, *Monitoring the World Economy*, Tables 2.6.

capital, factoring in first its quantity, then its character (residential or non-residential) and then its quality, with all of these significant as increases in the stock of non-residential capital are taken as the main vehicle for embodying new technology, which again should raise productivity. Weighting the labour and capital inputs we thus arrive at the total augmented joint factor input (item 4.4) of 1.76 per cent, this approximately equivalent to the TFI measure in Table 2.1. Given the estimated GDP growth rate of 3.03, we are thus left with a residual (the equivalent of TFP) estimated at 1.27. Maddison, however, does not directly measure TFP in Table 2.2, but instead tries to estimate the impact of the following factors which greatly enrich our understanding of the growth process:[6]

• the opening of economies to international trade, it being one of the major characteristics of the golden age that world trade expanded much more rapidly than did world output as trade liberalisation resulted in more open economies and created the potential for countries to benefit from economies of scale and specialisation of production;
• gains from structural change, in particular the transfer of resources from low to higher-productivity sectors, first from agricultural to manufacturing and later from manufacturing to services;
• accelerated technological diffusion from the lead country (mainly the US), facilitated by improved mechanisms for technology transfer (the postwar Marshall Aid programme, US overseas investment and much greater international communication, travel and information exchanges);
• economies of scale in domestic markets, these in addition to those embodied in the opportunities afforded by expanding international trade;
• energy effect, this capturing the impact of the oil price crises known as OPEC I (1973–4) and II (1979); and
• natural resource windfall, the effects of the discovery of North Sea oil and gas reserves, which boosted the British growth rate between 1976 and 1983 and also affected the Norwegian and Dutch economies.

Table 2.3 reports Maddison's most recent step-by-step growth accounting exercise for Britain and the leading G-7 economies from three continents for both the golden age and the subsequent period. From this we observe certain distinctive characteristics of Britain's growth record:

1. In both periods the rate of growth of labour productivity exceeded that of the US (item 3), as did the growth of the non-residential capital stock (item 4), but Britain was handicapped by falling productivity of its capital stock (item 5), although it should be noted that after 1973 it was relatively less disadvantaged by this factor than were the other G-7 economies.
2. Whilst Britain's TFP growth rate did fall after 1973, it fell far less than in the other economies.
3. During the golden age, and relative to both Germany and Japan, the British economy did not benefit as fully from the foreign trade, structural change and scale effects, but instead resembled more the growth path of the US economy.

Taken together these tables lead us to explore the factors underlying labour and capital productivity, and to ask in what respects and why the UK economy was distinctive. However, while growth accounting provides 'a very flexible device for organising evidence on causal influences affecting the growth process', it 'cannot provide a full causal story'.[7] We are thus still at the level of proximate and not ultimate causes of growth: registering the facts about the components of growth, but as yet unable to explain the elements of policy or circumstance, national or international, that underlie them. Thus, for example, comparing Britain with the three other countries, why was the TFI effect so much lower during the golden age? We have a further problem:[8]

> To use a sports analogy, growth accounting is like an attempt to describe the performance of a basketball or football team in terms of the particular performance of the individuals on that team, without taking account of the fact that the performance of any one player often is made possible by what the others are doing, and even that whether a particular action on the part of one of the players helps or hinders team performance has a lot to do with the extent to which it is complementary to what the others are doing.

Growth accounting thus relates to what is measurable and to the proximate elements in the growth process. It assists us with some

Table 2.4 UK and other G-7 states and EU, G-7 and OECD-17 averages: comparative macroeconomic performance, 1950–73 and 1973–97

| | | Canada | France | Germany | Italy | Japan | UK | US | Averages: | | |
									EU[a]	G-7	OECD-17
A. Annual average real GDP growth rate	1950–73	5.1	5.0	6.0	5.6	9.2	3.0	3.9	4.9	5.4	4.8
	1973–97	2.8	2.1	2.2	2.4	3.3	2.0	2.6	2.6	2.5	2.4
B. Average annual rise in consumer prices	1950–73	2.8	5.0	2.7	3.9	5.2	4.6	2.7	4.2	3.8	4.1
	1973–97	5.8	6.4	3.3	10.1	3.9	8.2	5.4	7.8	6.2	6.0
C. Average annual standardised unemployment rates	1950–73[b]	4.7	2.0	2.5	5.5	1.6	2.8	4.6	2.9	3.4	2.5
	1973–97	9.0	8.6	5.8	9.6	2.5	8.3	6.7	7.7	7.2	6.2
D. Average annual current account balance of payments surplus as % of GDP	1960–73[c]	(1.0)	0.9	(0.9)	1.0	0.5	(0.1)	0.5	(0.7)	0.1	(0.3)
	1973–97	(1.9)	0.1	(1.4)	(0.2)	1.7	(1.0)	(1.1)	(1.2)	(0.6)	(0.4)

Notes:
[a] Excluding Luxembourg (except panel D).
[b] 1960–73 for Greece, Ireland, New Zealand, Portugal and Spain.
[c] Data not available for 1950s.

Sources: Derived from Maddison, *Monitoring the World Economy*, Tables 3.17, 3.18, 3.19; OECD, *Historical Statistics, 1960–94*, table 6.15; and OECD, *Economic Outlook*, June 1998, Annex Tables 1, 16, 21, 52.

historical questions, such as why growth was faster during the golden age; with some questions affecting the behaviour of groups of countries, such as why did OECD countries converge on US productivity levels after the Second World War; but it leaves significant unexplained residuals (item 12 of Table 2.2 and item 10 of Table 2.3). Moreover, when we broaden our field of analysis from growth to the four macroeconomic objectives identified earlier, when interconnections and trade-offs become crucial and when even small differences in policy regimes and social capability can make a substantial difference, it becomes clear that if we are to progress to ultimate causality, a different approach is necessary. As can be seen from Table 2.4, which summarises the comparative macroeconomic performance of the UK, it was not just with respect to economic growth that the British economy might be distinctive and classified as underperforming. A first step in such an analysis is to examine the main economic trends.

2.2 Economic trends

2.2.1 Competitiveness

Competitiveness lies at the heart of the growth process. At the national level the OECD defines competitiveness as 'the degree to which [an economy] can, under free and fair market conditions, produce goods and services which meet the test of international markets, while simultaneously maintaining and expanding the real incomes of its people over the long run,'[9] although our preferred definition is 'the ability to sustain an acceptable rate of growth in the real standard of living of the population, while avoiding social costs such as high unemployment, excessive environmental damage, or extremes of inequality in the distribution of income.'[10] Underlying this aggregate concept, of course, lies competitiveness at the firm level, which can be defined as 'the ability to produce the right goods and services of the right quality, at the right price, at the right time [thereby] meeting customers' needs more efficiently and more effectively than other firms.'[11] Competitiveness is also a significant contributory factor in whether governments can attain their three other macroeconomic objectives:

- Full employment, this dependent upon there being sufficient demand for labour to absorb potential labour supply, with the demand for labour in turn a function of the level of aggregate demand for goods/services and of firms being sufficiently competitive to maintain/expand their output and thus employment.

- Price stability, this requiring mechanisms that generate co-operative bargains between workers and employers in terms of sustainable real wage growth (based on achieved productivity performance) and the share of profits in GDP needed to maintain high investment levels.

- Equilibrium in the balance of payments, this requiring that British firms be sufficiently competitive that export growth at least matches import growth at the target level of unemployment.

Table 2.5 Measures of competitiveness (%), selected years, 1950–97

	1950	1973	1979	1992	1997
A. Share of world manufactured exports	25.4	9.1	9.1	7.9	..
B. Share of foreign patents in US	36.0	12.6	10.8	7.5	7.7
C. R&D as % of GDP	1.7	2.2	2.1	2.2	2.0
D. Gross domestic fixed capital formation as % of GDP	14.9	18.3	19.4	17.3	17.1
E. 18 year olds with 2 or more 'A' levels	5.0	13.0	13.0	20.0	24.8
F. TFP growth in business sector[a]	..	2.8	0.7	0.6	1.2
G. Share of US-Japanese investment in EU	..	..	..	41.8	..
H. Long-term unemployed as % of total unemployed	..	..	28.8	35.7	38.6
I. Total taxes on corporate income as % of GDP[b]	..	2.8	2.6	2.5	3.8

Notes:
[a] 1973 = 1960–73; 1979 = 1973–9; and 1997 = 1979–97
[b] Estimates are for 1993 and 1996, not 1992 and 1997.
Sources:
(A)–(F): Crafts, 'The British economy', table 1.2 and more recent issues of sources cited;
(G): OECD, *International Direct Investment Statistics Yearbook* (Paris, 1996), pp. 164, 280;
(H): Middleton, *Government versus the Market*, Table 10.10; OECD, *Main Economic Indicators*, October 1993 and October 1998;
(I): 1973–9: OECD, *Revenue Statistics, 1965–1981* (Paris, 1982), Table 12; 1993 and 1996: OECD, *Revenue Statistics, 1965–1997* (Paris, 1998), Table 12.

Some standard measures of competitiveness are reported in Table 2.5, with these broadly confirming our earlier conclusion that relative decline was most evident during the golden age and abated thereafter. These standard measures comprise diagnostics of the economy's *current* success in international competition (its share of world exports) and of its *future* competitive capability, this, in turn, a function of the economy's potential to achieve continued productivity growth through comparative *success* in innovative activity, skills formation and cost control. Much of the appeal of this concept is its focus on the supply-side of the economy and its obvious compatibility with the league table approach to national economic performance. Indeed, since 1980 the World Economic Forum has issued an annual world competitiveness report, while in Britain competitiveness has attracted so much attention that government white papers on the topic have been issued periodically since 1994 and the Blair government has held a series of well-publicised high-level Downing Street seminars, at which leading experts expounded on the extent and form of past competitive weaknesses and how these might be overcome to improve growth potential.[12]

Some economists, however, and most notably Paul Krugman,[13] are deeply sceptical of this approach because it misconceives the nature of international competition as a zero-sum game (a 'win-lose' struggle) in which countries, like firms, compete for world markets rather than recognising that the foundation of international trade is a positive-sum game, with mutual benefits for all in the form of improved products and larger markets. For Krugman, the portrayal of national economic performance as a study of rivalries is not only potentially misleading, but dangerous because it often underlies the case for protectionist measures which would destroy international trade. With world trade expanding at nearly one and a half times the rate of world output growth during the golden age, and comfortably ahead thereafter, the role of international trade as an engine of growth is indisputable.[14] However, the competitiveness concept, and the debate it has engendered, are particularly relevant to the British case as policy-makers have typically perceived economic performance in terms of country rivalries, and have made constant reference to aspects of other countries' national economic behaviour and institutions which are more growth-promoting or at least less growth-inhibiting.

Accordingly, the diagnostics in Table 2.5 are very relevant, if frequently misunderstood. For example, the charge has been, and continues to be made, that much of British economic underperformance stems from weaknesses in its educational system. These need careful specification: first, distinguishing between education and vocational training; and, second, between the elite end of the education system and that serving the lower half of the ability range. Thus, in terms of 'A' levels and degrees, Britain does not now compare unfavourably to many competitors (the US included), but there are definite problems with the volume and quality of provision for vocational training, especially apprenticeships, and with the numeracy and literacy attained by the educationally less able. We can predict with some confidence that problems here have all lowered the human capital of the British workforce below potential and impacted adversely on the levels of productivity that can be attained with any given technology.[15] Research and development expenditures (R&D) are another indicator which is often misunderstood. British R&D levels were much higher after the war than before and, indeed, second only to the US as a share of GDP. But serious questions need to be asked about the effectiveness of much British R&D, and in particular of the consequences of it being dominated by government-financed military projects, which absorbed a substantial portion of the scientific and engineering community and had very limited spin-offs for the civilian economy.[16]

A range of diagnostics have been included in Table 2.5 to convey a sense of how the interpretation of competitiveness has evolved over the postwar period. Thus the share of inward investment is now seen as important, although the point is rarely made that throughout the postwar period, outward investment by British multinational companies exceeded routinely inward investment by other countries' multinationals.[17] Similarly, with the recent reaction against big government, high taxes are now seen as a clear disincentive to business activity, and yet taxes on corporate income are now higher than in 1973; indeed, total tax receipts are now a higher percentage of GDP than during the golden age.[18] Whilst we cannot provide estimates for all of our diagnostics for all of the years selected, we are able to show here no simple pattern of declining competitiveness before OPEC I and stabilisation thereafter. Moreover, the meaning of competitiveness and its significance depends upon the time horizon adopted. In the short-term a government may be able to improve international competitiveness, in the sense of lowering British costs relative to those of competitors, by devaluing the exchange rate. This should make British exports cheaper abroad, but imports more expensive at home, thereby improving the **balance of trade**. In the long-run, however, improved competitiveness depends upon securing productivity growth and this requires a mix of macro- and microeconomic policies which address deeply embedded features in the socioeconomic system, which are altogether more complex, which may take many years, if not decades, to yield benefits and which may produce unintended policy effects, for good or for bad.

From our cross-country knowledge of the growth process, we know that a country's international trade performance is both a cause and a consequence of its competitiveness. There is general agreement amongst economists that to sustain competitiveness requires improvements in long-term productivity performance, control of costs and attention to many aspects of national life which impact upon social capability. Weak competitiveness, however, can be shielded, both internally and externally, at least for a time. Indeed, one argument now being advanced forcefully by some economic historians is that low productivity during the golden age was a consequence of weak competitive pressures at home and the extent to which British firms were sheltered from the full force of competition in international trade, this being one consequence of Britain's delayed entry into the EEC (achieved in 1973 as against 1958 for the original member states). These arguments owe much to a view of British economic performance after 1979 as much improved because of the more rigorous enforcement of market disciplines on the private and public sectors, these the hallmark of the Thatcherite project, combined with globalisation and much more intense competition in international trade. Thus, Broadberry and Crafts, who initiated the most recent phase of this debate,[19] have argued that the postwar settlement of a managed-mixed economy in which the uncompetitive practices of both labour and capital were not confronted by governments – we discuss this more fully at pp. 71–2, 116, 118–19 – resulted in a suboptimal environment, in which British firms were not able to take full advantage of new technologies and working practices.

The culprits here are all long-standing components of the so-called

British disease: on the one hand, Britain's archaic industrial-relations system; on the other, poorly educated management within firms themselves operating in a weak competitive environment. These arguments will all be discussed later, but we introduce them here because it is important at this early stage to establish a central strand of the historical and current literature on the British economy: that economic underperformance was both long-standing and potentially remediable if different decisions had been taken right at the beginning of the postwar period. Moreover, these arguments combine weaknesses in both government and the market, another central theme in the literature. As we shall see, for both the political left and the right, the postwar settlement was flawed and with long-lasting results for the economy, as indeed for British politics.

The growth process has recently been likened to a mosaic, whereby there is no single vantage point that can encompass the full range of influences. However, whilst economists continue to disagree about important short-term issues such as the trade-off between unemployment and inflation, there is much fuller agreement about the necessary conditions – pro-education, pro-investment and pro-technology – if market economies are to deliver sustained long-term growth.[20] This leads us to highlight three particular characteristics of the postwar British economy which are potential problem areas: macroeconomic instability; low productivity; and poor incentive structures which weakened the means of remedying the productivity shortfall. We make a start on these by now examining the business cycle and then the other key economic trends of the postwar period.

2.2.2   The business cycle

One of the principal classes of explanations for Britain's slow growth has been that the incentive to invest was undermined by the amplitude and frequency of business cycles, these largely policy induced and known as Stop-Go. This view finds its fullest expression in Pollard's important book *The Wasting of the British Economy* (1984), in which he berates the Treasury for misplaced priorities, of finance above production, with consequent damage to Britain's real economy.

We represent the business cycle graphically in Figure 2.1 in terms of the variability of the annual growth rate of real GDP and the annual

Figure 2.1 Growth rate of real GDP and unemployment rate (%), 1948–97
Sources: Calculated from Appendix II Tables 1–2.

average unemployment rate. In both we detect a sharp break in the series which coincide with OPEC I, the first oil price shock. Before 1973 growth had fluctuated positively and there had never been a fall in GDP (although the 1957–8 recession came very close), while, by historical standards, cycles were of short duration (about four years peak-to-peak); similarly, unemployment had also been cyclical, but within very tight boundaries. After OPEC I the British economy experienced three serious recessions (1974–5, 1979–81 and 1990–2) and unemployment fluctuated much more sharply around a much higher average level. Indeed, during much of the 1980s and the early 1990s, the unemployment rate was much closer to the interwar average than to the levels seen during the golden age. In addition, of course, the average growth rate of GDP after 1973 was only two-thirds of that experienced during the golden age.

The British economy was thus much more unstable after 1973 than before. Moreover, and notwithstanding the Pollard thesis, there is strong evidence that during the golden age, the British economy was actually one of the most stable of the OECD. More successful economies thus experienced more pronounced business cycles (especially Japan), and there is no clear association between high growth and macroeconomic stability.[21] Similarly, there is no association between high growth and low-inflation economies, again with the Japanese case invalidating such simple propositions much favoured by politicians and other ideologues. Thus, although it did not appear so at the time, by historical standards, the British economy was exceptionally stable during the golden age. Conversely, after 1973 it has been exceptionally unstable, both relative to the golden age and to the general behaviour of the OECD economies.[22]

The Stop-Go thesis thus needs some modification, but is an adequate description for the course of the British economy for the whole of the period since the war. Cyclical movements were caused by changes in domestic demand at both the upper and lower turning-points, respectively the Stops and Goes of policy. Exports were, however, the most unstable element in aggregate demand. From panel B of Table 2.1 (p. 28), we can compare the average growth rates of the components of demand for each business cycle and for our two longer postwar phases, 1951–73 and 1973–97. In the former we observe that, as was characteristic of the golden age for all OECD countries, investment and international trade increased substantially, although we should note that throughout this period Britain experienced periodic balance of payments problems because – through weak competitiveness and other factors – export growth was insufficient to support a full-employment level of imports. We should also observe that during the golden age government expenditure, by this measure, increased significantly less than did GDP. This should make us wary of New Right arguments that big government was responsible for relative economic decline.

The investment boom of the golden age was not repeated after 1973, with the investment record particularly worrying during our transitional period 1973–9 and during the 1990s. In both of these sub-periods the British economy grew extremely slowly, and we should be wary with respect to the 1970s that we do not over-interpret this poor performance to portray this as the norm for the preceding period. Thus, it was part of the rhetoric of the Thatcher project that the dismal performance of the 1970s was the inevitable consequence of what came earlier rather than a period of special crisis, much of it to do with the oil shock and the breakdown in industrial relations that occurred under the Heath government of 1970–4.

2.2.3 The external account

It is the orthodoxy that before North Sea oil and gas came on stream in the late 1970s, Britain suffered from chronic balance of payments problems because of weak competitiveness and the authorities'

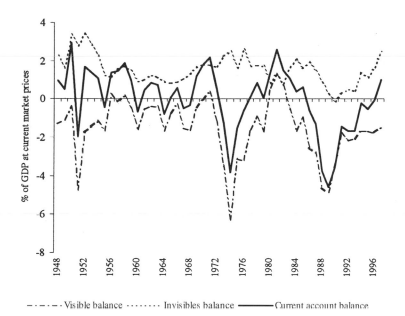

Figure 2.2 Current account balance of payments as a percentage of GDP, 1948–97
Sources: Calculated from Appendix II Tables 1, 3.

unwillingness before 1972 to manage the exchange rate more in line
with domestic economic capabilities rather than anachronistic notions
of sterling's global status and sustainable role. Certainly, the British
economy lurched from one balance of payments crises to another, but
what is cause and what is effect?

Figure 2.2 charts the **current account balance of payments** and its
two constituent elements: the balance on the visible trade account,
that is exports of goods less imports of goods, and the balance on
invisibles, namely exports of services less imports of services plus the
net balance on other items such as government expenditure overseas.
Britain has historically always run a deficit on its **visible trade balance**
which, typically, was more than compensated for by a surplus on the
invisible trade balance.[23] This reflected the pattern of its
industrialisation, its natural resource endowment and the structure
of its productive activities, whereby Britain was by the twentieth

Table 2.6 UK and comparators: distribution of employment by sector as a percentage of civilian employment, selected years, 1950–94

| | Germany | Japan | UK | US | Averages | | |
					EU	G-7	OECD
A. 1950[a]							
Agriculture	22.2	48.3	5.1	12.9	..	..	..
Industry[b]	43.0	22.6	44.9	33.6	..	..	..
Services	34.8	29.1	50.0	53.5	..	..	..
B. 1960							
Agriculture	14.0	30.2	4.7	8.5	21.3	17.3	21.6
Industry[b]	47.0	28.5	47.7	35.3	39.7	36.7	35.3
Services	39.1	41.3	47.6	56.2	39.0	46.0	43.1
C. 1974							
Agriculture	7.0	12.9	2.8	4.2	11.7	8.0	11.6
Industry[b]	46.7	37.0	42.0	32.5	40.4	37.1	36.2
Services	46.3	50.1	55.1	63.4	48.0	54.9	52.2
D. 1984							
Agriculture	4.8	8.9	2.6	3.3	8.7	5.7	8.9
Industry[b]	41.2	34.8	32.3	28.5	34.2	32.1	31.4
Services	54.1	56.3	65.1	68.2	57.1	62.2	59.7
E. 1994							
Agriculture	3.3	5.8	2.3	2.9	5.5	4.0	8.2
Industry[b]	37.6	34.0	24.1	24.0	30.1	28.4	27.5
Services	59.1	60.2	73.4	73.1	64.2	67.4	64.3

Notes:
[a] There are slight differences in the coverage of these sectors for 1950 as against 1960–94.
[b] Industry is defined as manufacturing plus construction and utilities.
Sources: Derived from Maddison, *Monitoring the World Economy*, Table 2.5; and OECD, *Historical Statistics*, Tables 2.9, 2.10, 2.12

century a nation with a small agricultural sector (necessitating substantial food imports), a medium-sized manufacturing sector (with a high propensity to import raw materials) and a comparatively large service sector (see Table 2.6), one element of which was the City of London whose trading activities (banking, finance, insurance and trade) produced significant net exports of services.

As with the business cycle, we observe a break in the series for the current account balance that coincides with OPEC I, although there has been no trend thereafter. Before 1973 the current account was on average in slight surplus, with deficits in years when the British economy was booming as domestic economic capacity was insufficient to meet demand, resulting in a surge in imports and the diversion to the domestic market of goods originally destined for overseas markets.

With the Stop-Go nature of policy, we observe that as the economy cooled and unemployment rose, import demand would fall off and the current account would return to slight surplus. There is general agreement that the balance of payments was a more pressing constraint in the 1960s than in the 1950s. However, throughout the golden age, and indeed beyond, balance of payments difficulties were magnified by two other forces: the first was that as a consequence of its perceived geopolitical status, Britain maintained a substantial military presence overseas until the late 1960s and this resulted in substantial government expenditures overseas, these equivalent in balance of payments terms to extra imports; and the second that as the postwar period progressed, British multinational companies increased their investments in overseas manufacturing capacity, this weakening the capital account of the balance of payments which, when combined with the very weak foreign exchange reserves position, often contributed to sterling crises.

As can be seen from Figure 2.2, the deterioration in the current account actually predates OPEC I and was, in fact, initiated by policy mistakes during the Heath government. After OPEC I we detect no trend: initially, there was an improvement which we associate with the heyday of North Sea oil and gas, although it should be noted that this also had a negative impact because it led to an appreciation of the sterling exchange rate which, together with other forces in operation stemming from the new Thatcherite policy regime, made British manufactured goods uncompetitive. Indeed, by the mid-1980s, and for the first time in more than a century, the balance of trade in manufactured goods was in deficit. The spectre of deindustrialisation (of a reduced share in total employment/output of the manufacturing sector) which had haunted policy-makers since the 1970s suddenly became very real, with these concerns most fully expressed in a widely debated, but alarmist House of Lords select committee report.[24]

Economists typically distinguish between positive and negative deindustrialisation: the former being a situation whereby the employment share is falling because a high rate of growth of manufacturing output is being outstripped by an even higher rate of growth of productivity; and the latter a situation whereby a low or even negative trend to output growth is exceeded by a mediocre productivity performance, resulting in a country growing relatively poorer compared with its competitors.[25] The background to both variants of the condition is that with economic maturity and affluence, consumers' expenditure is increasingly devoted not to food and manufactured goods, but towards services. Few doubted that Britain was experiencing the negative variant, but frequently the facts were not fully understood and there has been much misunderstanding about the relationship between deindustrialisation and the balance of payments. The share of employment in manufacturing had actually been falling since the 1960s with the trend more advanced than in the other large OECD economies, save the US (Table 2.6). This suggests that this structural shift is as much connected with economic maturity as with competitive weakness and, indeed, when the British case is compared with that of Germany and Japan, it is clear one reason why those economies were able to experience super growth in the 1950s and 1960s was because they had substantial scope to transfer resources from low productivity agriculture to manufacturing.

While the share of manufacturing output in GDP has also fallen, this is far less evident when GDP is measured at constant rather than at current prices, this indicative of the fact that, in common with other OECD economies, productivity growth in manufacturing has significantly exceeded that in services so that manufacturing prices fall more (rise less) than do services where more and more of consumers' expenditure is now being devoted. Moreover, the observation that manufactured imports were increasingly penetrating the British market is not decisive either: import penetration of manufactures has risen in all OECD states, as these economies increasingly trade manufactured goods between themselves on the basis of differing **comparative advantages**.[26]

While the view is now very deep-seated that enduring competitive weaknesses resulted in British deindustrialisation proceeding further than in other advanced economies, an alternative perspective is equally valid: that, in terms of structure, the British economy now more closely resembles the American than the European economies. Moreover, what should also be emphasised is that uniquely amongst the G-7 economies, Britain combined deindustrialisation with a falling proportion of its exports which were services over the period 1973 through to the early 1990s.[27] This suggests that competitive weaknesses affected both traded goods and services and, indeed, so far as internationally traded services are concerned, Britain has been losing world market share faster than in manufactures.[28] This is a very relevant consideration to put against what nearly became the orthodoxy in the City of London during the 1980s: that manufacturing no longer mattered because services would fill the gap. This argument was always suspect: there are limits to which services can be internationally traded; their employment-generation potential is far less than that of manufacturing; and, of course, to an important extent the service sector is servicing the needs of the manufacturing sector. Moreover, while concern about poor productivity performance in Britain focuses on manufacturing, the service sector ought also to be examined. As one recent survey commented: 'The once fashionable idea that the United Kingdom possesses a considerable comparative advantage [in services] is not really sustainable.'[29]

We conclude our treatment of the external account with a brief comment on the area and commodity composition of British trade, which has been quite transformed over the postwar period, and with a discussion of the price and non-price competitiveness of British exports. The background to our discussion here is fourfold:

1. The central role that the expansion of world trade (particularly in manufactured goods) played in the postwar growth of all of the OECD economies, with all as a consequence becoming more open – that is having a higher ratio of exports to GDP (the British figures were 18.6 per cent in 1948 rising to 28.5 per cent in 1997);
2. The exceptionally slow growth of British exports relative to other OECD economies, and particularly during the golden age when world trade was growing at an unprecedented rate; and hence
3. Since the end of the Second World War Britain has experienced a declining share of world trade, this particularly so during the 1950s and 1960s (Table 2.5); and that
4. For many historians, the difficulties experienced by Britain during the interwar period were because the structure of its export trade was biased towards goods and markets which were slow growing. Deficient postwar performance might then be a legacy of past trading relationships and economic structures.

The structure of Britain's visible exports and imports over the past 60 years (see Table 2.7, p. 48) may then hold the key to understanding poor trade performance and, from this, national economic underperformance. Looking first at the area composition, we see the

Table 2.7 Area and commodity composition of British exports and imports of goods (% of total), selected years, 1938–96

	Exports								Imports							
	1938	1952	1954	1956	1968	1978	1988	1996	1938	1952	1954	1956	1968	1978	1988	1997
A. Area composition:																
US	5.4	6.7	..	7.8	14.2	9.3	13.3	11.8	12.9	9.2	..	10.5	13.5	10.3	10.3	12.3
Canada	4.4	4.9	..	5.5	4.2	2.0	2.5	1.2	8.6	9.2	..	8.9	6.5	2.7	2.0	1.3
Latin America	8.7	7.8	..	7.0	3.6	2.5	1.4	2.0	11.4	7.7	..	9.8	4.0	1.9	1.4	1.9
Europe	41.8	33.3	..	35.7	46.2	55.7	61.5	64.5	34.0	30.6	..	31.9	43.7	60.7	68.2	63.9
of which original EC-6 states							39.5	40.5							44.1	41.5
Japan	0.4	0.3	..	0.7	1.5	1.5	2.1	2.6	1.0	0.8	..	0.6	1.5	3.1	5.9	4.8
Other	39.3	47.1	..	43.4	30.1	29.0	19.1	17.9	32.2	42.6	..	38.4	30.8	21.3	12.2	15.8
Total	100.0	100.0	..	100.0	100.0	100.0	100.0	100.0	100.0	100.0	..	100.0	100.0	100.0	100.0	100.0
B. Commodity composition:																
Food, beverages & tobacco	8.0	..	6.0	..	7.0	8.0	6.8	6.8	49.0	..	40.0	..	24.0	15.0	9.8	9.3
Raw materials and oil	14.0	..	11.0	..	6.0	9.0	10.4	8.3	30.8	..	41.0	..	27.0	20.0	10.0	7.3
Finished & semi-finished manufactured goods, *of which*																
Metals	11.5	11.0	12.0	..	12.0	8.0	..	..	5.4	..	..	..	..	..	..	..
Machinery	15.2	21.0	22.0	..	27.0	25.0	..	..	2.7	..	..	..	..	..	..	..
Vehicles	8.8	18.0	15.0	..	14.0	12.0	2.5	5.1	0.5	..	..	..	..	..	6.4	6.2
Chemicals	4.6	15.0	13.0	..	5.0	3.0	14.1	13.3	1.5	..	..	..	..	..	8.8	10.1
Textiles	21.7	5.0	5.0	..	9.0	11.0	..	..	2.7	..	..	..	..	..	..	..
Miscellaneous	14.2	14.0	14.0	..	17.0	21.0	..	..	7.0	..	..	..	..	..	..	..
Total	76.1	84.0	80.0	..	84.0	80.0	80.4	83.7	20.0	..	19.0	..	48.0	64.0	78.4	82.4
Unspecified	2.3	..	3.0	..	3.0	3.0	2.5	1.2	0.5	..	0.0	..	1.0	1.0	1.8	1.0
Total	100.0	..	100.0	..	100.0	100.0	100.0	100.0	100.0	..	100.0	..	100.0	100.0	100.0	100.0

Sources: 1938–78: derived from A. K. Cairncross and B. J. Eichengreen, *Sterling in Decline: The devaluations of 1931, 1949 and 1967* (Oxford, 1983) Tables 2.1–2.3; 1988 and 1996: ONS, *United Kingdom Balance of Payments*, 1997 edn, Tables 2.1, 6.4, 6.5.

growing importance of the Continental European market, and in particular those countries now comprising the EU. The question naturally arises what might have been the trend had Britain been a founding member of the EEC, with most commentators agreed that during the 1960s, Britain lost more market share than it would have done if trade had not been so focused on non-EEC countries which had below average growth rates or were pursuing import-substitution policies (such as many of the newly independent ex-British colonies). Some have even argued that as a consequence of structural change in British industry during the war years,[30] which created a new comparative advantage in technically advanced sectors such as aircraft, electronics and vehicles, that Britain was exceptionally placed at the beginning of the postwar period to prosper in international markets. The most significant explanation for why it did not was because of competitive weaknesses, both price and non-price.[31] However, as Foreman-Peck argues: 'It is easier to identify the symptoms than the causes of the British loss of competitiveness, but even that is by no means simple.' Competitiveness problems imply that British prices rose relative to the rest of the world, implying problems of domestic cost control and/or an exchange rate which did not depreciate in line with this characteristic of Britain's situation. The devaluation of 1967 undoubtedly helped in the short-run, but problems of competitiveness returned in the 1970s, even after sterling was floated in 1972 so that ostensibly the exchange rate was no longer a constraint. The deterioration of Britain's quality competitiveness has also been widely noted, with long waiting-times for British goods leading to foreign customers looking elsewhere for supplies, and a failure to improve the quality of manufactured goods in line with competitors. As a consequence not only was export growth below average for much of the postwar period, but beginning in the 1960s, British manufacturers were no longer able to dominate the home market as weak competitiveness resulted in rising import penetration. This inability of British goods to compete at home and abroad brings us back to the heart of the debate about Britain's economic performance, that of low productivity and low productivity growth.

2.2.4 *The labour market and prices*

We chart in Figure 2.3 the unemployment rate. We do so since records

Figure 2.3 Administrative unemployment rates (%), 1881–1997
Source: Derived from J. Denman and P. McDonald, 'Unemployment statistics from
1881 to the present day'; *Labour Market Trends*, 104 (January 1996), tables 1–2;
1996–7: *Labour Market Trends*; ONS, *Retail Prices Index – April 1998*, Table 14.

began in 1881 because a long-run context is vital here, and we use the
administrative unemployment rate because, in the first instance, our
focus is on how contemporaries measured and thus assessed
unemployment's significance. Accordingly, the behaviour of the
unemployment rate here reflects changes both in the pressure of
demand in the labour market and in how unemployment is measured
for administrative purposes, typically in Britain as a by-product of
the administration of the unemployment insurance system (now known
as job-seekers allowance).

The first salient fact about postwar unemployment is that during
the golden age it dropped to negligible proportions relative to any
other period before or since. None the less, for at least the first
generation of postwar economic managers and politicians, it was
interwar unemployment that was the searing influence and this made
them extremely sensitive to this issue, thereby ensuring that the 'Go'
phase of the cycle would always come before unemployment had risen
much above 2 per cent in the 1950s and 2.5 per cent in the 1960s.
Unemployment actually started to rise on trend before OPEC I and,
of course, rose massively after 1979 as the Thatcher government
became, in effect, the first administration willing to sacrifice
employment to discipline the labour force to lower inflation. We chart
in Figures 2.4 and 2.5 respectively the headline inflation rate (the
RPI, the retail price index) and the consequences of sustained inflation
over the century for the reduction in the purchasing power of a 1914

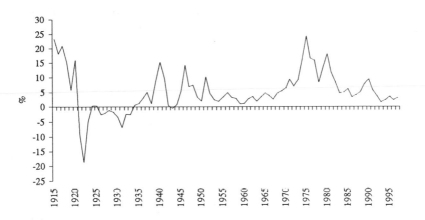

Figure 2.4 Annual change in RPI (%), 1915–97
Source: ONS, *Retail Prices Index – April 1998*, Table 14.

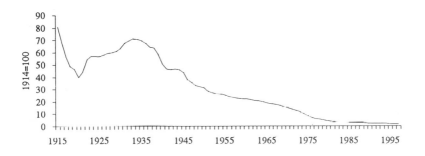

Figure 2.5 Index (1914 = 100) of purchasing power of pound, 1915–97
Source: ONS, *Retail Prices Index – April 1998*, Table 14.

pound (now worth less than 2p).

It is important that the trend of prices between the wars was downwards for this puts postwar experience in sharp relief. However, and as with unemployment, inflation only starts to move up from the late 1960s onwards so that during the 1940s, 1950s and most of the 1960s, the inflation rate was low – typically about 3 per cent – and indeed moderate inflation was deemed to *promote* economic growth. The average inflation rate then moved up to 13 per cent in the 1970s (peak of 24.2 per cent in 1975), before falling in the 1980s (average 7.4 per cent, peak 18 per cent in 1980) and again in the 1990s (averaging 4 per cent). Even before the current world recession economists were talking about the death of inflation,[32] and so, as a policy problem, it seems confined to the period *c*. 1965–90 and to quite particular global circumstances.

It is none the less the orthodoxy that for most of the postwar period, Britain has been considered a particularly inflation-prone economy and that before the 1979 policy shift, one of the defining characteristics of the British labour market had also been a very poor industrial relations record, which was manifest, visibly, in strikes and other forms of industrial protest and, less visibly, in low productivity as managers were unable to introduce new technologies and workplace organisation as they would have wished.[33] The comparative inflation record was reported in Table 2.4 (p. 34). This confirms that consumer prices did on average rise faster than against most comparators. Moreover, and potentially damaging for high growth, there is strong evidence that the amplitude of fluctuations in the inflation rate was significantly higher than in competitor countries, that is inflation itself was unstable and therefore unpredictable. For most economists, a number of implications (welfare costs) follow from the volatility of inflation, of which we highlight two as particularly relevant to the British case:[34]

1. Unanticipated inflation causes distortions in the allocation of resources because economic agents make mistakes in, for example, wage bargaining and investment appraisal, while taxation systems magnify these problems through their affects on incentives and relative prices; and
2. Inflation generates political conflict, especially if governments attempt to lessen inflationary pressures by prices and incomes policies.

The act of reducing inflation, however, is not costless for economically it invariably results in lost output and higher unemployment, with obvious consequent political ramifications. Moreover, the British inflationary record is not that dissimilar from the experience of some of the high growth OECD states (e.g. France, Italy and Japan). The lack of British exceptionalism applies also to industrial relations. While the statistics in this field are particularly difficult to interpret, academic – as against political – appraisals of the evidence have not found postwar Britain to be more strike-prone than its competitors, although its record was particularly and unusually bad in the early 1970s, when trade unions and industrial relations became uncommonly politicised and there was an exceptionally high number of disputes in one sector which has always been strike-prone (mining).[35] As Metcalf and Milner have argued:[36]

> Memories of the 1970s cloud much of the comment about the decline of industrial action in the 1980s, but the data suggest that it was the 1970s that was the peculiar decade, whereas the 1980s simply saw a return to the underlying trend of strike activity apparent since 1930.

Throughout the postwar period the greater part of British workplaces have been quite unaffected by strikes, but those that have been affected have been so very badly. In addition to mining, strike-prone sectors included iron and steel and shipbuilding, and, of course, motor car manufacturing where there were very particular problems associated with large-scale mass production and worker alienation combined with weak and inefficient management.[37] We reject absolutely then this crude version of the British disease, although we will return later to industrial relations problems and their impact on productivity. We complete this section with two further short discussions of important labour market characteristics.

First, we have the problem of regional unemployment whereby the outer regions have since the late 1950s experienced significantly above average unemployment rates, while London, the south-east and, at least during the golden age, the Midlands have been areas of well below average unemployment (see Table 2.8, p. 54). Although these spatial variations invoke memories of the mass unemployment of the outer regions between the wars, Britain's postwar regional problem has been somewhat different in character.[38] There is a similarity with respect to the decline of the staple industries (coal, cotton textiles, iron and steel and shipbuilding) and the problems created for the outer regions which, unable to generate or attract new employment, had by the late 1970s become some of the most depressed areas in the EU. These problems, however, need to be viewed in the context of the national and natural process of deindustrialisation, with its concomitant rise of the service sector; the trend towards new employment not in the cities, but in smaller towns and rural areas; the effects of Britain's EC entry; and the consequences of inward investment by foreign multinationals, which has led to new productive centres as, for example, in the renaissance of British car production in Japanese-owned plants in Swindon and Washington, Tyneside.

Table 2.8 UK regional unemployment rates (%), selected years, 1948–97[a, b]

	1948	1951	1964	1973	1979	1990	1997
London and south-east	1.0	0.9	1.0	1.3	2.9	4.0	3.5
East Anglia	1.0	0.9	1.0	1.6	3.7	3.7	4.2
South-west	1.4	1.2	1.5	2.1	4.6	4.4	4.4
West Midlands	0.6	0.4	0.9	1.7	4.7	5.9	5.5
East Midlands	0.7	0.7	1.1	1.8	3.8	5.1	5.0
Yorkshire and Humberside	0.7	0.7	1.1	2.3	4.7	6.7	6.5
North-west	1.9	1.2	2.1	2.9	5.9	7.7	5.1
North	2.6	2.2	3.3	3.9	7.3	8.7	8.4
Wales	4.3	2.7	2.6	3.0	6.3	6.7	6.4
Scotland	2.8	2.5	3.6	3.8	6.8	8.2	6.5
Northern Ireland	5.8	6.1	6.6	4.9	9.7	13.4	8.3
UK	1.6	1.3	1.7	2.0	4.7	5.8	5.6

Notes:
[a] Between the initial and terminal years the boundaries of most of these regions changed slightly.
[b] Between the initial and terminal years the definition of unemployment in relation to the workforce was subject to numerous administrative changes.
Sources: Middleton, *Government versus the Market*, tables 7.7, 10.10; Department of Employment, *Employment Gazette*, 99 (May 1991), Tables, 2.1, 2.3; and Department of Employment and Education, *Labour Market Trends*, 107 (January 1999), Table A.

Secondly, we need to comment on the changing structure of the employed population.[39] Looking first at the workforce, that is those in employment plus those unemployed,[40] the official statistics reveal a much lower rate of growth than that prevailing between the wars. Between 1950 and 1997 the workforce grew on average at just 0.3 per cent per annum, while the annual average growth rate for the workforce in employment was only 0.2 per cent. The gap between employment growth and the growth of potential labour supply is, of course, partially explained by the numbers unemployed being nearly six times higher in 1997 than 1950, but in addition there was a widening gap between total employment and the growth of employees in employment, as a significant expansion occurred in self-employment and second jobs, particularly over the last 15 years or so.[41] Indeed, in terms of employees in employment the numbers peaked in 1979, and thereafter have been on a downward, but highly cyclical path, with the 1997 figure equivalent to that last reached in 1964. Moreover, the nature of these jobs has changed: full-time jobs for men have contracted whilst part-time jobs for women have expanded, and in addition to the growth in the self-employed, there has been an expansion in those holding two or more jobs. The settled, largely industrial, male labour force of the immediate postwar years has thus given way to a much more fluid, mixed gender and flexible employment pattern.

At the aggregate level, therefore, there has been almost no employment growth in the British economy for nearly 40 years. Moreover, with the Thatcherite project of containing government growth and the effects of deindustrialisation, there have been very significant shifts in the occupational distribution of those who are employed.[42] We have, first, the public-private sector divide. In 1950 some 24.3 per cent of the workforce in employment were within the public sector, with the nationalised industries taking 40 per cent of this public sector share; by 1979, the overall public sector share had risen to 27.9 per cent, but with the nationalised industries contracted to less than 30 per cent of this share (see also Figure III.7, p. 166).[43] After 18 years of privatisations and public sector contraction and restructuring, the public sector share had by 1997 fallen to less than 20 per cent, and with the nationalised industries barely 7 per cent of this figure. We have then a transformation of the public sector: a withering away of its market and non-market provision of goods (the nationalised industries) and a concentration on non-market services (defence and general government), the traditional functions of the pre-First World War British state. Even so, the NHS remains Britain's – indeed Europe's – largest employer at about 1.1 million workers, that is almost one in twenty of employees in employment.[44]

Secondly, within both the diminished manufacturing sector and the much enlarged service sector there have been important compositional changes.[45] We report in Table 2.9 some post-golden age estimates that reveal which sectors have been expanding and which contracting in terms of value added, the labour input (adjusted for hours worked) and labour productivity. As is clear, manufacturing is now far less dominated by heavy industry, and is focused on much more technical products such as computing, pharmaceuticals, aerospace and electronics. We should note also that high value-added is associated with high labour productivity growth and that every single sector reported negative growth in its labour input (again measured in hours worked).

The service sector has also been transformed. It now supplies

Table 2.9 UK manufacturing: value-added and labour productivity (percentage rates of growth), 1970–92

	Value-added	Labour input	Y/L[a]
Total manufacturing	**(0.18)**	**(3.41)**	**3.23**
Computing	7.62	(1.77)	9.39
Pharmaceuticals	4.72	(1.61)	6.33
Aerospace	2.58	(2.03)	4.61
Instruments	2.16	(2.36)	4.52
Electronics	1.91	(3.29)	5.20
Chemicals	1.40	(2.22)	3.62
Rubber & plastics	1.24	(1.59)	2.84
Paper & printing	0.88	(2.15)	3.03
Electrical machinery	0.80	(3.51)	4.32
Chemicals nes	0.31	(2.96)	3.27
Fabricated metal	(0.01)	(3.65)	3.64
Food & drink	(0.23)	(2.35)	2.12
Other electrical	(0.31)	(3.71)	3.39
Timber & furniture	(0.71)	(2.49)	1.79
Metal goods nes	(1.01)	(3.79)	2.78
Motor vehicles	(1.22)	(3.71)	2.48
Other manufacturing	(1.38)	(3.92)	2.54
Textiles & clothing	(1.49)	(4.45)	2.96
Machinery	(1.54)	(4.01)	2.47
Non-ferrous metals	(1.93)	(4.80)	2.87
Minerals	(2.33)	(3.71)	1.39
Basic metal	(3.60)	(6.72)	3.11
Iron & steel	(4.20)	(7.41)	3.22

Note: [a] Labour productivity.
Source: G. Cameron, J. Proudman and S. Redding, 'Deconstructing growth in UK manufacturing', *Bank of England Working Paper*, no. 73, Table A.

nearly 70 per cent of GDP as against 53 per cent in 1970, and over the period 1970–97 its output grew at an annual average of 2.6 per cent, whereas manufacturing output growth averaged only 0.7 per cent.[46] It is also within services that women workers are heavily concentrated and outnumber male workers. There has been a contraction in employment in the traditional services such as the utilities (electricity, gas and water) and transport and communications, with moderate growth in the distributive trades and more rapid growth in the following: business services and finance; hotels, catering and entertainment; and the welfare services of education and health. However, the demarcation between manufacturing and service sector jobs is rather imprecise, with many employed in what are classified as the former sector actually performing service-sector type functions. The rise of the service economy has thus proceeded further than the raw numbers imply, and with all of this set against a background of profound shifts in consumers' expenditure, household and work organisation and personal lifestyles. In short, in terms of production and consumption (the ultimate objective of economic activity),[47] the British economy of the late twentieth century is hardly recognisable in terms of the structures and personal expectations of the early postwar years. One rather stunning statistic encapsulates the transformation: there are now more persons employed in Indian restaurants than in coal mining and iron and steel added together.

2.3 Explaining economic underperformance: a British disease?

Having established that during the golden age the British economy underperformed by somewhere between 0.5 and 1 per cent per year in terms of economic growth, and by rather less thereafter, we now need to examine the various classes of explanation that feature in the enormous literature on what constrained British productivity levels from matching those of competitors. We need first to draw a very sharp distinction between academic interpretations of economic underperformance and more popular/political interpretations. As Warwick put it:[48]

> What is clear is that the most general consensus is a negative one: it holds that the causal factors favoured among the general public and the world of popular journalism – the burdens of the welfare state, the recalcitrance of the trade unions, the high rates of taxation, the low levels of domestic investment – are erroneous or inadequate in themselves. But from this point, the paths to truth are multitudinous and diverse.

Secondly, the issue of timing is critical. Those who have tended to implicate government as the root cause of Britain's relative decline have concentrated on postwar economic policies,[49] while those who look further back have tended towards forces more deeply rooted in Britain's social and political structure. Only very recently have economic historians focused upon the state within a longer time perspective.[50] In addition, of course, the dominant view is now that, while relative decline began in the late nineteenth century, much of the early slippage is explicable in terms of the catch-up and convergence framework. In what follows we distinguish between three broad classes of explanation: those emphasising economic characteristics and explanations; those which focus on sociocultural explanations; and those which give prominence to political forces and economic policies. We outline each in turn, although the last class is treated more fully in Chapters 3 and 4.[51]

Economic explanations start from the premise that the British economy does not deploy its resources as effectively as its competitors, with the spotlight then focused on a variety of failures: in following best practice in the methods and materials of production; in innovation; in the inadequate levels of R&D and investment; in the inability to capitalise upon inventions to utilise the fruits of technical and scientific progress; in work organisation, with both management and shop-floor implicated; in price and non-price uncompetitiveness; and in undue reliance upon soft markets as a consequence of empire. The common threads throughout these arguments are those of widespread market failure; the fact that few of these explanations are amenable to quantitative evaluation; that many are ripe for ideological exploitation; and that there exists a strong possibility that cause and effect are being confused. For example, Britain's low rate of physical investment is long-standing, but is it a cause or a consequence of slow economic growth?[52]

The second class of explanations also encompass a myriad of possible contributory factors – from the nation's culture to elite attitudes – but share a common strand in maintaining that there is something distinctive about Britain's culture which is economically dysfunctional. This class forms the basis of the more popular accounts of Britain's economic failure, being particularly prominent in the 1980s because of the then Western belief that it was cultural factors that underlay much of the then spectacular economic success of Japan and other Asian economies.[53] Unfortunately, this class is also not amenable to quantitative assessment. It also suffers from the heuristic problem that 'Unless they can account for the origins of national attitudes by reference to the institutions that generate and reproduce them, they do little more than summon up a *deus ex machina* that is itself unexplainable and thus somewhat suspect.'[54]

Sociocultural explanations have thus typically been somewhat vague about the mechanisms through which cultural norms are translated into suboptimal business decision-making and often unaware that in other 'more successful' countries there are parallel literatures which emphasise cultural malaise. None the less, a number of potential problem areas have been extensively explored in the British literature. These include the cult of the amateur and the bias against practical skills, with consequences for the quality of the civil service and the status of engineers and technicians; a bias against industry because of a prevailing ethos of gentlemanly capitalism which weakened the quality and quantity of entre-preneurship; the hegemonic power of the City of London and the consequent domination of finance over manufacturing capital; the divisiveness of Britain's class structure, which impacted upon industrial relations and attitudes towards the market and education; and the widely-shared, but largely incorrect view that Britain had above average income and wealth inequalities and below average social mobility.

The third class of explanations comprise longer-term political forces and shorter-term issues of economic management. The principal focus of attention for the former has been Britain's global status, both real and as perceived by domestic political elites. Empire is now seen as having involved substantial welfare losses for the British economy, while the postwar great power delusion resulted in a defence effort beyond domestic economic capacity, which had serious implications for the balance of payments, exchange rate stability and national macroeconomic policies. Secondly, there exist long-running complaints of the British economy being handicapped by either too much or too little government. Thirdly, certain recurrent themes in British industrial policies have been identified, namely that the needs of short-term economic management and the amelioration of the social distress occasioned by structural changes in Britain's productive base have had a much higher priority than the promotion of long-run structural adjustments. As Mottershead says of the 1960–74 period, 'governments have intervened against market forces, rather than trying to improve the functioning of the market', with industrial policy 'limited to a peripheral role of tidying up at the edges of the economy, rather than providing any central thrust to alter and improve industry's performance and that of the economy as a whole.'[55] Fourthly, as we shall see in Chapters 3 and 4, the broader record of British economic management remains acutely controversial, with the literature replete with examples of inappropriate policy choices, forecasting errors, unintended policy effects and misguided policy objectives and instruments. Underlying these explanations is a view that government evolved in a manner in Britain which was unsuited to the economic management challenges of the postwar world: that Britain suffered from institutional sclerosis. This, O'Brien observes, 'has now replaced entrepreneurial failure as the centre of modern historiography concerned with the origins of long-term decline of the British economy.'[56] As political forces and economic management have become entwined this century, explanations of Britain's decline which appeal to political and institutional forces have necessarily become more pressing.

These three classes of explanation of Britain's economic failure all share one common strand of thought: that 'something in the organisation and operation of Britain's economy and society was fatally flawed.'[57] Whether this is a British disease, as some such as Allen have contended,[58] has now been encompassed within the debate about whether the Thatcherite project remedied whatever was distinctive about Britain's economic problems and thereby facilitated an economic renaissance. This presents a major problem of historical perspective: policies attempted in the 1980s and 1990s in reaction to perceived problems of longer-standing may not actually have been appropriate for the golden age years, let alone politically possible. What we attempt here, therefore, is to try and distinguish what was and, in certain cases, still is distinctive about the British case and what is frequently misunderstood about Britain's economic underperformance. In the process we come closer to the ultimate and fundamental causes of slow growth.

We first mention the Broadberry thesis, which is based upon a detailed cross-country and long-term evaluation of Britain's overall economic performance and of its manufacturing sector.[59] This yields the important conclusion that Germany and the US caught up on the British economy at the aggregate level not because of an emerging productivity lead in manufacturing, but by shifting resources out of agriculture and improving their relative productivity position in services. In other words, the US and, to a lesser extent, Germany had long-standing productivity advantages in manufacturing over Britain. Indeed, argues Broadberry, comparative productivity levels in manufacturing have been remarkably stable over the past 150 years or so. From this follows the important implication that to study Britain's long-run relative decline, one must examine why Britain experienced a loss of productivity leadership in services. This view does not dismiss problems with the manufacturing sector, problems which might have been remedied to close the aggregate productivity gap with the US and Germany, but it does refocus the debate on the service sector about which we know far less.[60]

We, second, identify a particular disadvantage long suffered by British manufacturing, but which proved particularly costly during the era, often labelled Fordism (lasting from c. 1920s–c. 1970s), when the dominant mode of manufacturing was characterised by automated production processes, mass production of ranges of relatively standardised products, the minute division of labour and all within the context of very large plants and supporting corporate bureaucracies. Three different types of studies provide insights here into the Britain's quite distinctive economic problem:

1. We have evidence of the concentration of strike activity and other industrial relations problems in a few key sectors, and within even these few plants, with these a consequence not of some broader British disease, but of local and particular circumstances to do with large-scale production and certain heavy industries.[61]

2. There is compelling evidence that in these key sectors, as elsewhere in British manufacturing, for production to be efficient it had to be on a large scale, but large plants are more strike-prone and thus many British firms were unable to attain the absolute productivity levels achieved by their competitors.[62]

3. There are a number of studies of the labour process in these 'problem' sectors, of how and why managers and shop-floor workers were unable to generate co-operative and mutually beneficial bargains about work patterns and new technologies, and how as a consequence American technology and production organisation could not be fully implemented to close the productivity gap.[63]

Some quantitative indication of the factors underlying the productivity gap are given in Table 2.10. These data derive from cross-country comparisons of productivity performance at the industry level and thus attempt, so far as is possible, to compare like-with-like in order to reveal the scope and scale of

Table 2.10 Estimates for 1967/8 and 1972 of the potential benefits had British manufacturing adopted best practice standards

**A. Predicted improvements in net output/head
from achieving best practice standards
throughout British manufacturing, 1967/8 (%)**

Eliminating capital shortfall	9.1
Removing sub-standard educational background of workforce	8.5
No adverse trade union problems	6.7
Correcting plant size	5.5
Making good R&D shortfall	4.7

B. Labour productivity comparisons in international companies: reasons for productivity differential, 1972	French advantage over UK (%)	German advantage over UK (%)	North American advantage over UK (%)
1. 'Economic' causes:			
Length of production run	1.5	5.5	20.5
Plant and machinery	5.0	5.0	6.0
Other[a]	2.0	2.0	6.0
2. 'Behavioural' causes:			
Strikes and restrictive practices	0.0	3.5	5.0
Manning and efficiency	5.5	8.5	6.0
Total differential[b]	15.0	27.0	50.0

Notes:
[a] Includes differences in product mix, capacity utilisation and quality of materials.
[b] The contributions to the total differential are multiplicative and not additive.
Sources: N. F. R. Crafts, 'Economic growth', in Crafts and Woodward, eds, *The British Economy*, Tables 9.7–9.8; S. W. Davies and R. E. Caves, *Britain's Productivity Gap* (Cambridge, 1987), Table 7.4; and C. F. Pratten, *Labour Productivity Differentials within International Companies* (Cambridge, 1976), Table 9.1.

underperformance. The results are revealing. The most important factors underlying the UK productivity lag were that British firms were trying to operate large plants, but failing to get the full advantage from them; workers were less educated, more highly unionised and bellicose than their American counterparts; managers had invested less capital per worker and were less committed to R&D. Clearly, the larger size of the North American market gave their firms a big advantage over their European counterparts, but these findings show that beyond that constraint, there were very significant behavioural, and thus potentially controllable, forces which impacted to the disadvantage of British firms.

The problems of British industry, however, can be taken too far. The historical literature is preoccupied with the failings of industry and rarely concerns itself with those sectors which achieved best standards and produced world-class companies, and why they were able to do so: it is as if British business history was British Leyland rather than GEC, ICI, BP or Cadbury Schweppes.[64] Moreover, in assessing the behavioural factors in Table 2.10, the point must be kept to the fore that the late 1960s and 1970s were a particularly disturbed era in industrial relations, one explicable as much in political as in economic terms.

The third distinctive element we identify in the British case concerns the role of the City of London and of problems associated with the financing of industry. Two main strands are stressed in the literature. The first concerns the influence that the City has supposedly long exercised in British economic policy with the consequence that macroeconomic policies have been unhelpful to the real economy.[65] The second relates to a complex of concerns: that British financial institutions do not adequately support and finance companies; and that with the decline of personal capitalism, British companies have become unduly affected by their institutional shareholders and as a consequence more risk averse and short-termist in their business strategy, thereby impacting negatively on investment and R&D. At the heart of both sets of concerns is whether there exists a dissonance between the interests and priorities of the City and those of domestic industry. This is very much an ongoing debate, not least because the very nature of the City and its diverse activities makes it an intractable subject for study, whilst its influence through personal-political networks is rarely made visible. This said, however, and like much else to do with the declinist literature, academics have tended to be less convinced of the City's sins than have less expert and, particularly, political opinions.[66] Even so, City institutions, and the weight of the financial services sector, have a prominence in British economic and political life which is neither matched in Europe nor North America.

Fourthly, and finally, we introduce a strand to the literature which has become known as the institutional rigidity school. This is particularly associated with a volume on Britain's decline which was edited by two American economic historians in the 1980s and which has since been much debated.[67] Strictly speaking, this is not really a school, more an approach to the problem of decline which emphasises and explores how past choices influence future possibilities. It is thus a variant of the early start hypothesis, but one that offers fresh supply-side insights into the complexity of relative decline and the conditions necessary for Britain to become a high growth economy. We start with Elbaum and Lazonick's contention that:[68]

> Britain's distinctiveness derived less from the conservatism of its cultural values *per se* than from a matrix of rigid institutional structures that reinforce these values and obstructed individualistic as well as collective efforts at economic renovation.

For Elbaum and Lazonick, as for others such as Hall, too much of the literature sees economic decline as somehow exogenous to the economy, as the problem laying with interference in 'the operation of British markets rather than [in] the nature of those markets themselves'.[69] Accordingly, such writers bring us back to how markets actually operated, why they were prone to failure and how government might have improved their operation by overcoming institutional resistances to modernisation. It also allows traditional problem areas, such as labour relations and low investment in physical and human capital, to be reinvestigated in terms of deficient incentive and penalty structures which affect the efficiency of labour, capital and goods markets.

Deficiencies in British business organisation and weak control over the labour process have, unsurprisingly, become the focus of much of this work. But such arguments are vulnerable to the counter-argument that there were demand-side reasons why new technologies were not introduced and full economies of scale unrealised, for these can, in certain circumstances, be seen to be rational responses to the real constraints on mass consumer demand of heterogeneous tastes and an unequal income distribution. Moreover, in much of these institutional arguments there is an implicit *dirigiste* counterfactual which is also vulnerable. From what we now know about government failure throughout the twentieth century, in both micro- and macroeconomic policies, it does not necessarily follow that if the British state intervened more forcefully to lessen institutional rigidities, the resultant failings of government would have been less than the prior failings of the market. We are thus left with the problem being less what the state did do, but rather what it did not. It is therefore now time to turn our attention to government policy and its effectiveness.

2.4 Summary and interim conclusions

The magnitude and causes of Britain's postwar economic underperformance remain highly controversial, but with the 'declinist' literature dominant. Indeed, decline has become so potent a motif that one reviewer of a recent contribution to this literature complained that 'Endemic pessimism and cynicism are hard to cure, especially among academics.'[70] His complaint was clearly the child of frustration that yet another group of academics did not appreciate the transformation of the British economy and of its prospects that had occurred because of the Thatcherite project. We are thus brought to the heart of the problem for today's historian. The objective facts show that, at best, relative decline was halted; and that any verdict about the efficacy of the Thatcher reforms has to balance the gains to economic growth – themselves probably rather modest, given the low average growth rate – against the social costs of higher unemployment and a much more unegalitarian distribution of income and wealth, which many now see as undermining Britain's social fabric. Moreover, even if the economy is now better equipped to take advantage of future growth possibilities, it is none the less the case that relative to comparators, the British economy has all the hallmarks of still being stuck in a low-growth low-investment cycle.[71] As a consequence, there is a serious risk that today's historians feel compelled to base their view of the past at least in part on a perception of what might transpire in the future.

We have stressed in this chapter that relative to earlier periods, the postwar British economy performed if not well, then at least adequately, and particularly so during the golden age. It is the politicisation of economic policy and the resulting fixation of politicians on the economy that underlies much of the pessimism about overall performance and the search for scapegoats, be they labour, managers or, by the 1970s, government itself. The league table approach to national economic performance, which has now become so integral a part of the competitiveness culture, also reinforces such pessimism. Of course, because we cannot yet know what the lasting effects of the Thatcher reforms will be for the British economy, any judgements must be provisional. None the less, for historical assessment it is probable that the fault line for debate will be constructed thus. On the one hand, there will be market optimists who take a rosy view of the positive effects of the Thatcher reforms and who emphasise that, whilst disadvantaged during the Fordist era, the British economy has inherent characteristics which position it well in relation to an economy dominated by its service sector, but also sustaining a small, high value-added and high technology manufacturing sector. Alternatively, there will be those pessimists who see the 1980s as a one-off catch-up exercise, with much of the productivity improvement illusory and merely a statistical artefact produced by the reduced size of the manufacturing sector, and who argue that the Thatcher years did nothing to remedy long-standing weaknesses, and especially so with respect to investment in physical and human capital. The content historian will be the one who quickly realises that there is no right answer to understanding decline, merely more or less profitable ways of attempting a grand narrative.

3

ECONOMIC POLICIES SINCE 1945

Since the Second World War British economic policies have typically sought to achieve simultaneous internal and external balance in the short-run and as rapid a growth of living standards as possible in the long-run.[1] In such a policy regime, internal balance is commonly defined as the lowest possible rate of unemployment consistent with an acceptable rate of inflation (i.e. a minimisation of the Okun discomfort index – the sum of the unemployment and inflation rates – as charted in Figure 3.1), external balance as some desirable level of the current account balance of payments (typically equilibrium, but recently as a sustainable deficit) and the standard of living as measurable by GDP per capita, no adjustments being made for quality of life considerations or the pre-tax distribution of incomes at this stage of the policy process. In practice, postwar British economic policy can be characterised as a succession of major conflicts between short-run macroeconomic objectives and longer-run growth-promoting supply-side policies.

In this chapter we discuss the evolution of economic policies from the end of the war through to 1997. This entails first establishing what the economic authorities' policy objectives were and why they came to have the priorities they did. The authorities' policy instruments can then be discussed and an analysis made of how and why the growing problem of policy trade-offs, especially that between full employment and price stability, forced successive governments to experiment to widen the range of policy instruments available to them. We reserve all questions of policy effectiveness for the next chapter, save when they impact in turn on the environment in which

67

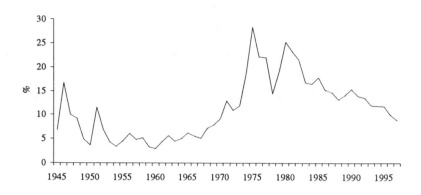

Figure 3.1 Okun discomfort index (%), 1945–97
Sources: ONS, *Retail Prices Index – April 1998,* Table 14; J. Denman and P. McDonald, 'Unemployment statistics from 1881 to the present day,' *Labour Market Trends,* 104 (January 1996), Tables 1–2; 1996–7, *Labour Market Trends.*

policies were being set (as in Section 3.1.2). This chapter is organised as follows. In Section 3.1 we cover some background material necessary for an understanding of the evolution of policy, principally the facts and characteristics of party political competition. The growth of the public sector is then discussed in Section 3.2 and the principal institutions and agencies responsible for economic policy in Section 3.3. We then outline the broad phases through which policy evolved in Section 3.4. Finally, in Section 3.5 we draw some preliminary conclusions.

3.1 Politics and policy since 1945

3.1.1 Political trends

Table 3.1 provides the basic political facts for postwar Britain: the dates of administrations, the results of general elections in terms of the governing party and initial Parliamentary majority, and the names of the 11 Prime Ministers and 20 Chancellors of the Exchequer who necessarily form the focal point for any discussion of economic policies.[2] The Conservative Party was the governing party for 34.7 of the nearly 52 years between the 1945 general election and the election of the Blair government, although if the line is drawn at 1979, the point at which there occurs a radical shift in policy regime, the Labour

Table 3.1 British political facts, 1945–97

Dates of governments	Party of government	Parliamentary majority at election[a]	Prime Ministers[b]	Chancellors of the Exchequer[b]
07/1945–02/1950	Labour	146	C. R. Attlee	H. Dalton (11/1947) Sir S. Cripps
02/1950–10/1951	Labour	5	C. R. Attlee	H. Gaitskell
10/1951–05/1955	Conservative	17	Sir W. S. Churchill	R. A. Butler
05/1955–10/1959	Conservative	58	Sir A. Eden (01/1957) H. Macmillan	R. A. Butler (12/1955) H. Macmillan (01/1957) P. Thorneycroft (01/1958) D. Heathcote Amory
10/1959–10/1964	Conservative	100	H. Macmillan (10/1963) Sir A. Douglas-Home	D. Heathcote Amory (07/1960) J. Selwyn Lloyd (07/1962) R. Maudling
10/1964–03/1966	Labour	4	H. Wilson	J. Callaghan
03/1966–06/1970	Labour	96	H. Wilson	J. Callaghan (11/1967) R. Jenkins
06/1970–03/1974	Conservative	30	E. Heath	I. Macleod (07/1970) A. Barber
03/1974–10/1974	Labour	(33)	H. Wilson	D. Healey
10/1974–05/1979	Labour	3	H. Wilson (04/1976) J. Callaghan	D. Healey
05/1979–06/1983	Conservative	43	M. Thatcher	Sir Geoffrey Howe
06/1983–06/1987	Conservative	144	M. Thatcher	Nigel Lawson
06/1987–04/1992	Conservative	102	M. Thatcher (11/1990) J. Major	Nigel Lawson (10/1989) John Major (11/1990) Norman Lamont
04/1992–05/1997	Conservative	21	J. Major	Norman Lamont (05/1993) Kenneth Carke
05/1997–	Labour	177	A. Blair	Gordon Brown

Notes:
[a] Over all other parties.
[b] Dates in parenthesis indicate end of tenure of office.
Sources: D. E. Butler and G. Butler, *British Political Facts, 1900–1994* (7th edn, 1994), pp. 21–45, 216–19; and, for 1997 election, <http://www.parliament.uk/commons/lib/state.htm>.

Party was actually slightly ahead of the Conservatives as the governing party with 17.1 years in office as against 16.7 years for its opponents. Between 1945 and 1997 there were 15 general elections, with the average period of incumbency approximately 3.7 years and with the periods 1951–64 and 1979–97 notable for the Conservatives winning three and then four successive elections. In terms of the length of the electoral cycle and the average duration of administrations, it appears that political competition and instability were no greater than in other OECD states, and much less than in some more economically successful ones (e.g. Italy).

It should also be noted, however, that between 1959 and 1983 no British government won re-election after serving a full term in office and this gives a clue to the fluidity and contestability of British politics for much of the postwar period.[3] Thus the Conservatives appear a more dominant party than was actually the case and, in their efforts to generate and sustain electoral appeal, especially amongst the lower socioeconomic classes, we observe how and why economic performance became politicised. Similarly, the Labour Party has always had to target higher socioeconomic groups to gain electoral success, with one of its strategies being to attract public sector professionals. The background to the development of economic policies thus accords with Harold Wilson's dictum that 'all political history shows that the standing of a Government and its ability to hold the confidence of the electorate at a General Election, depends upon the success of its economic policy.'[4] Accordingly, the maintenance of full employment and, from the mid-1950s when it became an explicit objective, economic growth became key benchmarks against which the electorate were deemed to judge the respective merits of the political parties. This clearly created potential for a dissonance between reality and the claims of politicians, whilst also providing incentives for governments to manipulate the economy to maximise the probability of their being re-elected: so-called political business cycles. At the 1959 general election, Gallup opinion-poll data recorded that economic issues came a poor second to foreign policy and defence. By the time of the 1966 election, however, economic issues had become 'the most urgent problem facing Britain today' for 48 per cent of respondents, a transformation which was completed in the 1970s when unemployment, inflation and industrial relations topped the list of responses to public opinion surveys.[5]

The evidence for political business cycles in postwar Britain is very ambiguous, as indeed it is elsewhere.[6] Governments had what economists call a reaction function, but the econometric evidence on the relationship between the key **dependent variables** (typically pre-election trends in real income growth, unemployment and inflation) and government popularity is highly ambiguous, leading Mosley to conclude from his extensive review of the literature that in Britain for 1953–81, 'The "vote function" relating popularity, inflation and unemployment is just too unstable to act as a menu for policy choice.'[7] This is actually an important finding for it can be argued that it was the very imprecision of the vote function which encouraged pre-election tax cuts and additional public expenditure to boost personal disposable income for they were unlikely to backfire in terms of subsequent electoral popularity, whilst politicians believed they were becoming more adept at the presentation of economic facts in a chosen favourable light.[8]

3.1.2 Consensus or adversarial politics?

This presentation of the political contest as wholly adversarial and with potentially serious disbenefits for economic policy, and thus ultimately economic performance, should be tempered by a consideration of what has become a very active debate amongst contemporary historians: whether, beginning during the coalition government of the Second World War and enduring right through to the disjunction caused by the first Thatcher government, there existed a cross-party consensus about major issues which moderated the actual level of party competition and ensured considerable continuity in policies between administrations.[9] For its proponents consensus stemmed from a postwar settlement between the two political parties which was sanctioned by the accommodation of organised capital and labour, and which comprised agreement in five core areas:[10]

1. The mixed economy: that the basic utilities, transport and communications be publicly owned and operated to meet national economic objectives of stability and growth.
2. Full employment: this to be achieved through Keynesian economic management of active monetary policies and the functional use of tax and expenditure policies to produce a budget deficit if unemployment threatened and a boost to demand was required.

3. Conciliation of the trade unions and relative freedom for private industry: that both organised labour and capital were acknowledged as part of the estate of the realm and that neither should be the subject of much government intervention and regulation.
4. The welfare state: based on the important Beveridge Report that there be a consolidation of existing health, unemployment insurance and other services to provide a universal national system.
5. Retreat from empire combined with the maintenance of a geopolitical posture commensurate with Britain's imperial history and victory in two world wars.

As a list of core values and policy goals which were held by the policy and political elites, this would not have been contentious or viewed as undesirable before the mid-1970s, when government itself begins to be seen as the cause of Britain's economic problem. To this extent, a broad consensus did exist, but it appeared more clear-cut than it actually was because of the way in which the first Thatcher government set out to dismantle the postwar settlement and portrayed consensus, in her words, as 'the process of abandoning all beliefs, principles, values and policies.'[11] For the New Right, consensus was wrong-headed and had brought Britain's economy and society to the brink of disaster. Thus consensus had to be abandoned and instead be replaced by a radically different and necessarily confrontational new policy regime which could remedy the damage wrought by the managed-mixed economy and welfare state.

Recent historical revisionism now emphasises the negative aspects of consensus (what government felt unable or unwilling to do) as much as the positive side; it has demonstrated that there remained substantial differences in the underlying values of the two main parties, which impacted upon economic policy as the Conservative Party was always striving to contain the growth of government and to create an 'opportunity state';[12] and with the opening of the official papers for the 1950s and beyond in the Public Record Office, it is now clear that the conversion to Keynesian policies of demand management was slower and less complete than had originally been thought. The term 'Butskellism' which has been applied routinely to describe consensus and continuity in the economic policies of the 1950s, and which was a construct of the names of the outgoing Labour and incoming Conservative Chancellors in 1951, is also now seen as unhelpful.[13] There were real differences between the parties which were manifest in

different choices in policy instruments and objectives, while as
Cairncross has shown: 'The Conservatives accepted in principle the
use of monetary and fiscal policy in managing the economy but they
were reluctant Keynesians and practised demand management only so
long as it did not conflict with what they took to be sound principles.'[14]

The verdict of recent work is that the existence of a consensus before
1979 appears only when looked at from a very broad perspective and
that, when examined at the level of key policy areas, the reality was
much more disagreement and discontinuity. As Pimlott has argued:
'consensus is a mirage, an illusion that rapidly fades the closer one
gets to it.'[15] Whilst historians have recently arrived at these
conclusions, there exists an earlier generation of political scientists
who had always emphasised the adversarial nature of Britain's postwar
politics and who have explored the costs of this for economic policy
and performance. Foremost here are Beer and Finer.[16] The adversary
politics thesis that has grown out of their early work has three
important variants. The first emphasises how political competition
results in frequent reversals in economic policy as each successive
government attempts to implement radically different policies from
those of its predecessor. The second relies less on ideology and more
on the compulsion to maximise votes, resulting in the generation of
excessive popular expectations about the ability of governments to
manage the economy. The third identifies adversarial politics as a
symptom of more deeply rooted problems in the British state, in
particular the high degree of centralised political authority which
'means there is not only considerable scope for arbitrary short-term
shifts in policy, but also that there are few mechanisms for reassessing
policies or challenging existing priorities.'[17]

The adversary politics thesis contains much appeal to those wishing
to understand Britain's economic decline. However, the seesaw nature
of policy has been greatly overstated, and probably derives from
ahistorical generalisations about the policy U-turn made half way
through the Heath government of 1970–4. Industrial policies and
planning, upon which there were long-standing differences between
the parties, form the only real candidates for adversarial politics in
the economic sphere. The outstanding features of the whole postwar
period, whether assessed in terms of government inputs (interest rates,
the PSBR, public expenditures) or economic outcomes (GDP growth,
distribution of income, employment, prices) is that successive
governments made little difference to the secular trend of

deterioration in economic performance. This led Rose, another leading political scientist, to conclude that 'British parties are not the primary force shaping the destiny of British society; it is shaped by something stronger than parties', and to reinstate consensus – albeit a moving one – as the best characterisation of the British case.[18] We concur and would argue that the recent reaction against consensus has been taken too far, and especially in economic policy where there was agreement about the broad policy framework which produced the four key macroeconomic policy objectives. The precise targets, the chosen trade-offs between objectives and the selection of policy instruments differed, but the fundamentals exhibited far more continuity than change.

One further set of arguments from political scientists, however, is appropriate here before progressing to examine the scale and scope of Britain's public sector. The role of politics in economic management needs also to be seen in the context of the overload or ungovernability thesis: that whilst there was the growth of government, this was not matched by an extension of its capacity to govern and, in particular, to regulate the economy in line with policy objectives.[19] On the one hand, popular expectations of government rose with affluence and full employment and also, in part, as politicians gave way to the temptation to compete in terms of what government could potentially deliver to the electorate. On the other hand, the ability of government to discharge these responsibilities declined as the number of dependency relationships (especially deference to authority) collapsed through growing noncompliance by market and government participants. The result of excessive demands combined with diminished capabilities was, in this view, stagflation, ineffective government, capitulation to interest groups and growing voter dissatisfaction. In short, the crisis of the 1970s – from which emerged the Thatcherite project and the necessity for the Labour Party to reinvent itself as New Labour and to finally accommodate capitalism and the market.

3.2 The public sector since 1945

The expansion of the public sector and the growth of big government have been common features of all twentieth-century states, whatever their economic and political systems.[20] The British case conforms broadly to the experience of other advanced capitalist countries, save in two important respects: its first critical phase of peacetime growth came in the 1920s, whereas in most other OECD states it was precipitated by the depression of the 1930s; and the distinguishing characteristic of Britain's public sector from the 1960s onwards has been its smallness relative to the major (more successful) European economies. In terms of a frequently used typology,[21] in Britain, as elsewhere, there was a transformation in all three functions of the public economy: that is adjustments to the *allocation* of resources produced by the market; actions to alter the *distribution* of income and wealth resulting from market activity; and policies to bring about the *stabilisation* of economic activity (the full employment objective).

The public finances pose eternal questions for politicians and their advisers: what public services should be provided, how should they be financed and what, if any, macroeconomic role should government play? In establishing the size and scope of the public sector we, by definition, delimit the private sector and the scope for the invisible hand of the market economy. We also come close to the priorities of the state, to its power relationships and the distribution of the cost/ benefits of big government. In short, in the modern world the budget replaced the barricades as the fault line of a class society, although the British also maintained a secondary interest in dysfunctional industrial relations for a significant part of the postwar period. Debate over the appropriate economic role of government, and of its size in terms of the balance between the market and non-market sectors, has always been central to the preoccupation with relative economic decline. For the greater part of the twentieth century, those seeking to restrain the growth of the public sector remained on the political defensive as progressive thought identified the state as the principal agent for the modernisation of Britain's economy and society. The election of the first Thatcher government in 1979 constitutes an important turning-point in this long-term trend of government growth. This is not so much because the first or subsequent Thatcher governments actually succeeded in rolling back the frontiers of the state, not at least in terms of public expenditure and taxation, but because the economic crisis of the 1970s, which engendered the New Right in Britain, shifted quite profoundly the conception of government's capacity to engineer economic and social advance.

We begin our examination of the public sector with the long-run

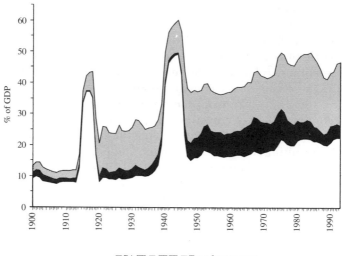

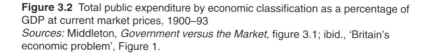

□ PACE ■ GFCF ▨ Transfer payments

Figure 3.2 Total public expenditure by economic classification as a percentage of GDP at current market prices, 1900–93
Sources: Middleton, *Government versus the Market*, figure 3.1; ibid., 'Britain's economic problem', Figure 1.

course of the expenditure ratio, the ratio of total public expenditure (TPE) to GDP, which is charted in Figure 3.2 and which is the conventional summary indicator of public sector size. This also shows the overall composition of TPE by economic category as between:

- current expenditure on goods and services (PACE), this a measure of the public sector's direct claim – and absorption – of national income (and equivalent to col. 2 in panel B of Table 2.1);
- gross fixed capital formation (GFCF), that is capital investment by the public sector (principally the nationalised industries); and
- transfer payments which comprise interest on the national debt and the greater part of welfare expenditures.

We have charted the expenditure ratio since the beginning of the century to illustrate that both world wars were associated with once-and-for-all

Table 3.2 Total public expenditure as a percentage of GDP at current market prices by functional classification, selected years, 1900–93

	1900	1913	1937	1948	1951	1955	1960	1964	1968	1973	1979	1984	1989	1993
Public administration and other	0.7	0.8	1.0	1.2	1.2	1.0	1.0	0.9	0.9	0.9	0.9	1.2	1.3	1.4
Debt interest	1.6	1.7	5.4	5.1	4.7	4.8	4.6	4.2	4.4	4.1	5.1	5.5	4.1	3.2
Law and order	0.4	0.6	0.5	0.5	0.6	0.7	0.7	0.8	0.9	1.0	1.2	1.9	1.9	2.3
External services	0.0	0.0	0.0	0.2	0.6	0.4	0.5	0.8	0.7	0.9	1.2	1.1	1.1	1.2
Defence	6.0	3.1	4.9	6.3	7.6	8.0	6.3	6.1	5.6	4.8	4.7	5.4	4.2	3.8
Social services	2.3	3.7	10.5	17.6	14.1	13.9	15.1	16.5	20.2	21.2	23.9	27.1	23.1	28.8
Economic services	1.6	1.4	2.7	4.8	7.1	6.2	6.9	7.1	7.8	6.5	5.7	5.0	3.4	3.9
Environmental services	0.5	0.6	0.9	1.3	1.7	1.9	1.9	2.5	3.4	3.6	3.1	2.7	2.3	2.2
Total	13.3	11.9	26.0	37.0	37.5	37.0	37.1	38.9	43.9	42.9	45.9	49.9	41.4	46.8

Sources: Middleton, *Government versus the Market*, table 3.2; ibid., 'Britain's economic problem', Table 1.

increases, but that public expenditure carried on rising faster than did GDP between the wars and, for reasons we will come to shortly, during much of the postwar period. From the breakdown of TPE by function in Table 3.2, it is clear that the growth of public expenditure has been most evident in social services which, by the 1990s, comprise over 60 per cent of TPE. At the beginning of the century, defence had been the largest single item; by the end of the century, it was relatively much smaller and equivalent in value to economic services, although it should be noted that for much of the postwar period, Britain maintained a defence effort significantly above that of competitor economies, and especially that of Germany and Japan.[22] None the less, as Judge shows, it was the relative decline in the defence budget between 1955 and 1974 which was the most important enabling factor in 'provid[ing] fiscal space for the development of the welfare state.'[23]

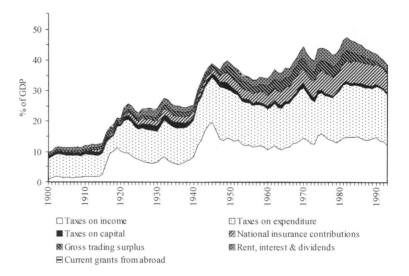

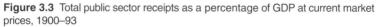

Figure 3.3 Total public sector receipts as a percentage of GDP at current market prices, 1900–93
Sources: Middleton, *Governemnt versus the Market*, Figure 3.5; ibid., 'Britain's economic problem', Figure 2.

The receipts ratio, together with the major heads of revenue, are charted in Figure 3.3. The upward trend, which prevailed through to the mid-1980s, resulted from increased rates on existing taxes and a widening of the tax base. Of the former, the transformation in income

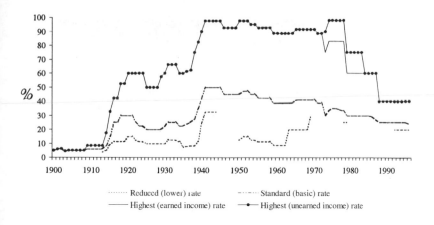

Figure 3.4 Rates of income tax, financial years (%), 1900–97
Source: Board of Inland Revenue.

tax was the most dramatic (see Figure 3.4), changing out of all recognition as a consequence of the First World War, and once more in the Second World War, as its coverage was extended through pay-as-you-earn (PAYE) to encompass the whole working population.

The rise to prominence of income tax and the development of national insurance determined the shift in the tax mix over the course of the century. Taxes on expenditure provided nearly 77 per cent of total tax revenue in 1900, but thereafter was gradually eroded down to a low point of 37 per cent in 1975, before recovering to 47 per cent by 1993 as part of a stated policy, pursued by Conservative governments after 1979, of reversing the trend towards increased reliance on direct taxation. Over the century as a whole, Britain's fiscal system was made more progressive, although the growing interaction of the tax and benefit systems created a host of problems for incentives at various points in the income distribution. From modest beginnings – the introduction of differentiation between earned and investment income (in 1907) and graduation (in 1909) – income tax emerged as a powerful revenue provider capable of underpinning the growth of big government. Rightly had Gladstone labelled the income tax a 'colossal engine of finance' which must not be permitted a permanent place in Britain's tax armoury if the minimal, *laissez-faire* state was to be preserved.

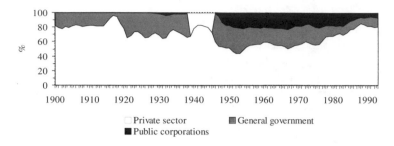

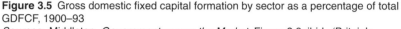

Figure 3.5 Gross domestic fixed capital formation by sector as a percentage of total GDFCF, 1900–93
Sources: Middleton, *Government versus the Market*, Figure 3.8; ibid., 'Britain's economic problem', Figure 6.

The respective shares of the private and public sectors in gross domestic fixed capital formation (GDFCF) comprise another suitable indicator of the growth of government (Figure 3.5), although here we observe that the phase of government growth which had begun with the First World War was exhausted by the early 1950s with the completion of the Attlee government's nationalisation programme. Thereafter, the private sector share rose, in part because high levels of capital formation were integral to the rapid growth of the British economy through to OPEC I, but also because from the late 1960s onwards, successive governments squeezed public sector investment programmes, an unsurprising result given the natural bias towards

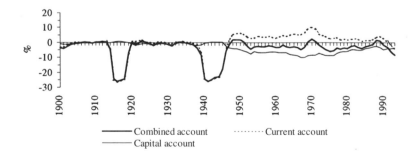

Figure 3.6 Public sector financial balances as a percentage of GDP at current market prices, current and capital accounts, 1900–93
Souce: Middleton, *Government versus the Market*, Figure 3.10; ibid., 'Britain's economic problem', Figure 7.

the short-term and the stronger political constituencies associated
with current expenditure programmes. Such has been the contraction
in public investment that by the early 1990s, the share of the private
sector in GDFCF now approximated to that prevailing in 1913.

A long-run view of the balance, and composition, of the public sector
budget is given in Figure 3.6. The two dips into substantial overall
deficit are, of course, associated with the world wars and had the
concomitant that the national debt rose very substantially during these
periods, with resulting long-term implications as the interest charge
on this debt had to be covered from current revenue (see Table 3.2)
and, at various points, governments sought to repay the principal of
debts accrued during wartime. None the less, the postwar period has
seen a trend reduction in the ratio of national debt outstanding to
GDP as the effects of inflation on the real value of that debt more
than compensated for the debt created under the new regime of
Keynesian economic management. One effect of this new policy regime
was to cast the national debt in a new light since debt expansion was
a necessary by-product of the commitment to full employment, and it
was argued that the debt would pose no serious subsequent problems
since public and private debt could be conceived quite differently,
namely through the doctrine of 'we owe it to ourselves'.

With the demise of the Keynesian system in the 1970s, which in
part followed from the very marked deterioration in Britain's public
finances, especially between 1973 and 1975, the issue of the
sustainability of the national debt once more reappeared with a
renewed emphasis on the effects of the debt burden on the supply
of capital and labour, and thus crowding-out issues which had
exercised public policy before the Second World War. Looking at
the postwar period as a whole, the public sector budget balance was
in deficit for all but seven years, but the current account was always
in surplus, even during the years of acute fiscal stress of the 1974–9
Wilson-Callaghan administration. Thus, under the Keynesian policy
regime, current receipts always covered current expenditure and
deficits reflected public sector fixed capital formation. Accordingly,
the deterioration in the public finances of the early 1990s, with
current receipts falling short of current expenditure from 1992/3
through to 1994/5, which was caused by the erosion of the tax base
in the mid- to late-1980s and the effect of automatic stabilisers with
the business cycle depression of 1990–2, thus constituted a clear break
with postwar trends.

We can now summarise postwar trends in Britain's public sector:

1. The Second World War caused far less of a displacement effect on the expenditure ratio than did the earlier conflict. Taking 1935/6 as the last peacetime (i.e. pre-rearmament) year, at which point the standard and highest marginal rates of income tax were 22.5 and 60 per cent respectively, the burden of personal taxation peaked during the war years (tax rates of 50 and 97.5 per cent) and then fell back very slightly to 45 and 92.5 per cent in 1949/50, only to rise once more to fund the Korean War. Very high marginal tax rates thus originate from the Second World War, which was, of course, followed by significant additional expenditure commitments associated with the Beveridge welfare reforms. Lastly, during this period we note a further extension of state ownership with the Attlee government's nationalisation programme.

2. There then followed a brief period of stability in the public sector lasting from the end of the Korean War until the resignation of the Chancellor of the Exchequer and his Treasury team in 1958, when the peace dividend could no longer contain the pressures for additional social spending (see pp. 87–8).

3. The ensuing phase of growth, according to Judge, exhibited 'no significant differences between the records of Labour and Conservative governments at the level of aggregate expenditures ... [rather] there seems to have been a steady acceleration in the rate of growth of state expenditures under both parties until the onset of recurrent crises in the mid-1970s.'[24]

4. The current phase of indeterminacy in which Britain's public sector moves is within parameters determined by the constant buffeting of the business and electoral cycles and externally imposed disciplines (markets and, more recently, Maastricht), but with an ideological convergence on a desirable expenditure ratio of approximately 40 per cent, making it on average 5–10 percentage points of GDP lower than its major EU partners.

3.3 The institutions and practice of economic policy-making

Our starting point is with the institutions or agencies responsible for British economic policy. It is important that these evolved in a very British fashion of *ad hoc* and piecemeal adjustments to new challenges and that there were no radical administrative innovations associated with government's now much enlarged economic responsibilities. Thus the Bank of England, although nationalised in 1946, retained significant practical independence, while the Treasury had grafted on to its traditional responsibility as the guardian of the public finances the new obligation to manage aggregate demand to ensure full employment and the other macroeconomic policy objectives.[25] Within Whitehall, the Treasury was and remains the most powerful of all departments, with its administrative reach extending into every area of public policy. By European standards, it is a hybrid department which combines responsibilities for finance and national economic management. According to its critics it excels in neither.

Criticism of the Treasury has been a regular feature of the postwar policy debate.[26] Labour governments, in particular, have wanted to counter Treasury power, so much so that on assuming office in 1964 they established a rival agency, the Department of Economic Affairs (DEA), which was charged with drawing up a national plan and with ensuring that supposed Treasury obsessions with finance and sterling did not act to the detriment of longer-term plans to improve the supply-side of the economy.[27] Institutional experimentation and a preoccupation with the supply-side actually predates this government and were part of the growing concern about relative decline and the necessity of boosting the growth rate. Thus it was the previous administration which first signalled a revival of interest in national economic planning with the establishment of two agencies for the purpose in 1962: the National Economic Development Council (NEDC), a tripartite corporatist structure where government, trade unions and employers could meet to discuss and produce consensual solutions to Britain's economic problems, and the National Economic Development Office (NEDO), a second-tier body which supported the work of the council and exercised an important informational role for the private and public sectors.[28] Both agencies survived until the 1990s when the Conservative government, always antagonistic towards legacies of the age of consensus, abolished them, justifying their actions that they were anachronistic and unnecessary now that Britain's economic decline had been halted.[29] The Wilson-Callaghan years of 1974–9 were also a significant period of institutional and policy experimentation, most notably with the creation of the National Enterprise Board in 1975 to orchestrate a new phase of industrial policy activism, entailing – through public ownership – both the restructuring of sunset industries and the promotion of sunrise sectors.

The centrality of the Treasury in British policy and politics should not detract, however, from the activities of other government departments and agencies which exercise considerable influence over economic policy, especially microeconomic policies. Within Whitehall, there are the departments concerned with trade and industry, sometimes separate and sometimes unified; departments with responsibility for employment, now unified with education, a change which indicates the evolving diagnosis of Britain's economic problem; and departments for the environment, for central-local government relations and for revenue-raising in the form of Customs and Excise and Inland Revenue. In addition, for much of this period there was a substantial nationalised industry sector which, to a greater or lesser extent, was a vehicle for national economic policies such as containing inflationary pressures or boosting public investment programmes for stabilisation purposes; and, from the early 1960s through to 1979, governments established, abolished and then re-established a series of agencies to persuade and/or statutorily enforce prices and incomes policies in their efforts to reconcile full employment with price stability.[30] Viewed in the round, the administrative machinery for economic policy was required to accommodate the complexity and interrelatedness of economic issues, provide co-ordination between the constituent strands of policy, demarcate conflicts between policies, set acceptable trade-offs between objectives and evaluate the effectiveness of policies. In short, policy can be viewed as a learning process in which policy-makers must puzzle about what to do and, in the process, balance what is thought technically correct against what is economically and politically possible.

One model of the economic policy process which has found favour amongst modern political scientists and has a number of applications to the British case is that of social learning.[31] This is usually represented as incorporating three main properties: current policies as a function of past policies, with strong elements of inertia in the system; experts as a guiding force in the learning process; and the state as exercising some measure of autonomy. These three properties, in turn, then operate on three central variables: the intermediate objectives of policy, such as securing a stable exchange rate; the policy instruments used to attain those objectives; and the precise settings of those instruments. Three types of change can then be established:

1. First-order: alterations to the setting of policy instruments (e.g. movements in interest rates).
2. Second-order: shifts in the hierarchy of policy instruments (e.g. the introduction of cash limits in 1976 to provide improved control over public expenditure in response to the perceived breakdown of the old control system) without major adjustments to the hierarchy of policy objectives.
3. Third-order: dramatic shifts in the hierarchy of policy objectives (e.g. the displacement of the full employment by the price stability objective in 1979–80) such as to constitute a transformation of the policy regime or paradigm (represented as the eclipse of Keynesianism by **monetarism**).

In our assessment of the evolution and character of British economic policies we will encounter policy shifts mainly of the first-order, less frequently of the second-order and only once of the third-order. Such a schema provides useful benchmarks for assessing the magnitude of change, its significance and the extent to which expertise inside the state, as against politicians and agents outside the state, dominated the learning process.

3.4 The phases of economic policy

We adopt the following eight-part periodisation for postwar economic policy, which we relate to background constraints and opportunities and to shifting perceptions of the economic problem. We report in Table 3.3 the four main macroeconomic indicators by government between 1945–97.

3.4.1 Recovery and reconstruction, 1945–51

Our first period runs from the end of the war through 1951.[32] This was the period which laid the foundations for the managed-mixed economy and welfare state. It was an age of austerity; of very slow decontrol and deregulation in which the economic authorities were

Table 3.3 Macroeconomic indicators, annual averages by government, 1945–97

Government	Time period	GDP growth rate (%)	Change in RPI (%)	Unemployment rate (%)[a]	Current account balance of payments (% of GDP)
Labour	1945–51	1.5	5.5	1.9	(2.1)
Conservative	1951–64	2.9	3.4	1.8	0.2
Labour	1964–70	2.5	4.6	2.1	0.0
Conservative	1970–4	2.8	10.4	3.0	(0.3)
Labour	1974–9	2.1	15.6	4.8	(0.9)
Conservative	1979–97	2.1	5.8	9.2	(0.6)

Note:
[a] Major change in definition at 1979. Estimates for 1979–97 on a consistent claimants basis.
Sources: Calculated from Appendix II Tables 1–3; ONS, *Retail Prices Index – April 1998*, Table 14.

fearful of a postwar slump as they managed the transition from a war to a peacetime economy. They were preoccupied with sterling problems, ones far from resolved by devaluation in 1949 from $4.03 to $2.80; mindful of the need to close the productivity gap that had opened up between British and American industry; and forever feeling their way, in effect experimenting, to find an acceptable balance between economic management, on the one hand, through permanent controls on demand and supply and, on the other, Keynesianism which impacted principally, but not exclusively on the demand side.

3.4.2 Consolidating the postwar settlement, 1951–8

Our second period begins in 1951 with the change in government and lasts through to 1958.[33] While the Conservative Party had, in opposition, to adjust its electoral programme to accommodate the full implications of the 1945 defeat, when returned to power in 1951 it none the less retained substantially different economic priorities and principles from those of Labour. It sought a different balance between government and the market, and we should thus expect – and do observe – first- and second-order shifts in policy, although initially these were somewhat delayed because involvement in the Korean War (1951–3) necessarily entailed the short-term maintenance of physical controls which otherwise they would have been predisposed to scrap immediately. At heart was what we would now label a supply-side strategy of reducing the size of the public sector. First, there would be retrenchment in public expenditure (assisted after 1953 by the peace dividend) and then tax cuts to improve incentives for work, savings and investment. The Conservatives thus portrayed their ambitions in terms of creating an 'opportunity state' and began to give an emphasis to affluence and the ability of governments to promote economic progress which, as we have seen in Section 3.1.1, would profoundly alter the nature of the political contest. Economic growth thus became an explicit policy objective by the mid-1950s, a consequence in part of the authorities now being confident that they had avoided a postwar slump, and from then on international comparisons of growth rates were becoming available which resulted in a new perception of economic decline taking root.[34]

Monetary policy was also used much more actively after 1951 than before. This followed from the ambition of curtailing public sector growth and the fear that Keynesian demand management might impart an upward bias to public expenditure growth because tax rates raised in times of boom might not be reduced in times of slump as expenditure would have grown in the interim to fill the gap, a socialist ratchet or so it was argued. Sterling and balance of payments problems, together with growing concerns about reconciling full employment with price stability, also preoccupied the authorities and it is during this period that Stop-Go became established. Our second sub-period thus combined a consolidation of the core values and practices established in the postwar settlement with efforts to rework that settlement into an economy which, by Conservative standards, was more dynamic and freer of governmental controls.

3.4.3 High Keynesianism, 1958–66

The third phase lasted from 1958–66, being, in terms of economic policy, a period characterised by more experimentation and innovation than in any peacetime period before or since.[35] It was also a period of deep frustrations as first the Conservatives and then Labour were unable to execute a modernising strategy, focused on the supply-side, which was not susceptible to continuing short-term problems of demand management emanating from ongoing weaknesses in the balance of payments. This phase begins in January 1958 with a unique political event: the resignation of the Chancellor of the Exchequer and his entire Treasury team of ministers on a matter of principle, ostensibly over the refusal of the Cabinet to back more restrictive monetary and fiscal measures to contain inflation and more closely match domestic economic capacity, but in reality as much to do with personality clashes, inflexibility and the normal wear and tear of high political intrigue.[36] None the less, this episode brought the Macmillan government to the brink of collapse. It also illustrates that this government contained many who were uncomfortable about how traditional Conservative virtues of 'sound' money were being compromised by the pursuit of consensus politics, and indeed many have seen this episode as a sort of proto-monetarist revolt.

The government weathered the storm and, indeed, won a convincing victory in the 1959 election (Table 3.1). None the less, it has become the orthodoxy that thereafter a combination of Stop-Go in the economy, crises and scandals (especially Profumo), but above all a sense that the Conservatives were unable to rise to the challenge of modernisation, all contributed to a speedy decline in fortunes. In reality, they only just lost the 1964 election, and this after Labour had in opposition done much to re-engineer its electoral appeal, and most visibly so in Wilson's claim that the party would harness the white heat of technology as part of a consistent and powerful modernising package for British economy and society. The economic record to 1964 was also perfectly respectable in terms of meeting the four macroeconomic objectives, with higher growth 1960–4 than in the business cycles immediately before or after (panel B, Table 2.1, p. 28). Moreover, between 1959 and 1964 the Conservative government had embarked upon an unprecedented phase of policy experimentation and economic-political reorientation: what Samuel Brittan called the 'great reappraisal'.[37] There was, first, the application to join the EEC in mid-1961, this for a complex of economic as well as geopolitical reasons.[38] Next, there were a number of initiatives from 1957 onwards to try and control wage inflation by brokering deals between employers' representatives and trade union leaders.[39] The early 1960s also saw a substantial reorganisation of the Treasury and of its functions for public expenditure control and national economic management.[40] Finally, there was the creation of the NEDC and NEDO.

These latter bodies gave a new emphasis to growth and to the supply-side within the context of high Keynesianism. Thus up to 1964 and, indeed, continuing under Labour through to the crisis measures of July 1966, the economy was managed at a very high pressure of demand in an effort to stimulate growth. However, there was the ever-present threat of overheating, with resultant balance of payments and sterling problems. Moreover, from the embryonic roots of the NEDC/NEDO, and the economic expertise they brought into Whitehall, there arose under Labour its flagship policy in opposition: that of the establishment of the DEA to formulate a National Plan which would underpin growth ambitions. Labour's modernising ambitions entailed also a much more active phase of industrial, regional and technology policies, all directed at a restructuring of British industry.[41]

3.4.4 A return to orthodoxy, 1966–72

Our fourth phase runs from July 1966 through to the Heath government's U-turn in 1972.[42] It was initiated by the failure of the 1964–6 Labour government to capitalise upon its flagship economic policies as, inheriting from the Conservatives a severely overheated economy, it suffered periodic crises as the markets tested the resolve of the new government to defend the $2.80 sterling exchange rate, whilst being politically unable to deflate the economy sufficiently to resolve these difficulties and thereby create sufficient spare capacity in which its supply-side policies might be able to prosper. Unfortunately, victory in the 1966 election had also 'increased the anticipation of progress ... [such that] When Labour's new dawn failed to materialize the optimism of 1964–6 was transformed into bitter cynicism.'[43] The scrapping of the National Plan in 1966 began this process of disillusionment, with the ensuing deflationary budgets and mini-budgets to try and defend the parity completing the collapse of fortunes, with this struggle itself eventually abandoned in November 1967 when sterling was finally devalued to $2.40.[44]

Throughout this fourth phase we observe a retreat from policy experimentation towards economic orthodoxy, although with the change of government in June 1970 there was also a short-lived shift in the direction of policy 'away from demand management towards less interventionist supply-side policies that, it was hoped, would stimulate growth and lead to an abatement of inflationary pressures'.[45]

This reaction against big government is known as the Seldon phase and has often been seen as a precursor of the more radical Thatcherite project. This is actually a misreading of the historical record, for while 'Heath was strongly motivated by the desire to improve the efficiency of the British economy, he was never a "whole hogger" on *laissez-faire*.'[46] None the less, what distinguished the early Heath years, as with the tail-end of the previous administration, was the beginnings of a diagnosis of Britain's condition that required industrial relations reform. The Wilson government had proposed moderate reforms in its 1969 white paper *In Place of Strife*, but had capitulated in the face of backbench and trade union opposition.

The new Heath government, however, pressed ahead and passed the Industrial Relations Act, 1971, which attempted significant reforms across a broad front. This would eventually result in the collapse of that government in the face of trade union opposition and the chaos caused by a miner's strike, but it is important that throughout this fourth postwar policy phase, both Labour and the Conservatives were drawn into conflicts with the trade unions.[47] The initial voluntary phase of prices and incomes policies gave way to a statutory phase between 1966–70, and while in opposition the Conservatives implacably opposed such detailed government intervention, when they attained government they practised a covert incomes policy between 1970–2 on public sector workers in the hope that this de-escalation of successively smaller nominal increases (known as 'N minus one') would influence private sector wage setting.[48] The actual results were limited (see Figure 2.4, p. 51), but what brought about the more profound shift in policy known as the Heath U-turn was the fear of rising unemployment in 1971–2 and the financial difficulties experienced by certain high-profile British companies which had to be bailed out by the government (e.g. Rolls Royce).

3.4.5 Corporatism and Keynesianism, 1972–9

Our fifth phase thus starts with the Conservative government being panicked into abandoning its previous disengagement in industrial policy, together with its commitment to tight monetary and fiscal policies, and continues through to the election of May 1979, although during the summer–autumn of 1976 policy was punctuated by a new and much more severe sterling crisis which had enduring effects.[49] The unifying characteristics of this phase were a resumption of corporatism, much looser monetary and fiscal policies (at least to 1976) and endemic political and economic crises: a phase thus, according to its critics, of last-ditch Keynesianism and of problems with the postwar settlement, which had long been in the making, finally coming to fruition. This phase also saw Britain finally attain membership of the EEC in January 1973, and in the previous year, as part of the generalised break-up of the **Bretton Woods** system of fixed exchange rates, choosing to float sterling in order to attain a more flexible approach towards weak competitiveness and continuing balance of payments problems.

We begin thus in 1972 with the most significant peacetime reflation of demand that the British economy has ever experienced. The resulting 'Barber boom' was characterised by unsustainably high growth by 1973, a rapid fall in unemployment (Figure 2.1, p. 41), but also a very pronounced deterioration in the current account balance of payments (Figure 2.2, p. 43), notwithstanding the floating exchange rate. Thus, at the point at which the OPEC I shock hit, Britain already had a seriously weakened external account. Moreover, this reflation made more urgent that the government have an effective anti-inflation strategy. The statutory controls of prices and incomes operated from November 1972 onwards was unequal to the task and there resulted growing conflict with employers and the trade unions, all of which culminated with the miner's strike of 1973–4, the ensuing three-day week and, finally, the calling of a snap election in late February 1974 over whether it was government or the trade unions who really governed Britain.[50]

The result of this contest was unclear (Table 3.1, p. 69), save that it was apparent that it was not the Conservatives who could govern or at least control the trade unions. The minority position of the new government produced a stasis in policy, with necessarily corrective action delayed until Labour had completed negotiations with the trade unions for voluntary control of wages in return for implementation of various manifesto commitments such as repeal of the much-hated Industrial Relations Act. This accord, known as the social contract, was a precondition for Labour making a further appeal to the electorate for a Parliamentary majority sufficient so that they could govern effectively. This they did not receive, with the consequence that right through to May 1979, Labour was dependent upon building coalitions with small and/or regional parties on particular issues. Long before this election, however, Labour was forced to change direction. The following speech by the Prime Minister to the 1976 party conference conveys a sense not just of a shift in policy direction for this government, but of the approaching end of an era:[51]

> We used to think that you could spend your way out of a recession, and increase employment by cutting taxes and boosting Government spending. I tell you in all candour that that option no longer exists, and that in so far as it ever did exist, it only worked by injecting a bigger dose of inflation into the economy, followed by a higher level of unemployment as the next step. Higher inflation followed by higher unemployment. We have just escaped from the [sic] highest rate of inflation this country has known; we have not yet escaped from the consequences: high unemployment. That is the history of the last 20 years.

This speech, which was shortly followed by stringent budgetary cuts and a tightening of monetary policy,[52] has been widely seen as marking a repudiation of the Keynesian conventional wisdom. In Holmes's assessment it 'reflect[ed] a decisive change in the intellectual climate ... devastat[ing] the philosophy of post-war Keynesianism in a way that had been previously unthinkable for any Prime Minister, Labour or Conservative.'[53] However, the speech's author (his son-in-law, Peter Jay, a financial journalist and a recent convert to the cause of monetarism) and ultimate audience (the foreign exchange markets) counsels caution about the timing of any third-order change from Keynesianism to monetarism. Accordingly, whatever the rhetoric, policy actually remained recognisably Keynesian in terms of policy instruments and objectives through to the election in 1979, while there was no conversion to the principles of monetarism by the Chancellor and his political and civil service colleagues.[54] What there was, however, was a new realism about government's capacity to manage the economy in a world of high inflationary expectations, greater uncertainty and sharper class divisions, themselves stemming from the age of high inflation.

Our fifth phase is thus punctuated by Labour confronting some brutal political choices which were a consequence of the OPEC supply-side shock impacting on an already unstable domestic economy, which was itself inflation-prone because of long-standing industrial relations problems. In addition, and what was distinctly new, given the substantial budget deficits of the time and floating exchange rate regime, the markets were now able to exercise a decisive influence on how the government would resolve its problems. Thus, as the summer gave way to autumn, the money markets showed increasing concern that public expenditure was growing out of control, while the foreign exchange markets were exercised that Britain's high inflation rate risked an uncontrollable depreciation of sterling which, through higher import prices, would in turn impact back on the domestic inflation rate.[55]

The choice appeared to be that between autarky or continued participation in the liberal world order. The political left championed what became known as the Alternative Economic Strategy (AES), this entailing further nationalisation, import controls and economic planning; the political right pursued the case for less and smaller government in all respects. The Labour Cabinet chose the (qualified) latter path and in the process prepared the ground for Thatcherism by acceding to IMF monitoring of the British economy, and with it the imposition of monetary targets; to a significant rise in unemployment; and to massive cuts in public expenditure, indeed the most significant retrenchment of the whole postwar period.[56] However, the government was not impotent for the remaining two and a half years of its term of office. Admittedly, there is the strong image of it finally collapsing in the spring of 1979 because of the so-called 'winter of discontent' when the government had tried and failed to enforce a final de-escalatory phase of its incomes policy. But, our historical image of this administration has been too much constructed by its successor, and more considered academic reappraisals are now emphasising that when Labour left office inflation was lower than in 1974, growth had been resumed, unemployment was falling and the balance of payments much stronger.[57]

3.4.6 The monetarist policy experiment, 1979–83

That both the Heath and Wilson-Callaghan governments collapsed because of industrial relations conflicts provided the text against which the incoming Conservative government sought to construct a very different economic policy regime. There would consequently be no statutory incomes policies, although public sector workers were inevitably so controlled as part of the fiscal retrenchment which was a central component in the manifesto pledge to tame big government. Our sixth phase, however, is better known for the monetarist policy experiment to which the British economy was subjected during the first Thatcher administration.[58] As Galbraith was to say, if monetarism had to be put to the test 'what better people to try it on than the British, whose famous phlegm will put up with anything'.[59]

There was, however, much more to Thatcherism than just monetarism. Indeed, elsewhere I have referred to it as a move to 'back to basics' in economic theory and policy.[60] For Thatcher and her New Right colleagues, what was necessary to save the British economy from further ruin through Keynesian economics and over-mighty trade unions was the reassertion and application of certain *universal* economic truths: of sound finance, through monetary rectitude, in macroeconomics; and of market incentives and disciplines, in microeconomics. Moreover, a move back to basics also related to concerns about overload and ungovernability: it was an attempt to downgrade public expectations of what governments can reasonably achieve, with consequent rewards being as much political as economic. In fact, the period of monetary fundamentalism was extremely short-lived, and it was market triumphalism that would become the enduring legacy of these years.

The years 1979–83 thus saw a short and ultimately unsuccessful experiment to secure lower inflation through a monetary disinflation comprising strict control of the money supply, high interest rates and an accommodatingly restrictive fiscal policy. The Keynesian policy objective of full employment was deliberately sacrificed in the effort to secure price stability, and throughout these years, there was a conscious and strident policy experimentation which introduced a new policy framework (the Medium-term Financial Strategy, MTFS) designed to engineer that disinflation; to downgrade expectations of government, by educating workers and managers about market disciplines through higher unemployment and bankruptcy (non-accommodation of wage and other cost-push pressures); and to prepare the ground for supply-side policies (privatisation, industrial relations and tax-benefit reforms) calculated to counter long-run decline.

The reasons why this experiment failed are analysed in Section 4.1. Here we observe that these changes constituted the only third-order shift of the postwar period, but even so the rhetoric of policy shift was typically much stronger than the reality. In any case, monetarism was pursued by the new government for additional reasons independent of a reordering of the price stability and full employment objectives. The appeal of monetarism was first that it appeared to depersonalise the economic problem since imposition of a monetary growth rule, combined with a view of the private sector as inherently stable providing government did not intervene, led directly to a minimal short-term role for government. Secondly, monetarism and the elevation of price stability above all other macroeconomic objectives was a veil behind which other neo-liberal agendas could be pursued: the contraction of the public sector, with reduced public borrowing (the PSBR) justified in terms of monetary disinflation; labour market reforms to reduce the **NAIRU** so that such disinflation did not result in permanently higher unemployment once agents accepted the credibility of the MTFS; and tax and benefit reforms which, in strengthening incentives, rejuvenated the supply-side and thus eased the public finances on both the receipts and expenditure side.[61]

3.4.7 After monetarism, 1983–92

The period of monetary fundamentalism soon gave way to our seventh phase: that of a progressive retreat from monetarist rhetoric, monetary policy restraint and even explicit money supply targets (abandoned in Britain in 1985) towards a much more pragmatic position, which would eventually result in what became known as exchange rate monetarism, this itself culminating in the ill-fated ERM episode of October 1990 to September 1992 when Britain sought to maintain a fixed, but overvalued exchange rate.[62] The background to the growing preoccupation with the exchange rate was twofold. First, there was the concern that, in seeking to contain inflationary pressures through monetary policy instruments (especially high interest rates), there must not be a repeat of the 1980–2 appreciation of the sterling exchange rate for this had severely damaged British exports and the manufacturing sector. Monetary policy should thus seek to stabilise the exchange rate. Secondly, the lesson was drawn from the previous phase that in Britain there was, in practice, no settled and durable relationship between growth in the money supply (however defined) and nominal incomes, while

the monetary authorities found themselves quite unable to keep
monetary growth within the targets set by the MTFS because of
the particular structure and propensity to innovate of Britain's
financial system. We will document these missed targets in Section
4.1.4.

The relaxation in monetary and fiscal policies that occurred after 1983
was made possible by the fact that inflation had fallen from its peak in
1980 and made necessary by the huge rise in unemployment that had
been the consequence of this monetary disinflation. Unemployment, in
fact, remained above 10 per cent through to 1987 (Figure 2.1), but while
the inflation rate had by the mid-1980s returned to levels not seen since
the late-1960s (Figure 2.4), it still remained significantly above competitor
economies, with competitiveness thereby being eroded unless there was
an accommodating depreciation in the exchange rate. It was early in
this period that Lawson, the architect of the MTFS and the most
important economic minister of the Thatcher years, enunciated a new
guiding principle which has since become the orthodoxy, that:

> instead of seeking to use macroeconomic (i.e. fiscal and monetary) policy
> to promote growth and microeconomic policy (of which incomes policy
> was a key component) to suppress inflation, the Government should
> direct macroeconomic policy to the suppression of inflation and rely
> on microeconomic (or supply-side) policy, such as tax and labour mar-
> ket reform, to provide the conditions favourable to improved perform-
> ance in terms of growth and employment.[63]

In macroeconomic policy, therefore, the aim was to generate and
sustain a credible anti-inflation strategy. Given their policy ambition
of reversing Britain's economic decline, we would expect the greater
part of policy innovation to be on the supply-side. The years 1983–
92 and, indeed, those through to the loss of power in 1997 thus see
the active promotion of privatisation; efforts to make markets more
efficient and to broaden the influence of market disciplines on public
sector activities; and adjustments to the tax and social security
systems in the name of strengthening incentives and such penalties
as thought appropriate. However, the background was one of very
marked macroeconomic instability, with the Lawson boom of 1987–
8 giving way to a sharp recession between 1990–2, while globalisation
was proceeding apace which lessened all countries' national
economic policy autonomy.

3.4.8 The search for policy credibility since 1992

The retreat from monetarism was completed with Britain's ejection from the ERM in September 1992.[64] The twin characteristics of this eighth and final phase was the emphasis on the long term and on policy credibility. The current policy environment might be described as combining pragmatic macroeconomic management, more coarse than fine-tuning, of closet Keynesianism within a disciplinary framework provided – or often not – by monetary policy credibility, with a continued commitment to longer run supply-side reforms directed at securing stable output and employment growth without reawakening inflationary pressures.[65] The stance of policy is well expressed in the Treasury's current mission statement which requires it:[66]

- to 'maintain a stable macroeconomic environment', entailing the 'objectives of low inflation, sound public finance, affordable public expenditure and an efficient and effective tax policy'; and
- to 'help strengthen the long-term performance of the economy and the outlook for jobs, in strategic partnership for others', this associated 'with a range of supply-side policies including efficient public expenditure management, privatisation and the Private Finance Initiative', but also with intangibles (predictability and stability) in reality deriving from the effect of macroeconomic policies on the general economic climate.

It is arguable that this final phase constitutes a very quiet revolution in British economic policy. Since the ERM debacle, government has designed a new framework to secure policy credibility with the centrepiece being an explicit domestic inflation target, initially 0–2 per cent per annum, currently less than 2.5 per cent. This was part of a process of institutional reform directed at greater transparency and openness to the setting of interest rates, which eventually culminated in 1997 in the transfer of operational control of monetary policy from the Treasury to the Bank of England. This stage of the process occurred under New Labour, and is thus beyond our remit, but it is relevant here. It marks the culmination of a long process in which politicians, after half a century of very active discretionary economic management, are ceding certain functions to rule-based systems operated by non-political agents. The much greater scrutiny of government policies is also evident with respect to the public finances, where New Labour has sought policy credibility through a greater audit and monitoring role for Parliament.

3.5 Summary and interim conclusions

Economic policy is the interaction between what governments come to believe they have to do to the economy and what they think economics and politics makes possible. Over the half-century since the Second World War both have been transformed, but not in any straightforward fashion. In 1945 the stock of government was high and the public broadly approving of highly interventionist economic policies. In war the state had proved its competency, whilst politicians had risen above sectarian concerns to pursue the public interest. However, after the 1950 election the norms of peacetime politics were quickly resumed and this undermined the consent for such *dirigism*. Whilst opinion poll evidence shows that the political salience of economic issues grew for another two decades or so, the early 1960s actually marked the high-watermark for governmental capacity, and after the 1966 election disillusionment set in and so much so that by the 1970s, government itself was widely being seen as the source of Britain's economic problem. This conditioned a major characteristic of the Thatcherite project, that of downgrading public expectations of what government can deliver. This has, of course, also characterised New Labour when in opposition and then in government.

The interaction between the capacity of government and its economic ambitions has been conditioned also by developments beyond the nation state. At the end of the war sterling was not convertible, capital was internationally immobile, much of British industry was protected behind tariff barriers and there were, as yet, few international treaty obligations which impacted on domestic economic policies. The opening up of world trade in the 1950s, the development of the Bretton Woods system, membership of EFTA and then the EEC (now the EU), other international treaty obligations, the freeing of domestic capital markets and liberalisation of international capital movements have all come to lessen the policy space within which British governments operate. With the disintegration of the USSR and the other Communist states the market has triumphed as both ideology and as the superior allocative mechanism. One manifestation of this has been the emphasis now given to globalisation and how this constrains what any national government can seek to achieve in terms of its own economic policies. It would be premature to comment on the likely durability of the current balance between market and government in Britain today, but it is appropriate to observe that after the reaction against big government in the 1970s and 1980s, the size and scope of government in Britain is now rather closer to the American than to the mainstream continental European model.

4

POLICY EFFECTIVENESS SINCE 1945

> There is in operation ... a law of the deterioration of British economic
> policies. Like the 'average' Russian harvest ('worse than last year's, bet-
> ter than next year's'), every government seems to have done more dam-
> age and to have succeeded in fewer things than the preceding one.[1]

In this chapter we test the validity of Pollard's Law, although we should
note that Pollard was writing in the early 1980s amidst a serious
depression he considered to be the consequence of government
policies, which were themselves a continuation of the 'contempt for
production' that he identified as having characterised Stop-Go since
the 1950s. The radicalism of the Thatcherite project was thus unclear
at that time, as indeed was the possibility that in the longer-run this
project might contribute towards arresting relative economic decline.
Since then, of course, the orthodoxy has emerged that, first, the
Thatcher policies did mark a decisive break with the managed-mixed
economy and welfare state established by the postwar settlement; and,
secondly, that the new policy regime did indeed turnaround the British
economy. In addition to Pollard's Law we should also introduce at
this early point a central characteristic of the historiography of postwar
British economic policy: that the story told is one of a series of missed
opportunities (1945 with the pursuit of a New Jerusalem; late-1950s
with Stop-Go and not joining the EEC; etc.), with attendant
counterfactual, alternative and potentially more efficacious policy
programmes.

Taken together we have then the central questions that we need to
ask about the policy debate and an automatic link to the benchmarks

100

against which policy effectiveness should be assessed:

• against stated policy objectives, with allowance made for constraints known, unknown or unknowable;
• against widely canvassed alternative policy objectives (both domestic and other country's) and the setting/selection of policy instruments; and
• against later policies that have produced results which have been accepted as welfare-enhancing and potentially applicable to earlier periods.

This chapter is organised as follows. We divide our assessment between macro- and microeconomic policies (Sections 4.1 and 4.2 respectively), this roughly equivalent to demand- and supply-side policies. In each we progress from the policy environment through to the constituent parts of policy; we pay attention to the selection and settings of policy instruments; and then make an assessment of policy effectiveness, both of the constituent parts and overall. We show how successive governments confronted the trade-offs they faced between the four main macroeconomic objectives, how these trade-offs worsened over time despite efforts to augment the range of policy instruments available, and how eventually there emerged a crisis of Keynesian conventional wisdom in the 1970s which precipitated the single third-order shift of the postwar era. We then investigate what was genuinely new, efficacious or otherwise, in the resulting policy regime inaugurated by the first Thatcher government.

Throughout we will emphasise two characteristics of postwar British policies:

• conflicts between short-run macroeconomic objectives and longer-run growth promoting supply-side reforms, with the former prevailing at the expense of the latter as policy progressed from one crisis to another; and
• a tendency for governments to act as if their supply-side reforms had none the less improved the underlying performance of the British economy and its capacity to respond to demand stimuli without risk of inflation and/or a deterioration in the current account balance of payments.

We will explore whether the claims made for the Thatcherite project can be substantiated and, in the process, consider whether an earlier application of many of these reforms would have been practical economics and/or politics. In assessing policy effectiveness we will stress that the institutional setting in Britain severely limits the policy space, a concept we introduced earlier (pp. 20–1) and which we here employ in the sense of the parameters of what is possible when politics and economics are themselves conceived as being 'normal', that is not in crisis. In its affect upon the definition of current policy problems, the perception of the range and efficacy of policy instruments, and the resulting room for manoeuvre, the policy space can be conceived as a form of path-dependency, a concept in turn introduced earlier in relation to economic performance (p. 14). From this we are led naturally to the conclusion reached by two political scientists that 'Governing today is not so much about making fresh choices; it is principally about living with the consequences of past choices. Most activities of government do not reflect today's decisions, but decisions made yesterday.'[2]

In addition to this limited policy space we will also draw attention to the characteristic that 'the adverse consequences of government policies have been largely the unintended and unexpected by-products of well-meaning policies that were adopted without looking beyond their immediate purpose or understanding the magnitudes of their adverse long-run consequences.'[3] Unintended policy effects have particularly impacted on market incentives and penalties. Finally, in Section 4.3 we draw some preliminary conclusions. In what follows the reader is referred back to Table 3.3 (p. 86), our summary of the four main macroeconomic indicators by government, and the underlying charts of these series (Figures 2.1, 2.2 and 2.4; pp. 41, 43, 51).

4.1 Macroeconomic policies

4.1.1 The policy environment

Our starting point is with the distinction between the ultimate and intermediate objectives of policy and the means of achieving those objectives. In economics the ultimate objective is taken to be the maximisation of national economic welfare, whereas in politics the objectives are typically defined as the maintenance of the nation state and the maximisation of the probability of the governing party maintaining power. The one need not necessarily conflict with the other, but frequently does as competition in the political market-place results in manipulation of the economy in a manner which actually maximises sectional rather than national economic welfare. The existence of Stop-Go and the emphasis given it in the literature strongly suggest that, in the British case, economic policy is politics by other means. This brings us to the intermediate objectives of economic policy: these are the ends to which policy is directed, such as stable exchange rates or a favourable trade balance which, in turn, are the means to achieve the ultimate economic objectives. Finally, we have the individual policy instruments which can be set and combined to achieve these intermediate policy objectives. What we thus think of as economic policy, such as adjustments to interest rates or the annual budget, are thus the bottom layer of a policy pyramid in which firstly policy-makers have to establish their objectives and then to chose, calibrate and co-ordinate their policy instruments. Table 4.1 (see over) details the evolution of macroeconomic policy through successive regimes and associated sets of policy objectives and instruments.

The story of British macroeconomic policies since the war is, first, a story of the management of the trade-offs between the four macroeconomic objectives, and secondly, an account of how short-term crises have overtaken longer-term microeconomic initiatives to improve the economy's supply-side. Brittan, in his enormously influential assessment of the Conservative's economic record between 1951-64, concluded that for much of this period, 'Chancellors behaved like simple Pavlovian dogs responding to two main stimuli: one was a "run on the reserves" and the other was "500,000 unemployed" – a figure which was latter increased to above 600,000.'[4] In fact, the maximum tolerable level of unemployment would be redefined in the 1970s and 1980s such that even 600,000 would constitute policy success, but the essential pattern of policy being buffeted from a preoccupation with unemployment to concern for the external position has been sustained through to the present day.

Whilst this appears a bipolar world, in reality the bread-and-butter of macroeconomic policy was the management of two interconnected trade-offs involving all four policy objectives. The first trade-off

Table 4.1 Macroeconomic policy regimes, selected years, 1945–97

Year	Government	Policy regime	Principal macro-economic policy instruments	Hierarchy of macro-economic policy objectives
1945	Labour	Early Keynesianism	Fiscal; also initially cheap money	Full employment-price stability; Balance of payments surplus
1951	Conservative	Keynesian demand management	Fiscal; Monetary	Full employment-price stability; Balance of payments surplus; Economic growth
1964	Labour	Keynesian demand management	Fiscal; Monetary	Full employment-price stability; Balance of payments surplus; Economic growth
1973	Conservative	Keynesian demand management	Fiscal; Monetary; Exchange rate	Full employment-price stability; Balance of payments surplus; Economic growth
1979	Conservative	MTFS	Monetary targets; PSBR targets	Price stability Disinflation
1997	Conservative	Anti-inflation policy credibility, especially monetary policy transparency	Interest rates; Inflation targets	Price stability Reduce output gap

Source: Adapted from Crafts, 'The British economy', Table 1.4.

became known as the Phillips curve, that portraying an inverse relationship between the level of unemployment and the rate of wage inflation (for a diagrammatic representation, see Figure III.5, p. 165). This appeared to offer policy-makers a settled menu of choices of so much unemployment bought at the price of so much inflation.[5] The second key trade-off was that between economic growth and equilibrium in the current account balance of payments, with above trend growth associated with a weakening of the visible trade balance due to import penetration and the diversion of goods to the home market which were previously destined for exports as domestic capacity was unable to fully supply the high level of domestic demand.

Table 4.2 The timing of and signals for 'Stop-Go' policies using the current macro-economic indicators, 1951–79.

Year	Policy phase	Real GDP growth rate on previous year (%)	Annual average unemployment rate in year of policy (%)	Change in RPI on previous year (%)	Current account balance of payments (£ millions)	Change in foreign exchange reserves on previous year (£ millions)
1951	Stop	3.5	1.2	11.8	(425)	(344)
1952	Go	..	2.0	6.7	170	(175)
1956	Stop	2.0	1.2	3.3	209	42
1958	Go	-	2.1	1.5	345	284
1962	Go	(0.5)	2.0	2.7	115	(183)
1965	Stop	3.3	1.4	4.7	(49)	246
1968	Stop	4.1	2.4	4.8	(271)	(114)
1971	Go	1.5	3.6	9.3	1,040	1,348
1975	Stop	0.0	3.9	24.2	(1,732)	..
1977	Go	(1.5)	5.7	15.8	(224)	..

Source: Derived from Mosley, *The Making of Economic Policy,* Tables 4.1, 5.3.

The timing of and signals for policy intervention using then current macroeconomic indicators are shown in Table 4.2 for the classic period of Stop-Go through to the late 1970s. As can be seen, both trade-offs became increasingly expensive as the postwar period progressed: thus a constant target rate of unemployment could only be bought by ever higher inflation by the 1970s, whilst a target growth rate could only be attained if the authorities were prepared to accept deepening current account deficits.[6] The Phillips curve relationship broke down altogether in the 1970s with the appearance of stagflation, thus a combination of stagnant output, rising unemployment and accelerating inflation which hitherto had been thought theoretically improbable. Stagflation would thus contribute immensely to the crisis of Keynesian conventional wisdom of the mid-1970s, while the growth-balance of payments trade-off would shortly thereafter be eased, but only temporarily, by North Sea oil and gas.

Initially Stop-Go followed from the dual commitment to full employment and the maintenance of a strong pound. It was conditioned by inflexible labour and goods markets and subject to the external constraint that we discussed in Section 2.2: of endemic weakness in the current account balance of payments and of an inadequate level of foreign exchange reserves. The underlying condition of inflexible labour and goods markets, of aggregate supply not responding quickly enough to the Go phase of the cycle, strengthened the urgency of improving the supply-side if demand management was itself to be more effective. Whilst the authorities thought that they had lessened the external constraint in 1972, when they took the decision to abandon a fixed exchange rate and instead float sterling, in practice balance of payments problems have continued to limit the macroeconomic policy space and the maintenance of a high exchange rate has periodically been targeted as one means of containing domestic inflationary pressures. In Pollard's formulation of Stop-Go, cycles were policy induced and trend growth inhibited because the incentive to invest was undermined by the instability of the economy. Whilst we have rejected the strong form of the Pollard thesis, for during the golden age the British economy was actually one of the most cyclically stable of the OECD states, there remains the issue of whether policy made fluctuations better or worse and whether there was something uniquely growth inhibiting about Stop-Go. We address the issue of the stabilising effectiveness of policy in Section 4.1.4, but here note that there is strong supporting evidence that frequent adjustments to policy instruments impacting on both consumption and investment resulted in firms quickly learning that the Go phase of the cycle would not be permanent and that they should moderate their investment plans. The poor supply response to demand management was thus learnt behaviour.[7]

4.1.2 Fiscal policy

Before Keynes provided a theoretical rationale for how and why governments should manipulate the budget to secure a high and stable level of employment, the traditional characteristic of fiscal policy was that the authorities sought to balance the budget at the minimum level of taxation deemed politically appropriate.[8] The component parts of the budget did, of course, impact on the economy via government purchasing goods and services, transferring purchasing power to economic agents and impacting on the overall allocation of resources and distribution of incomes via the incidence of taxation and its affect on prices, incomes and choices, but the budget was too small to have much impact on aggregate demand. However, with the growth in the size of the public sector as a consequence of the two world wars (Section 3.2) the budget came to have such an effect and the story of postwar fiscal policy is one of how the authorities sought to reconcile these allocative, distributive and stabilisation functions to promote growth and stability.[9] Four questions dominate the literature:

1. In what senses, if any, were postwar fiscal policies Keynesian until the mid-1970s?
2. If Keynesianism can be demonstrated, were such policies responsible for the achievement of full employment up to the late 1960s?
3. To what extent were fiscal policies stabilising?; and
4. Was it the case, as critics of big government maintained, that by the mid-1970s relative decline was due to the excess growth of Britain's public sector?

In time-honoured fashion, the answer to the first question varies according to how the problem is defined. If Keynesianism is taken as meaning a particular theoretical understanding of how the public and private sector components of aggregate demand interact, and how it is necessary for the public sector to compensate for fluctuations in private sector demand because capitalist economies are inherently unstable, then the period through to the mid-1970s was genuinely the age of Keynes. If, however, Keynesianism is interpreted in purer terms, such as the largely unqualified willingness to use budget deficits to stimulate employment and to give a higher priority to full employment than to any other objective, then we must be much more cautious. The active use of budget deficits for stabilisation purposes was delayed until the late-1950s and, with the exception of the Barber boom, the maintenance of low inflation and balance of payments equilibrium always took precedence over full employment.[10]

Our answer to the second question is less equivocal as we accept Matthews' analysis, recently confirmed by Broadberry, that full employment for the quarter-century or so since the war was due less to Keynesian fiscal policies than to the twin booms in world trade and investment.[11] However, an indirect Keynesian effect on the propensity to invest can be presumed for the golden age, with businesses taking seriously the commitment to full employment and thus being optimistic that there would not be a major slump which would make their investment plans unrealisable. Moreover, the distinguishing characteristic of the golden age was less the commitment to full employment than the fact that this commitment was never seriously tested, and when it was in Britain in the early 1970s, it quickly became evident that government lacked the capability to deliver on its commitment. Government does, however, re-enter the picture in terms of policies which were growth enhancing. Indeed, this leads us to what Maddison calls the system characteristics of the golden age.[12]

1. Managed liberalism in international transactions.
2. Government promotion of domestic demand buoyancy.
3. Policies and circumstances which moderated inflation.
4. A backlog of growth possibilities which made the supply response very sensitive to high levels of demand.

Clearly, the logic of relative decline was that Britain shared less in the super-growth of the golden age than did those economies with the greatest potential to realise the catch-up bonus. None the less, all four system characteristics applied to the British case, although in practice the second and third elements often proved more difficult to sustain than in other countries. Whilst it was a British government which was amongst the first to abandon the commitment to full employment in the wake of OPEC I, it is none the less clear from the comparative record for the four main macroeconomic objectives (Table 2.4, p. 34) that all OECD countries experienced a very marked deterioration in performance by these criteria.

This then brings us to our third problem: that of the stabilising effectiveness of fiscal policies. Dow's conclusion with respect to the 1950s, that 'As far as internal conditions are concerned ... budgetary and monetary policy failed to be stabilizing, and must on the contrary be regarded as positively destabilizing',[13] is typically taken as setting the theme for much of the remainder of the postwar period. His conclusions, although frequently construed as being rather stronger than he intended, have received support from more recent work on the 1960s and beyond.[14] But the evidence for systematic failure is by no means clear-cut. Particular policy failures, in terms of the timing and scale of budgetary (and monetary) interventions, have been well documented, but overall there is 'no support for the view that the periodicity in the British trade cycle is the product, whether by accident or by design, of discretionary budgetary policy.'[15] This leaves open the question of whether policy made fluctuations better or worse during the heyday of Stop-Go, and indeed a balanced verdict on this era is that, because fiscal policy was used not just for fine-tuning demand, but to try and break through supply constraints, it was unable to lessen cyclical instability because no means was ultimately found of attaining faster economic growth.[16] Moreover, even after active Keynesianism was abandoned in the crisis of the mid-1970s, and there was less of the appearance of budgetary policy lurching successively from expansion to contraction, fiscal policy was often destabilising: contributing towards the severity of the 1979–81 recession and – through unwarranted cuts in personal taxation – to the extravagances of the Lawson boom of 1987–9.[17]

Fiscal policy was often destabilising because of forecasting errors about the current position of the economy and of its most probable immediate prospects. Much effort was expended on improving official economic statistics and forecasting, on acquiring new policy instruments such as the regulator which acted more speedily on demand, and on attempting to reconcile full employment with reasonable price stability through incomes policies of various sorts. However, the decisive development for fiscal policy was that during the mid-1970s, the view began to gain ground as part of the monetarist counter-revolution that Keynesian demand management was not just unnecessary, but dangerous because it undermined the inherent stability of the private sector. Ultimately, therefore, any view about the effectiveness of fiscal policy has to be subservient to the prevailing policy regime and the climate of economic ideas.

It remains to consider the arguments, advanced as part of the reaction against big government which was gathering pace by the mid-1970s, that Britain's economic problem was due to the excessive growth of its public sector. That public sector expansion might be harmful to the private sector is hardly a novel thesis, and indeed was a commonplace of Adam Smith and the classical economists. But in Britain in the mid-1970s, it had a particular appeal because stagflation was associated with a rapid growth in government borrowing, which many monetarists argued was crowding-out private sector investment.[18] A second line of argument, one associated with the influential work of Bacon and Eltis,[19] was that public 'non-market' sector growth deprived the private 'market' sector of productive resources, thereby contributing to deindustrialisation and stagflation. This found much favour amongst those concerned that the high rates of tax necessary to fund public expenditure were undermining incentives to work, save and invest, but it cannot be said that the Bacon and Eltis thesis received much support amongst academic economists. Moreover, the distinguishing characteristic of Britain's public sector was not its large size, but its smallness in relation to other more successful European economies.[20] None the less, claims for crowding-out and variants of the Bacon and Eltis thesis proved extremely durable in the wider political debate which was preparing the ground for the monetarist policy experiment to which Britain was subjected between 1979–83.

4.1.3 Monetary policy

The evolution of postwar monetary policy almost exactly mirrors the changing perception of Britain's economic difficulties and the shift in policy objectives that this compelled.[21] Thus in our first period 1945–51, when the concern was postwar reconstruction and the avoidance of a slump, monetary policy was largely subordinate to fiscal policy and direct controls. The change of administration in 1951 heralded a period of more active monetary intervention, with credit restrictions and short-term interest rates typically employed as instruments to depress demand whenever the balance of payments and/or foreign exchange reserves were under stress. Monetary policy still remained subordinate to fiscal policy, a policy mix which gained added support from the influential Radcliffe report on the workings of the monetary system.[22] However, greater reliance came to be placed on monetary instruments to rectify external imbalance once balance of payments difficulties became chronic in the 1960s, with the first target for monetary aggregates being adopted in 1967 as part of the package of measures agreed with the IMF when sterling was devalued. Whilst the external constraint was then eased for the next few years, the 1970s saw monetary policy instruments and objectives assume a much higher profile, with some arguing that it came not just to supplement, but to supplant fiscal policy as the principal element in demand management. This is actually too catastrophic an interpretation of the crisis of Keynesianism during the 1970s, for the growing use of monetary policy instruments was justified in part by the need to establish a new anchor for policy now that there was no longer the monetary discipline imposed by a fixed exchange rate.[23]

The course of policy was conditioned by a number of forces and constraints: the exchange rate regime, within which should be included the degree to which sterling was overvalued at various times and the trend increase in international capital mobility; the needs of debt management; the fiscal stance; the balance between short- and longer-run policy objectives; changing beliefs about the channels through which monetary policy operated; the search for improved techniques of money supply control; and certain distinct ideological influences. No simple evolutionary path may be traced. Rather, the use of monetary policy, 'has been peculiarly subject to the whims of intellectual fashion in economic thought, in Britain perhaps even more so than elsewhere', but with some striking continuities since 1945: 'an ambivalence about the role of monetary policy and whether it should be assigned to domestic or external objectives; a preoccupation with the management of the national debt; and an apparent inability to control monetary growth'.[24]

The effectiveness of monetary policy, both as a stabilisation instrument and as a means of achieving longer-term goals, remains even more uncertain than that of fiscal policy. There is no agreement about the channels through which monetary policy operates, though Keynesian analyses naturally focus on interest rates and monetarists more on the money supply; it is difficult in practice to separate out the effects of monetary from other instruments when economic policy was increasingly being framed in terms of 'package deals'; and over the period as a whole, the objectives and relative standing of monetary policy vis-à-vis other instruments were quite transformed.[25] We can summarise the overall impact as follows. Until 1972 the fixed exchange rate regime implied that there was little scope for monetary policy independence, while in any case resort to monetary measures was generally prompted by sterling crises. Few would disagree that the substantial fiscal and monetary boost of 1971–2 produced the excessive Barber boom, but apart from this Artis's verdict on 1960–74 appears valid for the whole period through to 1979: 'it seems unlikely that monetary policy did very much for good or bad in this period; it did not do very much at all, and was not supposed to.'[26]

After 1979, of course, monetary policy had a very much higher profile as control of inflation replaced the maintenance of full employment as the principal macroeconomic policy objective. The supposed superiority of money supply control over Keynesian policy instruments as the means of combating inflation was at the core of the monetarist counter-revolution and the ensuing monetarist policy experiment. However, as one considered assessment has put it:[27]

> Amongst supporters and opponents alike, there was a general air of expectancy and a feeling that this experience would answer important theoretical questions about the design of macroeconomic policy.
>
> In the event, the experiment has proved, or rather disproved, nothing. Monetarists have denied that an experiment ever took place; they have developed new theories to explain the behaviour of the income velocity of circulation or blamed external shocks for structural shifts in the demand for money and the natural rate of unemployment. Non-monetarists, in contrast, have interpreted the Government's failure to execute its strategy as planned as evidence that the money supply cannot be controlled; the gyrations in the velocity of circulation have been taken as further proof that the demand for money is inherently unstable and the coincidence of mass unemployment and stable inflation has been used to attack the natural rate hypothesis.
>
> In a political sense, the 1979–82 experiment certainly did provide a test of practical monetarism and, if nothing else, it established that rigid monetary rules are not the panacea for inflation-free growth in a dynamic, open economy that the Government originally hoped. But in the economic sense of testing key macroeconomic theories, the experiment has merely served to illustrate once again the limitations of empiricism and to highlight the fact that the sources of controversy in economics runs far deeper than many of its practitioners would like to believe.

We have then a polarisation of opinion between those who contend monetarism did not fail because it was never really tried, and those who maintain that the depression it produced between 1979–81, the continuing problems with inflation thereafter and the lacklustre average growth over the 1980s and 1990s demonstrates that the experiment was intensely damaging and of no lasting purpose at the macroeconomic level.[28] The subsequent retreat to pragmatism in macroeconomic policy that we identified in Section 3.4.7 thus acquires a significance not just because the phase of monetary fundamentalism in Britain was so short-lived, but because for the Conservative government, and later for New Labour, the idea became firmly established that the route to salvation for the British economy no longer lay in macroeconomic policy.

4.1.4 The overall effectiveness of macroeconomic policies

The strong claims made by both the opponents of Keynesian demand management and of monetarism are not supported by the empirical evidence. Over the whole postwar period, policy tended to be pro-cyclical rather than contra-cyclical, with frequent mistakes on the whole due to forecasting errors, to the shortage of policy instruments in face of the multiple policy objectives, and to the frequency with which the timing and magnitude of policy interventions had to be matched to an electoral cycle which was unsynchronised with the economic cycle. The redefinition of the guiding principle of macroeconomic policy that occurred after 1983, with the new focus being price stability rather than high growth and full employment (Section 3.4.7), has acted to lessen the scope for macroeconomic policy failure, but it has not been accompanied by a reduction in the criticism to which governments have been subjected. Macroeconomic policy remains acutely political and thus controversial.

If we divide the postwar era at OPEC I, and judge policy effectiveness initially in relation to the four main policy objectives, we can draw the following conclusions:

- Full employment: the architects of the 1944 employment policy white paper would have been astounded by the low average rate (and low variability) of unemployment achieved through to the late 1960s. However, this owed less to stabilisation policies than to the overall environment established by government, and when, post-OPEC I, governments were not able to sustain that environment the unemployment record worsened markedly. Whilst unemployment was by the mid-1980s to reach levels not seen since the inter-war years, a decade later and British unemployment was very low by EU standards, a result which many ascribe to the labour market reforms of the Thatcher years (discussed at Section 4.2.3).
- Price stability: whilst more inflation-prone than the average experience of the EU, G-7 and OECD economies (Table 2.4, p. 34), other high-growth countries have fared even less impressively and the British record – as with strike activity – was only really awful during the 1970s.
- High economic growth: we have already commented extensively on the British record and rather than repeat these deficiencies

in performance, we here cite Cairncross's observation, one based upon directly observing Chancellors at work in the 1960s, that none 'had any real insight into the mainsprings of economic growth, especially if that is taken to mean growth in productivity; they simply assumed that if expansion was sufficiently prolonged, industrial productivity would move upwards to a new, steeper curve.'[29] Underlying this lack of insight was a more deep-seated institutional separation of growth-promoting macro- and microeconomic policies which, before the shift in policy regime in 1979 generated unemployment and spare capacity in abundance, in practice severely limited the policy space.

• Balance of payments equilibrium: whilst our policy narrative has been dominated by crises the objective facts of Britain's record is that Britain's external position was about average in relation to comparator economies, but more sensitive to market pressures because of the unique role of the City of London. Moreover, had a more realistic geopolitical posture been attempted earlier, then much of the balance of payments problems that gave rise to Stop-Go in the first place might have been avoided.

The effectiveness of policy with respect to our second set of benchmarks, those of widely canvassed alternative policies, is more difficult, although the broad parameters are well known. During the 1950s and 1960s a number of economists argued that had the authorities been willing to accept a marginally higher average rate of unemployment, then the balance of payments constraint would have been less pressing and the growth and inflation objectives accordingly easier to attain. Given that a permanent incomes policy proved economically and politically elusive this may, in retrospect, have been the only economically sensible policy, but such was the searing influence of interwar unemployment that even an additional half of one percent on the unemployment rate was viewed as political suicide.[30]

Another less widely canvassed alternative was that of monetarism. At its simplest this required a rebalancing of monetary and fiscal policy instruments, most notably the establishment of a monetary growth rule (that the money supply should grow no faster than a disinflationary target rate of growth of nominal GDP) to which the PSBR was subservient. However,

Table 4.3 MTFS: £M3 and PSBR targets and outturns, 1978/9–1983/4

	£M3		PSBR (£billions)	
	Target range (%)	Out-turn over target (% points)	Forecast	Out-turn
1978/9	8–12	10.5	8.3	9.2
1979/80	7–11	9.6	8.5	9.1
1980/1	7–11	19.1	10.6	13.5
1981/2	6–10	13.7	9.5	10.6
1982/3	8–12	11.1	8.2	7.5
1983/4	7–11	9.5	7.2	10 0

Sources: Oliver, *Whatever happened to Monetarism?*, Table 4.3; and Britton, *Macroeconomic Policy in Britain*, Table 14.6.

this could, and indeed would be viewed more fundamentally in Britain as the proposition that economies are not in practice stabilised, but destabilised by government's demand management policies. We have seen how, beginning in the mid-1970s and rising to a crescendo between 1979 and 1983, an explicit monetarist policy was pursued and we report in Table 4.3 the authorities' lack of success in hitting the money supply and PSBR targets. We are not encouraged that an earlier monetarist policy experiment would have been any more successful, although most economists would be comfortable with the proposition that the Heath government should not have allowed the loose monetary policy of 1971–3 that preceded the very high inflation rates that we now associate with the 1970s. Most would also now subscribe to the conclusion that the inflation that followed the Barber boom tells us less about monetarism and more about how any demand-fuelled 'dash for growth' was bound to confront the reality of a supply-side woefully inadequate for the task.[31] The end of the Keynesian era, therefore, is explained less by an empirical demonstration of monetarism's superiority than of an inability of the existing policy regime to sustain full employment and high growth without accelerating inflation.

This brings us to the third set of benchmarks where, in practice, the alternatives available were much more microeconomic in design and potential effectiveness than macroeconomic, although they have an aggregate aspect to them. We thus use them as a springboard to our discussion of microeconomic policy effectiveness, and we begin with an alternative economic strategy which exercised enormous influence amongst the left of the Labour Party right through to the early-1980s. Thus, from the time of Attlee governments onwards, the left assumed that further nationalisations and the permanent maintenance of a controlled economy were desirable, although there was some imprecision about whether this different balance between government and the market was to be argued on grounds of economic efficiency, social control or egalitarianism. Given what we know about the efficiency losses of superseding the market, and that, in practice, British nationalised industries economically underperformed because of the way in which successive governments limited their commercial freedom, we might not be optimistic about this particular counterfactual.

Similarly, given what we now know about the social costs of the Thatcherite project, and that markets as governments are prone to failures of many sorts, we would need to counsel caution about the likely effectiveness of a much more pro-market macroeconomic policy adopted earlier in the postwar era. Had governments, for example, not committed themselves to full employment, then the wider growth-promoting environment that Maddison identifies might not have taken root. This said, even when we discount the strong version of the Pollard thesis, it is apparent that if macroeconomic policies had been more stabilising, then the cyclical path of the British economy might have been smoother and there might have been benefits for the inducement to invest and thus economic growth.

Both these left and right counterfactuals combine the tenet that policy mistakes with enduring effects were made right at the beginning of the postwar era. However, the latter, pro-market counterfactual has been more thought through and has a much higher profile in the historical literature, most notably in the Barnett thesis of a 'lost victory', in which the Labour government chose to build a New Jerusalem of a welfare state rather than channel resources directly to the restructuring and modernisation of Britain's economy.[32] This thesis, although savaged by professional historians, retains an enduring political and popular appeal,[33] while more considered economic analyses of the flaws in the postwar settlement are now the focus for debate, in particular the consequences of dysfunctional labour-capital relations and the disincentive effects of maintaining wartime rates of taxation for so long.[34]

Table 4.4 Microeconomic policy regimes, selected years, 1945–97

Year	Government	Policy regime	Principal microeconomic policy instruments	Hierarchy of micro-economic policy objectives
1945	Labour	Autarky	Direct controls of factor, goods and capital markets	Close productivity gap; Decontrol and demobilisation
1951	Conservative	Opportunity state	Tax mix and rates	Decontrol and market liberalisation
1964	Labour	Supply-side activism	Indicative planning; Regional policy; Industrial policy	Increase size of manufacturing sector; promote R&D and high-technology sectors
1973	Conservative	Emergency supply-side activism	Regional policy; Industrial policy; Price-wage policies; Industrial relations reform	Contain inflationary pressures and consequences for labour and firms
1979	Conservative	Supply-side activism and smaller government	Tax mix; Privatisations Industrial relations reform	Price stability; disinflation; subject market and non-market sectors to market disciplines
1997	Conservative	Supply-side activism	Deregulation; Decontrol Educational reform	Subject market and non-market sectors to market disciplines; improve average human capital

4.2 Microeconomic policies

4.2.1 The policy environment

Over the half-century since 1945 Britain has moved from having a near command economy to one of the least regulated in Western Europe; indeed, the relationship between government, business and trade unions is now arguably one more characteristic of the US than of the majority of Britain's EU partners. As we saw in Section 3.4, this shifting balance between government and market did not progress linearly, and most assuredly not in terms of its translation into microeconomic policies, where activism in supply-side management was evident at various times under both the Conservatives (1958–64, 1979–97) and under Labour (1945–51, 1964–6, 1974–6) and was also combined with very different macroeconomic policy regimes. We here define supply-side policies as those directed at increasing the supply of the factors of production (principally capital and labour, their quantity, quality and price) and the efficiency with which they are combined,[35] and we note that such policies typically reach beyond the proximate sources of growth to impact upon the ultimate and fundamental causes. Details of the evolution of microeconomic policy regimes are provided in Table 4.4.

Skidelsky, in his chronicle of the crisis of Keynesian conventional wisdom, says that one characteristic of the Keynesian era had been the belief that 'if demand is right, supply will look after itself', but that this 'was particularly delusive for an economy, such as Britain's, suffering from structural obsolescence, and fed the natural inclinations of "over-loaded" post-war British governments to avoid making choices about Britain's future.'[36] We have shown that this is not wholly accurate, for during the active phases of the 1960s and 1970s policy-makers were acutely aware that the efficacy of demand management was limited by supply-side weaknesses. What limited their capacity, however, was that the postwar settlement, which underpinned Keynesianism, did not sanction detailed intervention in goods and labour markets and that when they did attempt such intrusions they quickly realised that no amount of administrative experimentation or 'beer and sandwiches at Number 10' was going to convince sceptical business and trade unions to behave other than as largely free-market agents. Politics thus dictated that supply-side measures be subordinate to demand management. However, as soon as government abandoned the full employment commitment in 1979, and later reversed the traditional association of demand-side policies with promoting growth and supply-side policies with combating inflation, the stage was then set for supply-side policy objectives and instruments to emerge as the dominant strand of contemporary economic policy in Britain.

Although supply-side policies are now directed at the heart of the factors determining competitiveness, they have in the past also addressed other governmental concerns such as the strategic importance of the nationalised industries. Supply-side policies also draw inspiration from a very wide range of economic ideas: from those on the left with what came to maturity as the AES and from those on the right who, in their pursuit of ever more efficient markets, seek a return of the state to its traditional nineteenth-century *laissez-faire* posture. The actual term 'supply-side economics' was first coined in 1976,[37] but we are not being anachronistic in applying it to earlier phases because it has now entered such general currency amongst historians and others, and especially because until challenged by the recent work of Tomlinson and Tiratsoo, the consensus was that 'the chance for a radical reconstruction of the supply side of the economy was lost' right at the outset by the Attlee governments.[38]

Supply-side policies lack the clear-cut categories offered by the component parts of macroeconomic policies and because their consequences, intended and unintended, can be so far reaching, in practice it is extremely difficult to delimit their scale and scope. Drawing a rough distinction between policies impacting upon labour and those upon businesses, including the provision of finance, we can distinguish the following conventional labels for the principal component parts of British supply-side policies:

1. Industrial policy, product market interventions and capital market policies: fiscal incentives for investment and R&D, technology and innovation policies, assistance to sunset industries whilst contracting and promoting sunrise sectors, competition policies, privatisation/nationalisation, national procurement policies, general and specific market regulation/deregulation.
2. Labour market policies: tax and benefit reform, price and incomes policies, education and training policies, industrial relations law, general and specific market regulation/deregulation.

Although adversary politics appeared to generate much to and fro movement in supply-side policies from the end of the war through the watershed in 1979, with incoming governments often abandoning the institutions of their predecessors and with much first- and second-order policy shifts, when closely examined it is apparent that the underlying pattern was more one of evolution and continuity.[39] The real divide is 1979 and we can use this to illustrate how the selection of supply-side policies requires that a view be taken on the appropriate choice between government and market, with this, of course, dependent upon the underlying conception of the inherent (in)efficiency of markets and governments. Thus the *dirigism* of Labour between 1945–51 was based upon a view of widespread market failure and of government potency, whereas our third postwar phase (1958–66) saw the Conservatives and then Labour trying *inter alia* to use government to improve markets and, especially with respect to the well-known problems of free-riders, informational/ coordination weakness and externalities.

Explaining each, in turn, in terms of an example which lies at the core of the policy debate, we have, first, the problem of training, where Britain has for a very long time had a relatively low proportion of young people acquiring vocational qualifications and one of the least educated managerial classes. Economic theory suggests that one reason for both phenomena is that businesses are reluctant to invest in raising the human capital of their workforces because of the potential risk that, while they bear the costs of this investment, they cannot protect themselves by blocking other firms' poaching their workers. One justification for public education and training is thus that it overcomes this free-rider problem.

Actions to address the informational and co-ordination weaknesses of markets have also been a staple of postwar supply-side policies. Whilst many economists would now contend that such policies result in non-market failures which exceed the original market failures at which they are directed, until 1979 successive British governments took the view that the so-called invisible hand of the market was in a mature capitalist economy unable to provide sufficient information (through prices and quantities) and co-ordination for investment to be socially optimal. Healey and Cook use the example that before a new high-technology car plant can be built, managers must be confident that there will be a vibrant demand for their product and that there will not be supply bottlenecks which hinder the initial equipment of the production line. A government commitment to full employment on the demand side, and co-ordination between different consumer and producer goods' sections of industry on the supply side, was deemed to provide the necessary corrective which would underpin sustained, high growth.[40] The apparent success of such indicative planning in France would spur the Labour government of 1964–6 to attempt to replicate these informational and co-ordinating functions in its flagship policy, the National Plan, which whilst effectively stillborn because of continuing demand management problems was none the less deeply flawed in its own terms.[41]

The existence of externalities has long provided a justification for government intervention and has been particularly used to underpin government promotion of R&D, innovation and new technologies. In these policy areas the standard argument was and remains that businesses may have a suboptimal level of investment because they are not able to retain the full private benefits of their activities, as for example in the fruits of an invention spilling over and becoming available to all firms irrespective of their innovative efforts and R&D expenditures. This is another type of free-rider problem. A further example within this broad category concerns government funding of fundamental, so-called blue sky, research which may be uneconomic for individual firms because the paybacks are so uncertain and potentially so long term. It should be noted, however, that with much government-funded R&D being for defence purposes, the scope for civilian spin-offs was often very limited and thus much of the stated justification for government intervention was quite specious.[42]

Whilst economic theory provides contested justifications for intervention and non-intervention, the political market-place is also relevant as many oppose government interventions justified on grounds of market failure because the political process itself encourages economic agents to lobby for sectional advantage through subsidies and tariff protection, lessens the incentives for firms to minimise costs and provides incentives for regulatory capture which undermine the capability of government to make market and non-market processes more efficient. In understanding the evolution of supply-side policies, therefore, the political process is potentially as important as the perception of the economic problem and how it ought technically to be remedied.[43]

4.2.2 Industrial policy, product and capital market interventions

From the end of the war through to 1979, the principal characteristic of British industrial policy was that it sought to foster investment-led growth, typically through public subsidies (or investment allowances) to capital accumulation. This followed from:

> One widely held but grossly over-simplified theory about low UK growth
> ... that because countries with fast growth rates tended to have high

ratios of investment in plant and equipment to GNP (hardly surprising
if these were both seen as the results of market success) then what the
UK needed to do in order to grow was to invest more heavily.[44]

In fact, numerous studies attest that, as a percentage of output, during
the golden age manufacturing investment in Britain was on a par
with that in Germany. The problem, as we saw in Section 2.1, was low
capital productivity (about half that of the German rate), with much
evidence of widespread overmanning compared with German
companies, resulting in the inefficient use of labour.[45] In addition,
as has been suggested by critics of the prevailing investment subsidy
strategy, benefits at the aggregate level received from subsidising
investment must be placed against significant microeconomic
distortions to the allocation of resources because the British tax
system was not neutral with respect to investment funded internally
from retained profits as against externally.[46] Whilst there exists the
theoretical possibility that a different tax regime might have lessened
the required rate of return of a prospective investment, evidence
from the CBI's quarterly industrial trends survey since 1985 suggests
that the two dominant factors constraining investment were the
'inadequate net return on proposed investment' and 'uncertainty
about demand.' In other words, what limited investment was
uncertainty on the demand side.[47]

The second major category of industrial policies were those to
promote structural adjustment: both measures to assist the orderly
scaling-down of sunset industries and those targeted at sunrise sectors
where, at least before 1979, governments indulged in trying to pick
winners. With respect to the former, the primary motive for
intervention was concern about regional unemployment, for initially
the declining sectors were those same industries that had produced
such massive unemployment between the wars in Scotland, the north
and other peripheral regions. Thus, beginning with the 1957–8
recession, regional policy was reactivated and later selective assistance
was developed for a wider range of declining sectors; indeed, by the
early 1970s government felt compelled to undertake the emergency
nationalisation of strategic firms (such as Rolls-Royce and British
Leyland) in an effort to stave off their bankruptcy and the consequent
knock-on effects for the wider economy. The holding company for
these new public sector acquisitions was the National Enterprise Board;
this also had the brief to pick winners, but in this as with earlier

industrial policies, it was always the financial needs of sunset sectors which prevailed.[48] Moreover, the purchase of bankrupt companies during the 1970s exacerbated the perception of nationalisation's failure and contributed to the broader reaction against big government which prepared the ground for the Thatcherite project.[49]

Policies to promote new, high-technology sectors connect also to two other characteristics of industrial policies before the 1979 watershed:

1. A weakness for prestige projects, most notably Concorde, which, together with the Advanced Gas-cooled Reactor programme (another supposedly civilian project which was actually motivated by military needs), constituted two out of the three most expensive policy mistakes of the postwar period.[50]
2. The promotion of economic growth through the encouragement of firms to merge into ever larger enterprises, with policy particularly active between 1964–70 when Labour established a Ministry of Technology and a new agency, the Industrial Reorganisation Corporation, for this purpose. Unfortunately, in Britain, as a number of studies have shown, whilst there is a financial logic to mergers, the newly enlarged enterprises rarely achieved the potential efficiency gains that ought to follow from scale economies.[51]

Our third class of measures are competition policies which should have a particular importance in Britain because by the 1970s, the UK manufacturing sector had become 'one of the most highly concentrated (if not *the* most highly concentrated) in the world'.[52] Increased concentration is usually taken as evidence of enhanced market power and thus, in turn, of potential X-inefficiency as the diminished pressures of competition reduce the incentives to minimise costs. Whilst there have been long-standing concerns about anti-competitive behaviour in Britain, official interest in the potential disbenefits of the growing concentration of British industry was tempered by the hope that mergers would promote economies of scale and thus, on balance, be welfare enhancing. None the less, British competition policies were transformed in the postwar period as against earlier official indifference towards imperfect competition. Postwar policy activism began under the first Labour government, with the establishment of the Monopolies and Restrictive Practices Commission in 1948, and thereafter developed pragmatically but tentatively. The overall result, as one respected survey concluded, was that policy had 'always been a case of "too little, too late"' with four major underlying factors inhibiting policy. These have a broader applicability to much else in British economic policy, macro- as well as microeconomic:[53]

> *Cultural pragmatism*: the distrust of *per se* doctrines and the desire to see each case treated on its merits; this meant that, inevitably, policy implementation was costly and slow.
>
> *Market dogmatism*: the belief that the market, even if it was composed of only one or two incumbents, knew best how to allocate resources; and where markets had demonstrable deficiencies, these could rarely be made good by non-market, official interventions.
>
> *Ignorance*: in the form of poor and dated statistical information on changes in market structure, conduct and performance; policy was consistently reacting to events rather than anticipating them.
>
> *Powerlessness*: the conviction that many anti-competitive developments were taking place out of reach of the authorities; in particular, where events were international in scope, the locus for policy action was unclear.

Finally, we have policies directed at improving the functioning of capital markets in order to increase the supply of available finance for British enterprises. Despite the largely clean bill of health given to British financial institutions in official investigations,[54] deficiencies in the supply of capital have proved a perennial critique of British economic institutions, as has their bias towards overseas investment.[55] Governments launched a range of new institutions to address specific deficiencies, and in particular the difficulties faced by small- and medium-sized enterprises in raising capital. On the whole, however, most government intervention in this area was not motivated by supply-side issues *per se,* but by the needs of greater financial regulation and supervision in an age of sustained financial innovation and potential macroeconomic instability.[56]

As we now turn to the broad stance and effect of supply-side policies since 1979, we must resist the temptation to see the Thatcherite project as merely the antithesis of these earlier policies. The rhetoric certainly points that way, but the reality is more complex, especially as Thatcherite microeconomic policies initially were rather hesitantly pursued. The broad purpose and effect is, however, clear: instead of subsidising investment, policy sought to strengthen market incentives and penalties.[57] Thus, so far as industrial and related policies were concerned, the years since 1979 saw a steady build up of reforms in the following areas:

- Privatisation, the return of previously nationalised industries in whole or in part to private ownership, with this combined with continued regulation of those utility sectors where there were concerns that unchecked monopoly power would lessen managers' incentives to innovate, contain costs and raise productivity.
- Deregulation: this, from one perspective, the healthy removal of burdensome and costly bureaucracy and, from the other, the rebalancing of rights between government, employers and workers.
- Encouragement of foreign direct investment as a vehicle for the diffusion of new technologies and production practices and for the creation of additional physical capital.
- Deindustrialisation accepted and, indeed, conditioned by a massive reduction in public subsidies to sunset and sunrise sectors which removed soft budgets and confronted managers with more intense market incentives/disciplines.
- Reduction and restructuring of corporate taxation.

We reserve comment on the overall effectiveness of these reforms until Section 4.2.4, but here note Boltho and Graham's observation that 'Fearful of the risks of "government failure"', [Conservative] government[s] ... apparently become oblivious to the well-documented risks of "market failure".'[58] Policy placed enormous reliance on private markets being technically efficient and was blind and deaf to the view that Britain's economic problem before 1979 stemmed from a combination of market *and* government failures. As we shall now see, this affected also its labour market policies.

4.2.3 Labour market policies

One possible characterisation of labour market policies before 1979 was that they tried to shield labour from the dislocations (principally unemployment) of structural change and sought to accommodate the growing unionisation of the labour force. Accepting for the present that such a view can, but need not be, ideologically inspired, we begin our analysis by distinguishing between policies that impact upon the efficiency and operation of the labour market without affecting supply (such as employment exchanges which match the unemployed to vacancies), and those that do affect labour supply (such as the interaction of the tax-benefit system). We also note that there are many public policies which are not explicitly supply-side policies which, intended or not, impact upon the labour market, such as social welfare legislation and expenditures. This category of supply-side policies are thus very prone to being undermined by other government policies, and especially social welfare programmes which adopt a different stance towards the equity-efficiency trade-off.

There has been much written on whether, as a consequence of growing unionisation and the non-corporatist style of British industrial relations, the labour market became less flexible in the sense that nominal and real wages did not respond speedily to demand and supply shocks, thereby limiting the potential for demand management policies to sustain high economic growth and full employment.[59] The evidence certainly supports the proposition that during the golden age, wages were less flexible in Britain than in other more successful economies.[60] The British case shows also that incomes policies, the principal new postwar policy instrument aimed at lessening the unemployment-inflation trade-off and thus at improving labour market flexibility, are not likely to be a long-term success when an economy is characterised by a decentralised union structure, the absence of co-ordination between employers and no political consent for corporatist solutions to national economic problems.[61]

There is evidence also that policies to improve the occupational and regional structure of employment produced very limited benefits, with regional policies, in particular, criticised for their lack of clear objectives and frequent changes in policy regime. Labour mobility policies have also received generally unfavourable assessments; indeed, more generally by the 1970s there were widespread concerns about labour market flexibility as a consequence of developments in employment law, collective bargaining and the operation of welfare benefits. Failures with respect to vocational education and training were also particularly evident, and should be seen in the context that the general thrust of policy was to compensate workers for the loss of a job rather than to equip them with new or enhanced skills which would increase the probability of re-employment.[62]

Whilst labour market policies do become more active, interventionist and integrated from the early 1960s onwards, their effectiveness was handicapped by a number of factors: first, the tradition of voluntarism in British industrial relations made government reluctant to intervene in a whole range of areas from industrial training through to trade union law; and secondly, the searing influence of interwar mass unemployment made policy-makers extremely sensitive to job losses. As the diagnosis took root in the 1960s that Britain's economic problem in part derived from a dysfunctional industrial relations system, reform did become possible, but it was badly mishandled by the Heath government such that its Industrial Relations Act generated a level of trade union protest not seen since the troubled early 1920s. The general rise in unemployment from the late 1960s onwards (Figure 2.3, p. 50) acted initially to make government even more sensitive to job destruction such that by the 1970s, there were in place selective employment subsidies and a variety of training schemes which took the unemployed – especially youths – off the register. These, however, merely served to heighten the growing sense that labour market policies in Britain had not improved the average quality of the labour force in terms of human capital, employability and flexibility with respect to macroeconomic shocks.

In terms of whether supply-side policies promoted economic growth, particular reservations have been expressed about the commitment to and effectiveness of education at all levels: from school through vocational education and training to higher education.[63] Both input (educational expenditures) and attainment (educational qualifications) measures show a generalised failure which long predates the Second World War and which has been much examined by historians, generally within the cast of the cultural classes of explanations for relative economic decline (Section 2.3).[64] None the less, amongst policy-makers the belief in the virtues of expanding educational provision as the route to faster economic growth prevailed on the whole from the early postwar years, with developments thereafter shifting attention from quantitative (how much is spent in aggregate) to qualitative concerns, such as the structural mix of expenditures between sectors (further/vocational versus higher education), subjects (science/technology versus the humanities) and the general problems of creeping credentialism. What constrained the overall effectiveness of educational and training policies was undue

Table 4.5 Estimates of the NAIRU for males and decomposition of the rise in unemployment, 1956–79.

	1956–66	1967–74	1975–9
A. Unemployment rates (%):			
NAIRU	1.96	4.12	7.8
Actual	1.96	3.78	6.79

	1956–66 to 1967–74	1967–74 to 1975–9
B. Changes in unemployment due to (% points):		
Employers' labour taxes	0.42	0.67
Benefit-replacement ratio	0.54	(0.09)
Union wage mark-up	0.84	0.86
Real import prices	(0.36)	1.01
Mismatch	0.14	0.18
Demand factors	0.47	0.82
Incomes policies	-	(0.31)
Total predicted change	2.05	3.14
Total actual change	1.82	3.01

Source: Derived from P. R. G. Layard and S. J. Nickell, 'The causes of British unemployment', *National Institute Economic Review*, 111 (1985), Tables 6–7.

reliance on the market, rivalries between the different sectors of education and the continuing ideological conflict over educational choice, standards and ultimate purpose that is embodied in the problem of the so-called public schools and, before the reforms of the 1990s, the elitism of higher education.[65] One set of statistics brings out the British problem by the later 1970s and provides a clear link to weak competitiveness: by that time only 5.7 per cent of 18-year-olds in Britain were in non-higher technical and vocational education compared with 51.8 per cent in Germany, resulting in two-thirds of the British industrial labour force having no vocational qualifications as against one-third in Germany.[66]

Extending our net somewhat wider than labour market policies impacting on the supply-side, we report in Table 4.5 some estimates for why the NAIRU rose between the 1950s and 1970s. Taking as our baseline the average unemployment rate between 1956–66, we observe from panel A that the NAIRU had risen fourfold by 1975–9, and from panel B what factors underlaid that deterioration. We observe a mixture of supply-side factors such as the union wage mark-up and the benefit-replacement ratio which seek to measure respectively the extent to which labour supply is reduced by the activities of trade unions and the disincentive effects of unemployment benefits. We note, however, the importance of demand-side factors and from this progress to our general conclusion that labour market policies didn't do much during the era of full employment, but that once high unemployment returned their potential beneficial effects were swamped by the demand-induced fall in employment.

As we now turn to the content and effects of policy since 1979, we take as our starting point the collapse in demand for unskilled, especially male, workers and how this places a premium on labour market policies which improve human capital and employability. Indeed, many now argue that there has occurred a paradigm shift in the rules of international competitiveness such that national skills now form the sole long-term source of competitive advantage.[67] Policies since 1979 have had the following objectives:

- To reduce trade union power by increasing the rights of individual workers and, especially, the ability of employers to hire and dispose of labour, as required, at the lowest possible cost.
- To increase the incentives to work through reform of the structure and a lowering of the rates of welfare benefits and personal taxes.
- To free the labour market of restrictions and to increase the dispersion of earnings to strengthen incentives (including the abolition of minimum wages in scheduled trades).
- To promote individual enterprise and self-employment, including a culture of self-improvement through individual responsibility for education and training.
- To reduce government's direct impact upon the labour market via privatisation.
- To promote investment in human capital through the introduction of nationally benchmarked vocational qualifications and the expansion of higher education.

The subsequent economic record in terms of each one of these objectives has proved controversial, and especially so with respect to whether the trade union legislation of the 1980s underlaid the catch-up exercise in manufacturing productivity of that decade. In a widely cited article Brown and Wadhwani were deeply sceptical about such causality for in their view the expected employment and wage effects did not ensue.[68] In addition, there is a widespread view that the 1979–81 recession resulted in a one-off reduction in overmanning and the closing of marginal plants such that those remaining necessarily had above average levels of productivity. By contrast, Oulton's later survey of industry- and firm-level studies has found much evidence that the productivity improvement in manufacturing in the 1980s was positively correlated with high levels of unionisation in the 1970s, while other studies have shown that the decline of multi-unionism in large plants did much to reduce the disadvantage that had handicapped the achievement of scale economies in British manufacturing.[69] Few would now dispute that if the benchmark be minimising X-inefficiency, then the trade union reforms of the 1980s were a step in the right direction. Whether they would have been practical politics earlier seems unlikely as part of the political success of the Thatcher governments was that they learnt from the mistakes of their predecessors and did not attempt one grand industrial relations act, but instead a series of piecemeal reforms with each approximately calibrated not to pass the threshold of invoking deep political opposition.

The effects of the post-1979 rebalancing of the efficiency-equity trade-off in labour market policies also remains highly controversial. Whilst marginal rates of personal income tax have been transformed, falling from 98 per cent in 1978/9 to 40 per cent a decade later (Figure 3.4), the years since 1979 have seen an unparalleled – historically and in relation to the OECD states – shift in the income and wealth distribution towards greater inequality. This was due to a complex of factors in which adjustments to the tax and benefit systems to improve incentives were only one explanatory variable. In addition, the rise in unemployment, the increased private rate of return on education and the shift in the demand for labour away from the unskilled also played their part. The net effect was that in terms of inequality, the UK is now more like the US than Europe.[70] Whether this is desirable or not is a normative question and one which requires a benchmark of some alternative policy which would have delivered the same results for economic efficiency, but with less inequality. We will return to this in Section 4.3, our conclusion.

Most economists would agree that the UK labour market is now much more flexible than in 1979: that the shift in the balance of power towards employers has made labour supply more elastic; that frictional and structural unemployment have been reduced because the costs of job search have fallen and there are greater facilities for workers to augment their skills; and that workers are, on the whole, better off in work than unemployed.[71] Indeed, such has been the transformation of the UK labour market that British politicians have, in recent years, been claiming that high unemployment countries such as France, Germany and Italy ought to imitate the British reforms. As is often the case with British politicians, such claims ignore the reality that British unemployment was, in part, lower than that of the big EU countries because the British economy was at a more advanced stage of recovery in the business cycle, but even such a neutral source as the OECD secretariat has been complimentary in its assessments of the legacy of the Thatcher reforms for Britain's growth prospects.[72] None the less, significant problem areas remain: firstly, there is limited evidence that the reforms succeeded in reducing the NAIRU;[73] and secondly, despite the improvement in educational attainments at all levels, too high a proportion of school-leavers still have no qualifications and the current market-non-market mix of technical and vocational education is not augmenting British human capital to the extent required for the new facts of international competition.[74]

4.2.4 The overall effectiveness of microeconomic policies

The net effect of these industrial and labour market microeconomic reforms is hotly debated. For supporters such as Crafts, the 'Errors were more of omission and incompleteness than of misdirection', whereas for critics such as Graham, the overall project of Conservative capitalism failed because ideology dominated over analysis in policy-making.[75] We have thus, on the one hand, a critique that the Thatcherite project did not press ahead sufficiently with pro-market reforms, with the following weaknesses highlighted: insufficient competition in the utility sectors; weak antitrust competition policies; and, despite the rhetoric, a failure to reduce taxation. On the other hand, Graham and the greater number of academics who remain critical of these years have maintained that market triumphalism resulted in microeconomic policies which were 'extraordinarily ignorant of market failure and that, as a result, gross errors were made in policy towards industry, education, training, and research and development' while, moreover, 'supply-side reforms were not only sometimes poorly designed, but were further undermined by the lack of aggregate demand.'[76] Once more, therefore, we come back to competing economic ideas and how they influence policy for better or for worse. This divide, between government and market, between those who emphasise market efficiency over government failure and those who are unconvinced that markets should be privileged in all situations, continues as the fault line for British economic policy.

What unifies the years before and after the 1979 watershed is that the effectiveness of growth-promoting supply-side reforms cannot be judged in isolation from macroeconomic policies impacting on aggregate demand. The real counterfactual for the 1979–97 period is thus what might have happened if the incoming Conservative government had been able to break inflationary expectations without the recession of 1979–81 and then avoided the sort of macroeconomic instability which produced the Lawson boom and the subsequent 1990–2 recession. Future historians are also likely to make much of the Thatcher reforms coinciding with a new phase of globalisation, which itself made more intense the market incentives and penalties to which those reforms were directed.

4.3 Summary and interim conclusions

Whether judged in terms of governments' stated objectives, or some alternative set of widely canvassed policies, the effectiveness of British economic policy since the Second World War remains highly contested. Such judgements emerge from the interaction of actual governmental capacity and the expectations held about what that capacity ought to be, with Labour administrations typically subject to harsher popular-politically motivated judgements than Conservative administrations, and with the opposite tendency so far as academic assessments are concerned since these are more attentive to the economic situations that Labour inherited upon taking office: all moments of acute stress, namely the immediate aftermath of war (1945) and the grossly overheated economies of 1964 and 1974. The economic situation in 1997 is thus unusual as the one postwar occasion in which Labour has assumed office and not been immediately challenged by an economic crisis.

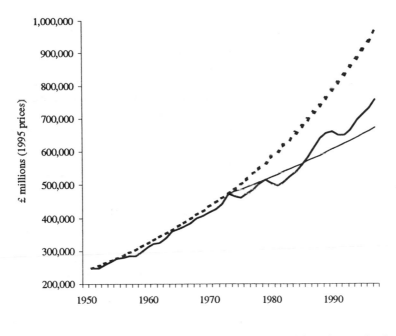

Figure 4.1 Real GDP: actual, 1951–97, and 1951–73 and 1973–9 trends extrapolated
Source: Calculated from ONS, *Economic Trends, Annual Supplement*, 1998 edn, Table 1.3.

In exploring the effectiveness of macro- and microeconomic policies we have emphasised how the latter were often disrupted by crises affecting the former. This did not stop after 1983, the watershed we identify when demand and supply-side policies were transposed, but it has abated and from this have come arguments that the Thatcher project brought about a halt to relative economic decline and thus vindicated those who, at an earlier point, questioned the postwar consensus on economic policy. The fact that the project was not practical politics, and that there were problems particular to large-scale manufacturing industry which are now largely superseded, has typically not been allowed to get in the way of a good story. The same applies also to the fact that the National Audit Office recently set the sustainable non-inflationary growth rate for the British economy in the range 2–2.25 per cent.

Those who claim an economic renaissance since 1979 need then to explain how the reforms delivered only an increment to the annual growth rate of 0.5–0.75 percentage points, or alternatively why the sustainable growth rate is still so far short of the, by OECD standards, very modest growth rate achieved during the golden age. A quantitative perceptive on their quandary is provided in Figure 4.1. If we take as our benchmark the troubled 1970s, real GDP in 1997 was 12.6 per cent higher than the level that would have obtained if the 1973–9 business cycle growth rate had been sustained through to the end of our period. On conventional welfare criteria this is a useful addition to national income, being some £84.5 billion in 1995 prices or approximately twice times the budget of the NHS. Alternatively, if our reference point is a more testing counterfactual, that of the 1951–73 growth rate extrapolated through to 1997, then real GDP in 1997 was 21.5 per cent below potential. This equates to a potential shortfall of over £207 billion at 1995 prices, sufficient to easily abolish the income tax and transform public spending. Not too much should be claimed for an exercise such as this, but it does illustrate the parameters within which historical judgements will have to be made.

The increment to GDP that may be ascribed to the shift in policy regime since 1979 needs also to be set against the more pronounced macroeconomic instability, which many economists judge to have been growth retarding,[77] the higher level of unemployment and poverty, and the resulting damage to the social fabric, as Britain has become a much more inegalitarian country.[78] In making a judgement about the overall effectiveness of economic policies since 1945, we have highlighted how supply-side reforms have consistently been handicapped by macroeconomic policy weaknesses. Policy-makers have been unable to secure the better quality economic intelligence needed for more accurate forecasting; they have had insufficient policy instruments to set against their multiple policy objectives; and for the greater part of the postwar period, they were unwilling to downgrade their overseas commitments and geopolitical posturing in line with the diminishing capability forced by relative economic decline, with enduring significance for the balance of payments, Stop-Go and thus the long-run growth prospects of the British economy.

Governments since 1979 have been as error prone as those before this policy watershed. There is much continuity in terms of the propensity to gamble with macroeconomic policy, with the last such episode being the ill-fated membership of the ERM between 1990–2, but there are also major differences which strengthen the significance of the shift in policy regime. We saw in Chapter 2 that during the 1980s, the British economy underwent a somewhat delayed catching-up exercise which went some way towards closing the productivity gap with Germany, Japan and the US. From our review of policy in this and the proceeding chapter, we confirm the diagnosis that slow growth during the previous golden age is substantially explained by institutional factors which constrained productivity growth and which were politically difficult to reform because they were so long established. The Thatcherite project challenged, as perhaps nothing else could, the market environment in which investment decisions were made and bargains struck between management and their workers. But was there an alternative, a less painful one and/or a more efficient one? In a substantive sense this is unknowable, but, more importantly, in posing the question we reach the limits of the economic historian's remit: the comparative advantage in exploring this question lies with political scientists and their judgements of what was possible.

5

CONCLUSIONS

In this book we have but touched the surface of the debates on British economic policy and performance since 1945, but hopefully we have done so sufficiently to convey a sense of the complexity of those debates, how they might be navigated and why there is no consensus about the most convincing explanation for such deficiencies in the British record as may be identified. Indeed, as Coates has put it, the debate is now rather 'like some Newtonian law of physics, in which each argument attracts an equal and opposite argument': too much government, too little government, and so on.[1]

In preceding chapters we have portrayed the development of Britain's economic problem as deriving from a complex web of mutually reinforcing market and non-market failures.[2] In the process we have surveyed the enormous academic literature generated by economists, political scientists and others to explain relative decline. The results of such academic enquiry, in sharp contrast to populist interpretations by journalists and many politicians,[3] produce few unambiguous answers.

The pursuit of some grand explanation or set of explanations of relative economic decline is a false trail if what is sought is a remedial political programme. Thus, few would disagree with Alford's verdict that 'the British economy still awaits a convincing diagnosis of its ills',[4] but the use of medical metaphor – measurement and observation leading to diagnosis and cure – provides a clue to the problem: there never can be a unique value-free diagnosis, and socioeconomic systems, rather like the human body, are, in practice, altogether more complex than is admitted by the non-holistic Western tradition of medicine. Moreover, too much of the declinist literature encourages simple-minded policy choices (Keynesian versus monetarist, big versus small government), while the short time-horizon of politicians predisposes them to experimentation with ill-regard for spill-over and unintended policy effects.

This approach might be thought overly fatalistic, but the purpose is not to argue that policy analysis has nothing to offer, nor that change is impossible, or even – if the social costs be accepted – that relative economic decline could not be halted and indeed reversed. Rather it is to argue that what is required is some clarity about what we are trying to explain. Decline itself has become an ideology, a pathological preoccupation. Supple distinguishes three concepts of failure, each with their own history: the 'humiliation of the loss of international power, the insecurity of deindustrialization, and the frustration of felt needs and aspirations'.[5] Since relative economic decline has taken place against the background of unparalleled absolute improvements in material life, we should be sensitive to the shifting relative weights of economic, political and psychological imperatives as between these concepts of decline and their relative standing over the last century or so.

In economic terms, there may in fact be little to explain, especially in the absence of suitable benchmarks of what would have constituted economic success - not fourteenth in terms of GDP per capita amongst the OECD-17 by 1997, but perhaps fifth (Germany's ranking)? This would have entailed an income gain of just 13 per cent over the level actually attained (Table 1.1, pp. 4–5). The problems may therefore be largely political and psychological, a failure to adjust to a world in which Britain is no longer top nation. For example, the ease with which the first Thatcher government embarked upon the Malvinas/Falklands War, in face of the clear risks of military disaster, certainly suggest that the need to believe in Britain as an eternal great power runs deep within the British consciousness. As a recent study of postwar British society has concluded:[6]

> British society is a complicated affair, full of loose ends and bits that don't fit. This may be a good thing for the people who live in it, but it is a source of frustration for those who study it and try to understand it. Every attempt to sum it up in a simple formula – as a 'class society' or whatever – has proved to have so many exceptions and qualifications that it was more trouble than it was worth. The first thing to understand about British society is that there are no short-cuts, no master keys.

Such a conclusion would also be appropriate for the postwar British economy and needs to be placed in the context that, after a century of relative decline and after the loss of the largest empire since the Romans, Britain none the less remains firmly within the clubs that constitute the world's economic elite (EU, G-7 and OECD). For the historian, therefore, the task is not just to make sense of the facts of that relative decline, and of the underlying competing explanations, but to confront why there has been the compulsion to write recent British economic – and other varieties – of history as inverted Whiggism.

APPENDIX I
GLOSSARY

balance of payments a tabulation of the credit and debit transaction of a country with other countries and international institutions during a specified period, with strict accounting rules the balance on the current account (**q.v.**) and capital account summing to zero, but in practice requiring a balancing item as balance of payments statistics are notoriously incomplete. A summary of Britain's balance of payments for 1997 follows:

A. Current account	(£ millions)
A1. Trade in goods	
Exports of goods	171,798
Imports of goods	183,590
Visible trade balance	(11,792)
A2. Trade in services	
Exports of services	56,904
Imports of services	45,744
Service balance	11,160
A3. Balance of trade	(632)
A4. Other transactions (net)	
Compensation of employees	83
Investment income	12,085
Central government current transfers	1,287
Other sectors' current transfers	(4,817)
A5. Current account balance	**8,006**
B. Capital account	
B1. Investment: direct, portfolio and other	
Investment overseas by UK residents	256,247
Investment in the UK by overseas residents	248,135
B2. Capital account balance	**(8,112)**
B3. Balancing item	**106**
C. Balance of payments	**0**

Source: Derived from ONS, *Economic Trends, Annual Supplement*, 1998 edn, Tables 1.18–1.19.

balance of trade the difference between a nation's exports of goods and services and its imports of goods and services, this a key component of the current account balance of payments (**q.v.**).

Bretton Woods an international agreement reached at the 1944 Bretton Woods conference which established the IMF and the World Bank, and which inaugurated a period of stable exchange rates based on the dollar as the world's major reserve currency.

ceteris paribus a term meaning 'other things being equal', which is much used by economists wanting to separate out the effects of one variable on another when changes in other contributory factors also intervene to complicate matters.

comparative advantage the proposition that economic agents should specialise in the production of those goods/services where their relative efficiencies are superior to others. This leads to an important conclusion, one central to international trade theory, that even if an economic agent by absolute standards is inefficient at an activity, perhaps worse even than all other agents, it will still be profitable to pursue that activity if they are even more inefficient in other activities.

crowding-out the process whereby government actions may reduce private expenditures, as for example in government borrowing which raises interest rates reducing private sector interest-sensitive expenditures (e.g. investment).

current account balance of payments the standard measure of a country's external balance in trade and payments, being defined as the sum of the visible trade balance (**q.v.**) and the invisible trade balance (**q.v.**).

demand the willingness and ability to offer a sum of money for a set volume of a good/service.

denominator the lower element in a fraction or calculation of a quotient; *see also* numerator.

dependent variable a variable whose value is conditional on the value of another variable; *see also* independent variable.

endogenous refers to that which is caused inside the specific system being examined; *see also* exogenous.

European Economic Community/European Community/European Union originally a free trade area with a common external tariff (a customs union) comprising 6 original member states at foundation in 1958, enlarged to 9 members in 1973 (with the accession of Denmark, Ireland and the UK), to 12 in the 1980s (Greece, Portugal and Spain) and to 15 in the 1990s (Austria, Finland and Sweden).

exchange rate the rate at which one currency is exchanged for another.

exogenous refers to that which is caused outside the specific system being examined. The weather used to be seen as a classic exogenous factor, but with global climate change even this is now seen as affected by economic behaviour and thus more properly as endogenous.

externality consequences for economic welfare not fully accounted for in the price and market systems, as for example in a factory's smoky chimney where the pollution costs (ill-health, nuisance, etc.) are born by those proximate to the factory.

factors of production the inputs in the productive process: land (typically also encompassing natural resources), labour and physical capital.

GATT the agreement initiated at Bretton Woods in 1946, and enhanced in successive 'rounds', to reduce tariff and other barriers to multilateral international trade.

GDP Gross Domestic Product, the conventional measure of national income, defined as the total flow of all goods and services exchanged in a society over a specified time, normally a year. Table 1 in Appendix II shows annual estimates of GDP calculated by the expenditure method, which sums the different classes of domestic expenditure and the net effect of exports and imports.

GDP deflator an index of prices which can be applied to the nominal (**q.v.**), that is current price, estimates of GDP (**q.v.**) over time in order to remove the effects of changes in the general level of prices, with the resulting series providing a more accurate measure of movements in the physical or real (**q.v.**) output of goods and services.

globalisation defined by the OECD as the geographical dispersion of industrial and service activities and the cross-border networking of companies, with manifestations of the phenomenon being the increasing openness of economies to international trade, increasing international capital mobility and the growing importance of multinational companies.

human capital a measure of the stock of knowledge accumulated over time and of the quality of the labour force.

independent variable a variable from which the value of other variables are derived; *see also* dependent variable.

inflation increases in prices which reduce the purchasing power of money, usually measured by the RPI (**q.v.**).

invisible hand the term employed by Adam Smith to describe the principle whereby a beneficent and efficient economic outcome emerged as the unintended aggregate consequence of the pursuit of individuals' self-interests.

invisible trade balance a key component of the current account balance of payments (**q.v.**) which measures exports of services less imports of services plus the net balance on certain current transfer payments made by the private and public sectors.

labour productivity output per unit of labour input, the latter either measured in hours worked or numbers of workers employed.

macroeconomic the aggregation of individual economic agents to comprise a whole economic system, typically the national economy and the determination of national income; *see also* microeconomic.

managed-mixed economy relating to an economy in which aggregate demand (and sometimes supply) are actively managed and a significant part of the productive sector is owned and operated by government or its agents.

microeconomic the individual economic agents, both consumers and producers, that comprise the whole economic system, with microeconomics focusing on the choices made by these individual agents; *see also* macroeconomic.

monetarism a macroeconomic theory, often associated with the Nobel prize-winning Chicago economist Milton Friedman, which claims that increases in the money supply are a necessary and sufficient condition for inflation.

NAIRU non-accelerating inflation rate of unemployment, the balancing point of the labour market at which level of unemployment wage rises are just consistent with a stable rate of inflation. This is often known as the natural rate of unemployment, a concept which was central to monetarism (**q.v.**), that Keynesian demand management policies were inflationary because they tried to keep the actual level of unemployment at too low a level, but which is now broadly accepted amongst economists as a description of the minimum level of unemployment attainable given the characteristics of the labour market.

nominal the valuation of some variable (wages, national income) at then current prices; *see also* real.

non-linear in a graph a straight line expressing the relationship between one variable and another is classed as linear, that is a change in one variable produces a constant proportionate change in the other variable. A non-linear relationship is thus the opposite case, as for example in the U-shaped function typically observed in the relation between average costs of production and output levels.

numerator the upper element in a fraction or calculation of a quotient; *see also* denominator.

optimum the best value which a variable can take with reference to some particular objective. Economists often use the term *Pareto optimal* with respect to the allocation of resources, this being where it is impossible to make any one economic agent better off except by making at least one other agent worse off.

pro-cyclical where variables move in the same direction over the business cycle, whereas if variables move inversely, they are described as contra-cyclical.

public good a commodity, the consumption of which has necessarily to be decided at the society rather than the individual level. Defence is a classic public good which embodies the three intrinsic characteristics of such commodities: non-rivalrous consumption, non-excludability and non-rejectability.

real distinguished from nominal (**q.v.**), that is a money value adjusted for changes in prices, as for example when money wages may rise by 5 per cent over a year, but because prices have increased by 3 per cent there has only been an approximately 2 per cent rise in the purchasing power over goods and services of those wages. To convert money values to constant price or real values requires that data at current prices be adjusted by an appropriate deflator, typically the RPI (**q.v.**) or the GDP deflator (**q.v.**).

RPI the official British index of changes in consumer prices.

stagflation the antithesis of the Phillips curve trade-off between unemployment and inflation where there is the simultaneous existence of 'high' unemployment and inflation.

supply the quantity of a good/service which the seller offers for sale at a given price.

terms of trade the ratio of export prices to import prices, with an 'improvement' in the terms of trade being where export prices rise faster (fall slower) than import prices so that for any given volume of exports a higher level of imports can be sustained.

visible trade balance a key component of the current account balance of payments (**q.v.**) which measures exports of goods less imports of goods.

APPENDIX II
KEY ECONOMIC STATISTICS

The following three tables form the basis for many of the tables and figures in the text together with a number of the worked examples detailed in Appendix III. These are the latest available estimates produced by the Office for National Statistics (ONS); they therefore differ very often – and sometimes substantially so – from the data with which contemporaries had to work in framing policy and assessing its effectiveness. For example, Mosley has calculated that during the 1960s and 1970s, the average range of revisions to the GDP and current account balance of payments series has been 1.2 per cent for the former and £268 million for the latter, with the revisions upward for the former in 17 out of the 20 years enumerated and improvements in the latter in eighteen years. He has also estimated that between 1951 and 1984 on average the Treasury underestimated the public sector financial deficit by 0.5 per cent of GDP, this being about half the average amount by which Chancellors sought to fine-tune demand through the budget, and with no tendency for the accuracy of forecasting to improve through time.[1] As a former Permanent Secretary to the Treasury has indicated when asked to reflect on the golden age years:[2]

> Anyone trying to recount the history of a period in which he was active, relying on memory and the material available at the time, would be totally astounded to find that most of the figures for the period produced ... 20 or 30 years later were quite unrecognizable. The most important instrument lacking was a position-finder to tell us exactly where we were at any given moment.

Table II.1 GDP by category of expenditure at market prices (£ millions), 1948–97

A	Consumers' expenditure ABPB+ABNV	General government final consumption NMRK	Gross domestic fixed capital formation NPQX	Increase in stocks & works in progress + net acquisitions of valuables ABMP+NPJO	Exports of goods and services KTMW	Imports of goods and services KTMX	Statistical discrepancy GIXM	GDP at market prices YBHA	Implied GDP deflator at market prices (1995=100) YBGB	Real GDP at 1995 market prices ABMI
	B	C	D	E	F	G	H	I	J	K
1948	8,465	1,810	1,502	175	2,191	2,407	61	11,797	5.3	224,486
1949	8,823	2,034	1,662	65	2,489	2,669	129	12,533	5.4	232,340
1950	9,314	2,125	1,799	(210)	2,988	3,046	102	13,072	5.5	239,480
1951	10,060	2,491	2,011	575	3,639	4,299	82	14,559	5.9	246,108
1952	10,594	2,956	2,265	50	3,750	3,899	52	15,768	6.4	247,168
1953	11,300	3,088	2,540	125	3,677	3,798	(49)	16,883	6.6	256,712
1954	11,987	3,167	2,741	56	3,827	3,922	13	17,869	6.7	267,730
1955	12,920	3,235	3,026	300	4,166	4,439	(101)	19,107	6.9	275,997
1956	13,590	3,491	3,315	259	4,586	4,510	(190)	20,541	7.4	278,707
1957	14,332	3,650	3,600	238	4,823	4,731	(241)	21,671	7.6	283,589
1958	15,125	3,722	3,724	111	4,688	4,535	(250)	22,585	7.9	284,625
1959	15,925	3,970	3,980	178	4,836	4,834	(178)	23,877	8.0	296,958
1960	16,710	4,205	4,368	562	5,134	5,499	14	25,494	8.1	312,850
1961	17,570	4,542	4,889	279	5,366	5,459	(216)	26,971	8.4	320,636
1962	18,611	4,868	5,049	(8)	5,500	5,554	(196)	28,270	8.7	324,608
1963	19,826	5,127	5,295	161	5,852	5,971	(67)	30,223	8.9	339,893
1964	21,156	5,458	6,279	700	6,183	6,768	28	33,036	9.2	358,498
1965	22,497	5,993	6,804	461	6,596	6,925	148	35,574	9.7	367,501
1966	23,769	6,531	7,261	288	7,148	7,215	77	37,859	10.1	374,597
1967	24,987	7,225	7,945	286	7,370	7,814	(116)	39,883	10.4	383,186
1968	26,901	7,685	8,728	452	8,962	9,329	(171)	43,228	10.8	398,858
1969	28,554	8,048	9,066	537	10,064	9,886	158	46,541	11.4	407,101

	B	C	D	E	F	G	H	I	J	K
1970	31,143	9,079	10,036	382	11,489	11,052	91	51,168	12.3	416,793
1971	34,923	10,346	11,243	114	12,890	12,095	(341)	57,080	13.4	425,404
1972	39,534	11,791	12,347	25	13,587	13,658	313	63,939	14.5	440,444
1973	45,236	13,455	15,227	1,529	17,027	18,840	(75)	73,559	15.6	472,701
1974	52,183	16,812	18,134	1,045	22,831	27,007	(819)	83,179	17.9	464,842
1975	64,207	23,270	21,856	(1,354)	26,803	28,655	(1,130)	104,957	22.7	461,605
1976	74,675	27,270	25,516	901	35,018	36,483	(2,565)	124,332	26.2	474,508
1977	85,270	29,760	28,201	1,824	43,210	42,262	(1,163)	144,840	29.8	485,673
1978	98,328	33,698	32,208	1,804	47,379	45,234	(1,084)	167,099	33.3	502,201
1979	116,686	39,086	38,211	2,162	54,894	54,165	(195)	195,589	38.1	516,083
1980	135,454	49,192	43,238	(2,572)	62,495	57,449	(775)	229,383	45.5	504,751
1981	150,391	55,667	43,331	(2,768)	67,355	60,243	(1,449)	252,244	50.6	498,314
1982	164,694	60,600	47,594	(1,188)	72,579	67,631	(597)	275,851	54.4	507,293
1983	181,047	65,934	51,490	1,465	79,751	77,428	(735)	301,524	57.3	526,285
1984	193,935	69,831	58,698	1,296	91,569	92,577	406	325,098	59.9	539,009
1985	211,950	78,792	64,463	821	101,926	98,723	0	354,229	63.3	559,525
1986	235,071	79,262	68,718	658	97,781	100,893	0	380,597	65.3	583,154
1987	258,136	85,077	78,924	1,096	106,437	111,449	0	418,221	68.7	609,023
1988	291,527	91,658	96,076	4,382	107,434	124,657	0	466,520	72.8	640,587
1989	319,995	98,982	111,033	2,686	121,883	142,690	0	511,889	78.2	654,315
1990	347,247	109,535	114,314	(1,913)	133,501	148,198	0	554,486	84.2	658,480
1991	368,232	120,799	104,680	(5,013)	135,365	141,117	0	582,946	89.9	648,639
1992	387,312	128,269	100,278	(1,901)	143,291	150,667	0	606,582	93.5	648,975
1993	412,398	130,565	101,230	320	162,078	168,774	0	637,817	96.1	664,018
1994	433,829	135,536	107,390	3,844	178,767	183,330	0	676,036	97.5	693,177
1995	454,171	140,406	116,360	4,420	202,412	205,221	0	712,548	100.0	712,548
1996	485,418	146,111	125,675	1,586	220,303	224,492	0	754,601	103.3	730,767
1997	519,190	147,406	133,710	2,882	228,702	229,334	(494)	801,972	106.1	756,144

Sources:
Cols B-I: ONS, *Economic Trends, Annual Supplement*, 1998 edn, Table 1.3
Col. J: (GDP deflator) calculated from col. I/col. K * 100.
Col. K: ONS, *Economic Trends, Annual Supplement*, 1998 edn, Table 1.2.

The latest estimates thus imply a historical record often far more rosy than was experienced by contemporaries, and never more so than in the case of balance of payments data where policy interventions were often made which would have been unnecessary if the contemporary estimates had not been so inaccurate.

The data in Tables 1–3 all begin in 1948, the first normal peacetime year and the first year in which the Central Statistical Office (CSO), the antecedent of the ONS, began publication of the key macroeconomic series. Where possible, in each of these three Tables the four-letter ONS code is given after a description of each series, that is YBHA in Appendix III Table I col. I is GDP at current market prices. This should help the reader to identify from other ONS publications the series being used and to update these Tables for post-1997 estimates.

These three Tables, together with the data in Appendix III, are available for downloading as EXCEL 97 worksheets from the author's website: **< http://info.bris.ac.uk/~hirm/rmhome.html >**

Table II.2 Unemployment, unemployment rate and RPI, 1948–97

	Numbers unemployed (m.)	Unemployment rate (%)	RPI (Jan 1974=100)	Annual change in RPI
A	B	C	D	E
1948	0.331	1.8	33.3	
1949	0.338	1.6	34.4	3.3
1950	0.341	1.6	35.1	2.0
1951	0.281	1.3	38.7	10.3
1952	0.463	2.2	40.5	4.7
1953	0.380	1.8	41.5	2.5
1954	0.318	1.5	42.3	1.9
1955	0.265	1.2	43.7	3.3
1956	0.287	1.3	45.8	4.8
1957	0.347	1.6	47.3	3.3
1958	0.501	2.2	48.7	3.0
1959	0.512	2.3	49.2	1.0
1960	0.393	1.7	49.8	1.2
1961	0.377	1.6	51.2	2.8
1962	0.500	2.1	53.0	3.5
1963	0.612	2.6	54.0	1.9
1964	0.413	1.7	55.8	3.3
1965	0.360	1.5	58.4	4.7
1966	0.391	1.6	60.7	3.9
1967	0.599	2.5	62.3	2.6
1968	0.601	2.5	65.2	4.7
1969	0.597	2.5	68.7	5.4
1970	0.640	2.7	73.1	6.4
1971	0.797	3.5	80.0	9.4
1972	0.876	3.8	85.7	7.1
1973	0.619	2.7	93.5	9.1
1974	0.619	2.6	108.5	16.0
1975	0.978	4.2	134.8	24.2
1976	1.359	5.7	157.1	16.5
1977	1.484	6.2	182.0	15.8
1978	1.475	6.1	197.1	8.3
1979	1.390	5.7	223.5	13.4
1980	1.795	7.4	263.7	18.0
1981	2.734	11.4	295.0	11.9
1982	3.119	13.0	320.4	8.6
1983	3.105	12.2	335.1	4.6
1984	3.160	11.5	351.8	5.0
1985	3.271	11.7	373.2	6.1
1986	3.293	11.8	385.9	3.4
1987	2.953	10.5	401.9	4.1
1988	2.370	8.3	421.6	4.9
1989	1.799	6.3	454.5	7.8
1990	1.665	5.8	497.6	9.5
1991	2.292	8.0	526.7	5.8
1992	2.779	9.8	546.4	3.7
1993	2.919	10.3	555.1	1.6
1994	2.636	9.4	568.5	2.4
1995	2.306	8.3	588.2	3.5
1996	2.103	7.5	602.4	2.4
1997	1.586	5.7	621.3	3.1

Sources:
Cols B-C: J. Denman and P. McDonald, 'Unemployment statistics from 1881 to the present day', *Labour Market Trends*, 104 (January 1996), Tables 1–2; 1996–7: *Labour Market Trends*.
Col. D: ONS, *Retail Prices Index – April 1998*, Table 14.
Col. E: calculated from col. D.

Table II.3 Balance of payments, current account (£ millions), 1948-97

A	Exports of goods LQAD	Imports of goods LQBL	Visible trade balance LQAD+LQBL =LQCT	Exports of services KTMQ	Imports of services KTMS	Service balance KTMQ+ KTMS	Goods and services balance KTMY	Other invisible items, credits HMBQ+ KTND	Other invisible items, debits HMBP+ KTNF	Invisible trade balance	Current account balance HBOG
	B	C	D	E	F	G	H	I	J	K	L
1948	1,663	1,815	(152)	528	592	(64)	(216)	590	(262)	264	112
1949	1,891	2,028	(137)	598	641	(43)	(180)	500	(257)	200	63
1950	2,293	2,347	(54)	695	699	(4)	(58)	733	(289)	440	386
1951	2,779	3,471	(692)	860	828	32	(660)	742	(369)	405	(287)
1952	2,817	3,089	(272)	933	810	123	(149)	829	(417)	535	263
1953	2,729	2,973	(244)	948	825	123	(121)	794	(438)	479	235
1954	2,829	3,039	(210)	998	883	115	(95)	761	(472)	404	194
1955	3,127	3,442	(315)	1,039	997	42	(273)	738	(547)	233	(82)
1956	3,439	3,389	50	1,147	1,121	26	76	786	(577)	235	285
1957	3,573	3,602	(29)	1,250	1,129	121	92	795	(575)	341	312
1958	3,470	3,436	34	1,218	1,099	119	153	908	(635)	392	426
1959	3,587	3,703	(116)	1,249	1,131	118	2	880	(648)	350	234
1960	3,801	4,205	(404)	1,333	1,294	39	(365)	900	(706)	233	(171)
1961	3,967	4,111	(144)	1,399	1,348	51	(93)	916	(701)	266	122
1962	4,065	4,169	(104)	1,435	1,385	50	(54)	1,002	(707)	345	241
1963	4,395	4,518	(123)	1,457	1,453	4	(119)	1,087	(746)	345	222
1964	4,632	5,183	(551)	1,551	1,585	(34)	(585)	1,246	(921)	291	(260)
1965	4,983	5,246	(263)	1,613	1,679	(66)	(329)	1,364	(997)	301	38
1966	5,348	5,459	(111)	1,800	1,756	44	(67)	1,326	(1,041)	329	218
1967	5,329	5,930	(601)	2,041	1,884	157	(444)	1,376	(1,121)	412	(189)
1968	6,537	7,245	(708)	2,425	2,084	341	(367)	1,599	(1,379)	561	(147)
1969	7,373	7,587	(214)	2,691	2,299	392	178	1,894	(1,518)	768	554

Year											
1970	8,266	8,284	(18)	3,223	2,768	455	437	2,086	(1,612)	929	911
1971	9,190	8,985	205	3,700	3,110	590	795	2,208	(1,762)	1,036	1,241
1972	9,587	10,323	(736)	4,000	3,335	665	(71)	4,345	(3,930)	1,080	344
1973	12,091	14,664	(2,573)	4,936	4,176	760	(1,813)	6,173	(5,274)	1,659	(914)
1974	16,546	21,787	(5,241)	6,285	5,220	1,065	(4,176)	7,656	(6,659)	2,062	(3,179)
1975	19,451	22,696	(3,245)	7,352	5,959	1,393	(1,852)	8,302	(8,015)	1,680	(1,565)
1976	25,404	29,334	(3,930)	9,614	7,149	2,465	(1,465)	10,501	(9,763)	3,203	(727)
1977	32,041	34,312	(2,271)	11,169	7,950	3,219	948	11,484	(12,225)	2,478	207
1978	35,331	36,865	(1,534)	12,048	8,369	3,679	2,145	14,570	(15,282)	2,967	1,433
1979	40,849	44,175	(3,326)	13,955	9,990	3,965	639	22,459	(23,010)	3,414	88
1980	47,493	46,164	1,329	15,002	11,285	3,717	5,046	30,023	(31,903)	1,837	3,166
1981	51,034	47,796	3,238	16,281	12,447	3,834	7,072	46,290	(46,813)	3,311	6,549
1982	55,657	53,778	1,879	16,922	13,853	3,069	4,948	54,552	(55,393)	2,228	4,107
1983	60,984	62,602	(1,618)	18,767	14,826	3,941	2,323	53,094	(52,118)	4,917	3,299
1984	70,565	75,974	(5,409)	20,944	16,603	4,341	(1,068)	64,057	(61,780)	6,618	1,209
1985	78,291	81,707	(3,416)	23,635	17,016	6,619	3,203	64,935	(65,911)	5,643	2,227
1986	72,997	82,614	(9,617)	24,784	18,279	6,505	(3,112)	58,633	(57,806)	7,332	(2,285)
1987	79,531	91,229	(11,698)	26,906	20,220	6,686	(5,012)	61,627	(62,198)	5,115	(5,583)
1988	80,711	102,264	(21,553)	26,723	22,393	4,330	(17,223)	72,011	(72,325)	4,016	(17,537)
1989	92,611	117,335	(24,724)	29,272	25,355	3,917	(20,807)	92,360	(95,044)	1,233	(23,491)
1990	102,313	121,020	(18,707)	31,188	27,178	4,010	(14,697)	98,979	(103,795)	(806)	(19,513)
1991	103,939	114,162	(10,223)	31,426	26,955	4,471	(5,752)	99,209	(101,831)	1,849	(8,374)
1992	107,863	120,913	(13,050)	35,428	29,754	5,674	(7,376)	86,740	(89,446)	2,968	(10,082)
1993	122,039	135,358	(13,319)	40,039	33,416	6,623	(6,696)	92,684	(96,606)	2,701	(10,618)
1994	135,260	146,351	(11,091)	43,507	36,979	6,528	(4,563)	96,129	(93,024)	9,633	(1,458)
1995	153,725	165,449	(11,724)	48,687	39,772	8,915	(2,809)	111,336	(112,272)	7,979	(3,745)
1996	167,403	180,489	(13,086)	52,900	44,003	8,897	(4,189)	123,956	(120,377)	12,486	(600)
1997	171,798	183,590	(11,792)	56,904	45,744	11,160	(632)	125,477	(116,839)	19,798	8,006

Source: ONS, *Economic Trends, Annual Supplement,* 1998 edn, Table 1.18.

APPENDIX III
USING AND INTERPRETING
ECONOMIC STATISTICS

III.1 Introduction

In the following we use examples, drawn from tables and figures in this book, to explain the purpose, derivation and envisioning of some basic statistics which are used routinely by economists and which if you master will add greatly to your understanding not just of the subject matter discussed here, but of all debates – historical and contemporary – which draw upon numerical data. Indeed, once you are so equipped you will be a more effective citizen as you will be able to question how opinion-formers deploy statistics in their efforts to persuade you of the merits of their case.[1] Accordingly, you are encouraged to replicate the calculations here on your own calculator or by using a spreadsheet, and to assist the latter (preferred) route to greater numeracy, the data in Appendices II and III are available for downloading as EXCEL 97 worksheets from the author's website: **<http://info.bris.ac.uk/~hirm/rmhome.html>**. Each worksheet contains notes sufficient to guide you through the procedures detailed below.

For those of you who are particularly resistant to economics and to graphs, tables and all the other apparatus of quantitative analysis, you may need to read this Appendix more than once and/or refer back to it as you read through the main chapters of this book. Indeed, if you have not grasped all that is in this Appendix on a first reading, this may actually be to the good as it demonstrates that you are trying to engage with the concepts and tools needed to fully understand the debate and not, as so many historians do, flicking through numerical matter as if it is not only distasteful, but an unnecessary distraction to *real* historical analysis.

Our enthusiasm for quantitative analysis must, however, be tempered by the knowledge that, as one critic has put it, many 'use statistics as a drunk uses a street lamp, for support rather than illumination'.[2] Accordingly, the use of statistics does not necessarily make any study more objective, rigorous or scientific. Rather, quantitative analysis provides a means – not an ends – to:

- test theories and explanations through a creative confrontation with the empirical evidence;
- summarise larger bodies of data into smaller collections of typical values;
- confirm that relationships observed in data did not happen merely because of chance or random error;
- discover new relationships in data; and
- describe, in a basic factual role, what occurred.

This Appendix divides into three further sections: Section III.2 briefly, but, hopefully clearly and without being intimidating, takes the novice user of economic statistics through some basic summary statistical measures used in this study; section III.3 offers guidelines on the potential perils and pitfalls of economic data, with the aim of providing a checklist for good practice in using and interpreting such data; and Section III.4 provides some basic guidance on charting data and seeking relationships between variables.

III.2 Some basic summary statistics explained

III.2.1 Quotients and percentages

When examining an economy's structure we typically begin by wanting to know the size of one variable in relation to another: its share, the fraction or more precisely the quotient. For example, in the following we calculate the share of exports in relation to national income for 1951 and 1973, taking this as a measure of the degree to which the British economy was engaged in foreign trade over the period known as the 'golden age' (see p. 3). Using Appendix II Table 1 (cols F and

I), we can see that in our initial year exports were valued at £3,639m. as against GDP at £14,559m., while the figures for 1973 were £17,027m. and £73,559m. respectively. We proceed as follows: to produce the quotient of exports to GDP, we construct a fraction in which, for each year, we divide the value of exports by that of GDP. NB: the top part of the fraction is known as the numerator (3,639 in the example for 1951) and the bottom part as the denominator (14,559). We can then transform the quotient into a percentage by multiplying it by 100. We thus obtain the following:

Statistic	Calculation for 1951	Calculation for 1973
Quotient	(3639 / 14559) = 0.250	(17027 / 73559) = 0.231
Percentage	(3639 / 14559) x 100 = 25.0%	(17027 / 73559) x 100 = 23.1%

From these results we can deduce that since the share of exports in GDP fell from 25 to 23.1 per cent, then exports must have grown slower than national income, and thus the British economy became less engaged in foreign trade during the golden age.

III.2.2 Growth rates

Consideration of percentages leads directly to the next basic statistical measure: the percentage growth rate of a variable between two periods expressed as a percentage of the value in the initial period. In the example given above for exports and GDP we provide the following two methods for calculating the percentage growth in these variables between our initial and terminal years (the second method involves less keystrokes for the numerator):

Calculation for exports	Calculation for GDP
((17027 – 3639) / (3639)) x 100 = 467.9%	((73559–14559) / (14559)) = 505.2%
((17027 / 3639)–1) x 100 = 467.9%	((73559 / 14559)–1) x 100 = 505.2%

This confirms that GDP did indeed grow more than exports over this period, suggestive that economic growth was not export-led over the golden age.

Typically, the economist might then calculate the annual average growth rate for the two series between 1951 and 1973, this to provide a sense of how much each year on average export growth fell short of GDP growth. Such a calculation, however, is not straightforward. Whilst intuitively it would seem that the average growth rate is the average of the growth rates from year to year for each year between 1951 and 1973 this would actually overstate the growth rate for growth is necessarily cumulative and what we require is a measure which expresses each year's growth as a percentage of the value of the previous year. There is a formula for this:

$$r = \sqrt[m]{(X_N / X_T)} - 1) \times 100$$

where r is the annual average – or compound – growth rate, X_N the value for the terminal year, X_T the value for the initial year and **m** the number of years between the initial and terminal years. Do not be put off by this formula, for fortunately such a calculation can be achieved rather more easily: many calculators have an X^Y function, or alternatively you can use the EXCEL 97 worksheet ESHCALC1.XLS which, as with the datasets we are here using, is available from the author's website together with full instructions on how to do the calculation.

III.2.3 Index numbers

The challenge posed by calculating compound growth rates leads directly to another basic tool of statistical analysis: index numbers. These are, in effect, a form of ratio, which can be defined as the inverse of the numerator and the denominator in the fraction that produces the quotient (thus in our example for 1951 the ratio of exports to GDP is 1:4). Index numbers are a vital element in a statistician's toolkit as they allow us to transform a variable or variables into a new series (or series) which can be expressed – typically – as a proportion of the base value or year. Thus continuing with our example of exports and GDP between 1951 and 1973, we chart (with base 1951 = 100) the growth of these two variables which, you will remember, start from very different positions and then grow differentially. That differential growth becomes much clearer once charted as index numbers:

The most widely known economic index number in public use is the Retail Price Index (RPI), although, typically, public discussion of

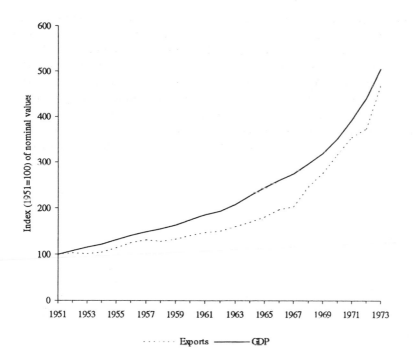

Figure III.1 Index (1951 = 100) of exports and GDP at current market prices, 1951–73

the RPI is in terms of the percentage change in prices over the previous year without making visible that this statistic derives from index numbers. The connection between the index number series and the percentage change from year to year is shown in Figure III.2 where the underlying index number series is charted on the left-hand Y axis and the headline inflation rate on the right-hand Y axis.

This index number series has a base of January 1974 = 100, so that if we read from the underlying data that the value for 1997 is 621.3, we can infer that prices were 521.3 per cent higher in 1997 than in January 1974. To calculate the change from year to year we of course have to calculate the percentage change for each individual year in relation to the appropriate preceding year. Whilst it is possible to do this with a calculator it would be tedious, and thus another good reason for learning how to use a spreadsheet. NB: whilst we can calculate the annual percentage changes for this dataset, we need to be wary that we do not confuse per cent with percentage points, a misunderstanding which is rife even amongst financial journalists. Thus for example, in September 1992, as the then Conservative government made a desperate and ultimately unsuccessful attempt to defend the value of sterling against foreign speculators and thus to remain within the Exchange Rate Mechanism (ERM), interest rates were temporarily increased from 10 to 15 per cent. Next day's newspapers reported this as a 5 per cent increase: it wasn't, it was a 5 percentage points (i.e. 15–10 per cent) or a 50 per cent increase (i.e. ((15 / 10) – 1) x 100). Index numbers are frequently encountered when examining

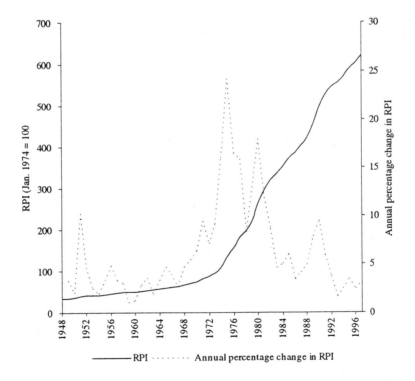

Figure III.2 Retail price index (January 1974 = 100), 1948–97

comparative economic performance, as in the following which uses Maddison's data on aggregate productivity to detail the stage of development attained by the G-7 countries in relation to the level of US productivity, both in relation to a benchmark of 1950 for each country (panel A) and in relation to the US level for each year (panel B). As is discussed elsewhere (pp. 6–9), such exercises form an important component of the catch-up and convergence arguments which now dominate discussion of Britain's postwar economic performance.

	1870	1913	1938	1950	1973	1992	Compound annual % growth rate 1950–92
A. Indices 1950 = 100							
Canada	16.5	43.0	53.8	100.0	195.2	258.9	2.3
France	24.1	50.4	94.7	100.0	314.5	524.2	4.0
Germany	36.2	80.1	110.8	100.0	380.8	630.4	4.5
Italy	24.1	48.8	88.6	100.0	364.0	574.5	4.3
Japan	22.7	50.7	107.9	100.0	549.3	986.2	5.6
UK	33.2	56.0	76.1	100.0	202.5	305.1	2.7
US	17.9	40.4	68.2	100.0	185.2	229.9	2.0
B. US level at each date = 100							
Canada	71.2	82.2	60.9	77.3	81.4	87.0	n.a
France	60.2	55.7	61.9	44.6	75.8	101.8	n.a
Germany	69.9	68.4	56.0	34.5	71.0	94.7	n.a
Italy	45.6	40.8	43.9	33.8	66.4	84.5	n.a
Japan	20.4	20.1	25.3	16.0	47.5	68.8	n.a
UK	115.5	85.9	69.2	62.1	67.9	82.4	n.a
US	100.0	100.0	100.0	100.0	100.0	100.0	n.a

Source: Derived from Maddison, *Monitoring the World Economy*, Table J-5; format from C. H. Feinstein, 'Benefits of backwardness and costs of continuity', in A. W. M. Graham and A. Seldon, eds, *Government and Economies in the Postwar World: Economic policies and comparative performance, 1945–85* (1990), Table 14 1

III.2.4 *Averages*

The RPI, being a measure of movements in consumer prices, is also an average, more correctly a weighted average since it represents a typical basket of goods and services purchased by the average household. The term 'average' is actually one of the most misunderstood and misused of all statistical concepts, in part because most journalists who report numerical data are themselves very sloppy in their use of the concept. There are many different sorts of averages, with the following covering the main cases which you will encounter:

- The arithmetic mean: defined as the sum of a series in a list of numbers divided by the number of cases in that list.
- The mode: the value within a list of numbers which is most frequently present.
- The median: the middle value within a list of numbers.

The arithmetic mean is what most people understand as the average, but when the term average is used to mean typical, as is often the case, it may well be that the mode or median would be a more appropriate measure as there is no reason why the mean, mode or median will be identical unless they conform to what statisticians call the normal distribution.

III.2.5 Nominal and real values

With inflation ubiquitous since the Second World War, it is important that when examining a variable over time we have a means of distinguishing its nominal, monetary value from its real value, that is its value when adjusted for the effects of inflation which acts to reduce the purchasing power of money. In Figure III.3 we demonstrate the importance of inflation adjustment using our GDP series which, for convenience, we have transformed into index numbers with a base of 1990 = 100, which is also the base for the price deflator which we use to move between nominal and real values.

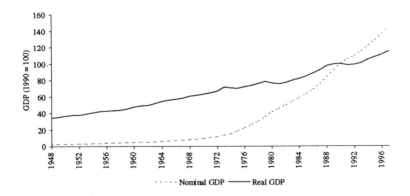

Figure III.3 Index (1990 = 100) of nominal and real GDP, 1948–97

As can be seen the greater part of the growth in GDP is actually illusory, being merely the effects of inflation. Thus the index (1990 = 100) of nominal GDP grew from 2.1 in 1948 to 144.6 in 1997, an increase of 6,698.1 per cent, whereas that for real GDP grew from 34.1 to 114.8, an increase of 236.8 per cent.

The relationship between the real and nominal values for the GDP series are as follows:

$$\text{GDP deflator} = \left(\frac{\text{GDP at current prices}}{\text{GDP at constant prices}} \right)$$

With the appropriate price deflator any variable expressed in current monetary values can be converted into real values, and *vice versa*.

III.3 The pitfalls and potentialities of economic data

Economic data is full of possibilities, but also potential pitfalls for the neophyte, not least that other more advanced consumers and producers of statistics may have a mission to persuade not shared by those less aware of the intricacies of the media. Thus data, as with the written word, has rhetorical potential and rarely more so than with the deeply ideological nature of the debates over the performance of the twentieth-century British economy.

The student of the British economy must, accordingly, be vigilant at a number of levels. First, they must be a good historian, watching for the selective use and interpretation of historical evidence, whether it be graced by numbers, or diagrams or neither. Secondly, and relatedly, they must test the arguments against the potential charge of self-interest by the authority being examined. Thirdly, they must be conscious of the important distinction in economics between positive and normative propositions: the former, ostensibly scientific and objective ('this is how the economy behaves') as against the latter's non-scientific and subjective characteristics ('this is how the economy should behave'). Fourthly, and more specifically with relation to data, the following ten guidelines offer a minimum checklist of concerns which ought to inform the users of economic data:

1. ALL data are incomplete and inconsistent, and, accordingly, potentially subject to revisions.

2. Read the small print: look at the sources/notes to a table/figure to see what the source of the data are and to what degree it might have been processed.
3. Why, how and for what purpose was the data collected?
4. Be clear that you understand what units of measurement are being used.
5. Be aware that the longer the time span of the data the more probable that there are discontinuities and differences of definition in the data which lessen its reliability.
6. In cross-country comparisons there are very serious problems associated with exchange rates and differing statistical conventions in different countries. In addition, of course, there are the effects of inflation and you need to be clear that all important comparisons over time and between countries are conducted in terms of real values.
7. Avoid spurious accuracy: do not become too enthusiastic about small differences in, for example, growth rates or unemployment rates of countries, which may well be within the margins of error of the data.
8. Have in mind appropriate reference points and comparators. Thus, for example, economic growth should be measured from peak-to-peak in the business cycle (not from trough-to-peak, as is the wont of many politicians), while the British case ought to be compared with appropriate other countries.
9. When using statistics, and in particular when writing essays, it is rarely useful to employ a raw numerical value (e.g. British exports increased by £13,388m. between 1951 and 1973) and much to be preferred if you express the change as a proportion of some other variable – normally GDP is the most useful here.
10. Look for datasets which have been used by authorities which draw very different conclusions about the performance of the British economy.

In developing a sense of doubt about data you are actually equipping yourself to use data: only from an understanding of the pitfalls can there come a sense of the potentialities.

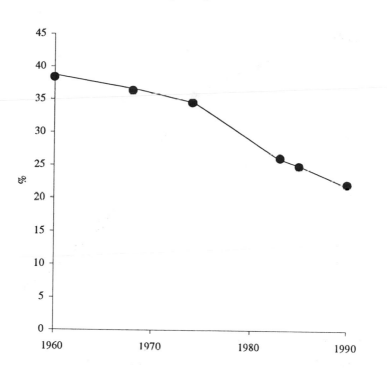

Figure III.4A UK: employment in manufacturing industry as a percentage of civilian employment, 1960–90 (full Y-axis)

III.4 Charting data and seeking relationships between variables

III.4.1 Introduction

The visual presentation of data and the search for relationships between economic variables forms a central part of the process of examining and making judgements upon economic performance. Both are potentially fraught activities: graphs and tables are usually pretty reliable from academics, but much less so from financial journalists and others where scales can be controlled to suggest much more dramatic changes than is in fact the case, as for example in Figures III.4A-B where,[3] just by the simple device of truncating the Y-axis, so that it runs only from the minimum to the maximum value, and

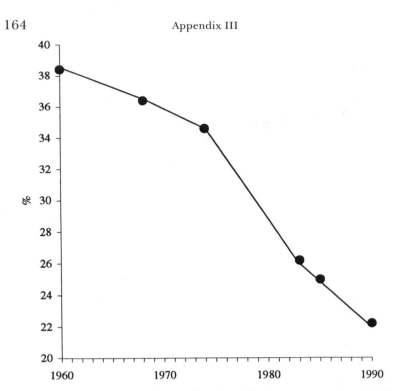

Figure III.4B UK: employment in manufacturing industry as a percentage of civilian employment 1960–90 (truncated Y-axis)

compressing the X-axis, one can make the relative contraction of Britain's manufacturing sector appear even more dramatic.[4]

III.4.2 Types of charts/figures

The main types of chart – all here produced from EXCEL 97 and within the capability of a novice within a few hours of getting to grips with the software – are as follows, with all of the data drawing upon the worksheets underlying Appendices II and III:

- Line Chart: as in Figures III.4 A and B, and one of the main visual displays for time series. Here the X-axis is time and the Y-axis can be any monetary or physical unit, or index number series.
- X-Y or Scatter Chart: a form of Line graph but where the X-axis can display a variable, and is particularly useful for testing asso-

ciations between variables (see Figure III.5 which charts the relationship between Britain's inflation rate and unemployment rate for the golden age, a relationship – known as the Phillips curve – important to policy-makers who believed there was a trade-off between these variables).

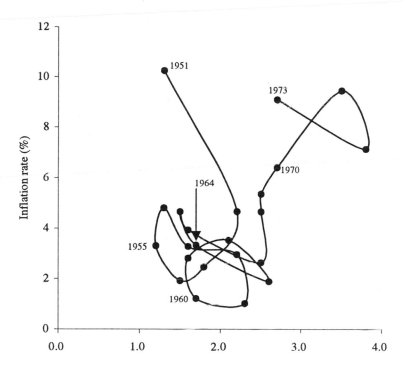

Figure III.5 Inflation and unemployment rates (%), 1951–73

- Column Chart: as in Figure III.6, which has uses for time series or category data, and with various derivatives – such as area charts – allows the representation of change over time in the total and shifts in the composition of that total. NB: reverse the axes and a column chart becomes a bar chart, with the bars either displayed side by side for each series or stacked one on the other to display the total and composition, thereby achieving the same effect as in Figure III.6.

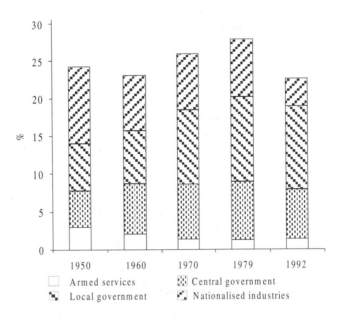

Figure III.6 Public sector employment as a percentage of total employment, selected years, 1950–92

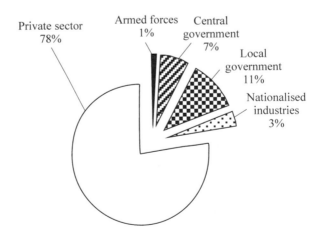

Figure III.7 Total employment by sector (%), 1992

- Pie chart: as in Figure III.7, this permitting the representation in greater detail and more forcefully the composition of variable, in this case the observations for 1992 used in Figure III.6 but with the addition of the private sector employment share.

III.4.3 Associations and causation

The principal subject matter of this book, as with economics and history themselves as academic disciplines, is about seeking relationships between variables. Consider some of the hypotheses examined in the main body of the text: that Britain's low level of productivity relative to other OECD economies was due to the behaviour of trade unions, or to the excessive size of the public sector, or to the low level of investment. Each one of these is amenable to testing of various sorts.

In asking whether a relationship exists our purpose is to identify whether two or more events are entirely independent of each other, or whether there is an identifiable statistical connection which is sufficiently strong for us to be reasonably confident that we have specified the appropriate causal connection(s). In hypothesis testing – the formal name for the testing of relationships – three questions are asked:

- Does there exist a statistical relationship between variables?
- What is the strength of any such relationship so identified?
- What can be inferred about the form of the relationship?

There exists a large body of statistical measures and techniques which are used for hypothesis testing and you will frequently encounter statements along the lines of 'the econometric evidence suggests ...', a reference to a sub-discipline of economics known as econometrics which is the application of mathematical and statistical techniques to economic problems. Try not to be intimidated by such evidence, for whilst you are inevitably handicapped by not having a training in economics and econometrics, this does not mean you cannot ask solid historical questions of the technical evidence being invoked:

- What is being measured and is it appropriate for the questions being asked?

- How reliable are the data underlying the econometrics?
- Are there alternative explanations which, had the economist/ econometrician been better informed about the historical record, ought to have been tested?

Above all, are we able to distinguish between association and causation? In interpreting the econometric results invoked by historians and economists you need to know that, in reality, whatever

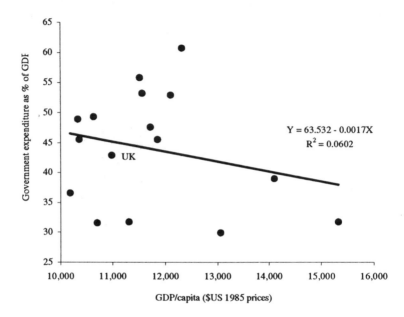

$$Y = 63.532 - 0.0017X$$
$$R^2 = 0.0602$$

Figure III.8 OECD-16: real GDP per capita and general government expenditure as a percentage of GDP, 1979
Source: Middleton, *Government versus the Market,* Figure 1.2.

economics' aspirations to be a science, economics and econometrics are practised in a manner which rarely produces definite empirical tests. Consequentially, whilst many historians of the British economy place strong reliance on econometrics, others use a method called colligation, an advanced form of story-telling defined by Blaug as: 'the binding together of facts, low-level generalizations, high-level theories, and value judgements in a coherent narrative, [all] held together by a glue of an implicit set of beliefs and attitudes that the author shares with [his/her] readers.' As Blaug concludes: 'In able hands, it can be extremely persuasive, and yet it is never easy to explain afterwards why it has persuaded.'[5]

The absence of clear-cut empirical results will be encountered time-and-time again in the main body of the text, but as with the potential pitfalls of data identified earlier, this should not lead us to abandon quantitative analysis but instead sharpen our analytical senses of what needs to be undertaken.

For example, consider Figure III.8 – an X-Y graph – which charts for the OECD-16 countries the level of GDP/capita, a conventional measure of the 'success' of an economy, against the ratio of general government expenditure to GDP, a proxy for the relative size of government. This exercise is conducted for 1979, the year in which a new Conservative government took power committed to reversing Britain's economic decline and believing that a central feature of that decline was the excessive size of Britain's public sector. For this scatter plot, we have calculated what statisticians call the linear trend. This is sometimes referred to as the line of best fit and is a procedure for drawing a line as closely as possible through the data points where the best fit is attained by minimising the difference between the Y values as represented on the trend line and the Y values existing as data points .

As can be observed this trend line has a negative slope, suggesting that countries with higher levels of GDP/capita do indeed have smaller governments. But is this an association or causation? Notice that the negative slope of the line is very slight and that the data points are very widely dispersed around the linear trend, which suggests that we should not have much confidence in our estimated trend line and therefore in the hypothesis that for the OECD-16 countries, there is actually an inverse relationship between government size and economic success. This doubt is then confirmed by the very low value for the R^2 which is reported above the trend line. This is a statistical measure of the goodness of fit and you will often see it reported in discussions of econometric evidence (if all the data points lay exactly on the trend line, the R^2 value would be 1).

We need, therefore, to ask more refined questions in seeking the relationship between government size and economic performance, although we should note at this stage that contrary to contemporary debate at that time, Britain did not have an especially large public sector. Thus in Chapter 3 we examine the composition as well as the total of government expenditure; we discuss taxation and its affects on profitability and incentives; we investigate the non-spending and taxing activities of government (regulation); and, of course, we consider that deficiencies in economic performance may actually have stemmed from problems with market agents, not government activities. In short, through data and its envisioning we are drawn to ask more complex questions of the historical evidence.

NOTES

Please note that unless otherwise stated all works cited are published in London.

Preface

1. P. F. Clarke, *The Penguin History of Britain*, vol. 9, *Hope and Glory: Britain, 1900–1990* (1996), p. 3; see also for similar sentiments relating specifically to postwar Britain, K. O. Morgan, *The People's Peace: British history, 1945–1989* (Oxford, 1990).
2. Words emboldened in the text are explained in Appendix I, the Glossary.
3. D. E. H. Edgerton, *England and the Aeroplane: An essay on a militant and technological nation* (1991), p. xv.
4. See R. J. Evans, *In Defence of History* (1997), for a recent spirited defence of this 'traditional' approach to history.
5. For attempts to answer the question what is economic history, see J. Gardiner, ed., *What is History Today?* (1988), ch. 3; see also D. C. Coleman, 'History, economic history and the numbers game', *History Journal*, 38 (1995), pp. 635–46, on the relation between economic and other branches of history.
6. K. H. Jarausch and K. A. Hardy, *Quantitative Methods for Historians: A guide to research, data and statistics* (Chapel Hill, 1991), p. 2. See also R. C. Floud, *An Introduction to Quantitative Methods for Historians* (2nd edn, 1979); R. Solomon and C. Winch, *Calculating and Computing for Social Science and Arts Students* (Buckingham, 1994); and for a really approachable 'how-to guide' which uses spreadsheet and database management software, M. J. Lewis and R. Lloyd-Jones, *Using Computers in History: A practical guide* (1996).
7. There are a huge number of texts that might be recommended for those wishing to acquire some basic economic theory. From experience, G. R. Hawke's *Economics for Historians* (Cambridge, 1980) and A. Dunnett's *Understanding the Economy* (4th edn, 1998) and *Understanding the Market* (3rd edn, 1998) are well suited for such purpose, while *The Economic Review* (a magazine for 'A' level students published four times per year by Philip Allan) contains many articles which apply economic

171

theory to postwar British experience in a most accessible manner.

8. A guide to further reading is provided at pp. 188–9.

9. The institute of Contemporary British History is the main professional body providing resources and guidance for the study of postwar British history, see its web site **<http://ihr.sas.ac.uk/icbh/>**; B. Brivati, J. Buxton and A. Seldon, eds, *The Contemporary History Handbook* (Manchester 1996); and, within its Making Contemporary Britain series, A. K. Cairncross, *The British Economy since 1945: Economic policy and performance, 1945–1995* (Oxford, 2nd edn, 1995).

10. See, however, the essay by N. F. R. Crafts, 'The golden age of economic growth in postwar Europe: why did Northern Ireland miss out?', *Irish Economic and Social History*, 22 (1995), pp. 5–25, on what the principal issues might be in such a history; see also V. K. Borooah, 'Growth and political violence in Northern Ireland, 1920–96', in S. Borner and M. Paldam, eds, *The Political Dimension of Economic Growth* (1998), pp. 266–77.

11. A. Maddison, *Monitoring the World Economy, 1820–1992* (Paris, 1995). The countries comprising the OECD-17 are detailed in Table 1.1.

12. R. Rose et al., 'Witness seminar: periodisation in post-war Britain', *Contemporary Record*, 6 (1992), pp. 326–40.

1 Introduction

1. Taken from J. M. Keynes's introduction to H. D. Henderson's *Supply and Demand* (Cambridge, 1922), p. v, one of the early volumes in the Cambridge Economic Handbooks series.

2. Maddison, *Monitoring the World Economy*.

3. One of the principal contributors to this literature has been Moses Abramovitz. See his *Thinking about Growth and other Essays on Economic Growth and Welfare* (Cambridge, 1989), esp. ch. 7; see also C. H. Feinstein, 'Benefits of backwardness and costs of continuity', in A. W. M. Graham and A. Seldon, eds, *Government and Economies in the Postwar World: Economic policies and comparative performance, 1945–85* (1990), pp. 284–93; and for a critical position on this hypothesis, see B. W. E. Alford, *Britain in the World Economy since 1880* (1996), ch. 10.

4. World Bank, *World Development Report, 1997: The state in a changing world* (Oxford, 1997), pp. 214–15.

5. Notice that this is a negative number because imports exceeded exports in this year.

6. Hawke, *Economics for Historians*, p. 4.

7. See R. Middleton, *Government versus the Market: The growth of the public sector, economic management and British economic performance, c. 1890–1979* (Cheltenham, 1996), pp. 46–8, for a discussion of the economic case for the supremacy of markets over alternatives.

8. See ibid., pp. 54–64.

9. P. A. David, 'Historical economics in the long run: some implications of

path-dependence', in G. D. Snooks, ed., *Historical Analysis in Economics* (1993), p. 29.

10. R. J. Barro, *Determinants of Economic Growth: A cross-country empirical study* (Cambridge, MA, 1997), p. 119.

11. S. Rebelo, 'Long-run policy analysis and long-run growth', *Journal of Political Economy*, 99 (1991), p. 520.

12. Labour Party news release, 'New policies for the global economy', 26 September 1994. The press reception afforded this speech illustrates the dangers faced by politicians who embrace new economic ideas too openly, and is a warning of the extent to which the formulation of economic policies calls upon informal economic expertise as much as the ideas of academic economics and economists. These and other issues are explored in the author's *Charlatans or Saviours?: Economists and the British economy from Marshall to Meade* (Cheltenham, 1998), esp. ch. 2.

13. See Barro, *Determinants of Economic Growth*, pp. 19–22.

14. See N. F. R. Crafts, *Can De-industrialisation Seriously Damage your Wealth?: A review of why growth rates differ and how to improve economic performance* (1993); with C. R. Bean, 'British economic growth since 1945: relative economic decline ... and renaissance?', in N. F. R. Crafts and G. Toniolo, eds, *Economic Growth in Europe since 1945* (Cambridge, 1996), pp. 131–72; *Britain's Relative Economic Decline, 1870–1995* (1997); and 'The British economy: missing out or catching up?', in B. J. Foley, ed., *European Economies since the Second World War* (1998), pp. 1–24.

15. See A. W. M Graham, 'Objectives and instruments', in D. J. Morris, ed., *The Economic System in the UK.* (Oxford, 3rd edn, 1985), pp. 251–71; J. D. Robertson, 'Guiding and making policy: ideas and institutions', in J. L. Waltman and D. T. Studlar, eds, *Political Economy: Public policies in the United States and Britain* (Jackson, MI, 1987), pp. 16–43; and J. E. Stiglitz, 'The role of government in the contemporary world', in V. Tanzi and K.-Y. Chu, eds, *Income Distribution and High-Quality Growth* (Cambridge, MA, 1998), pp. 21–53.

16. See Middleton, *Charlatans or Saviours?*, p. 59.

17. See, in particular, S. Pollard, *The Wasting of the British Economy: British economic policy 1945 to the present* (2nd edn, 1984).

18. Stiglitz, 'The role of government', p. 22.

19. D. N. McCloskey, *If You're so Smart: The narrative of economic expertise* (Chicago, IL, 1990), p. 44.

20. See I. Budge, 'Relative decline as a political issue: ideological motivations of the politico-economic debate in post-war Britain', *Contemporary Record*, 7 (1993), pp. 1–23; and J. D. Tomlinson, 'Inventing "decline": the falling behind of the British economy in the postwar years', *Economic History Review*, 49 (1996), pp. 731–57.

21. See Clarke, *Hope and Glory*, pp. 401–4 for what might have been.

22. Crafts, 'The British economy', p. 21.

23. Maddison, *Monitoring the World Economy;* and C. H. Feinstein, *National Income, Expenditure and Output of the United Kingdom, 1855–1965* (Cambridge, 1972).

24. Maddison, *Monitoring the World Economy*, table J-6.

2 Economic Performance since 1945

1. The business cycle troughs are taken to be 1952, 1958, 1962, 1967, 1971, 1975, 1981 and 1992.
2. R. C. O. Matthews, C. H. Feinstein and J. C. Odling-Smee, *British Economic Growth, 1856–1973* (Oxford, 1983).
3. See ibid., chs 3–4.
4. See his *Dynamic Forces in Capitalist Development: A long-run comparative view* (Oxford, 1991), ch. 5; and the more recent *Monitoring the World Economy*, ch. 2.
5. The negative figure for the gender balance reflects a combination of the labour market characteristics of women, which are reflected in their lower earnings (propensity to undertake part-time work and lower average skills levels) relative to men and the consequences of discrimination against them. It should be noted that one of the strong assumptions of the growth accounting exercises we noted above is that wages fully reflect the productivity of labour.
6. See Maddison, *Dynamic Forces*, pp. 147–57.
7. Maddison, *Monitoring the World Economy*, p. 44; and *Dynamic Forces*, p. 133.
8. R. R. Nelson, *The Sources of Economic Growth* (Cambridge, MA, 1996), p. 3.
9. *Competitiveness: Helping business to win*, Cm. 2563 (1994), p. 9.
10. R. Landau, T. Taylor and G. Wright, 'Introduction', in R. Landau et al., eds, *The Mosaic of Economic Growth* (Stanford, CA, 1996), p. 8.
11. *Competitiveness: Helping business to win*, p. 9.
12. See, for example, the report 'Productivity: the British disease revisited', *The Economist*, 31 October, pp. 31–2; and S. Brittan's 'A lop-sided debate', *Financial Times*, 12 November 1998, p. 30. Both articles make reference to a report, 'Driving productivity and growth in the UK', by the McKinsey Global Institute, an influential international consultancy company which seems to be setting the terms of the current British policy debate. This consultancy is a known extreme advocate of the benefits of the market and of the disbenefits of government intervention. Accordingly, the accusation has been made that its report and lobbying overstate the extent of Britain's productivity disadvantage so as to promote the case for further market deregulation, while ignoring the fact that the European countries supposedly so far ahead of Britain (France and Germany) have now more regulated market economies than has Britain – see L. Elliott, 'McKinsey's waste output', *Guardian*, 30 November 1998, p. 19.
13. P. R. Krugman, 'Making sense of the competitiveness debate', *Oxford Review of Economic Policy*, 12 (Autumn 1996), pp. 17–25.
14. Maddison, *Monitoring the World Economy*, p. 73.
15. See S. J. Prais's detailed historical and cross-country study of this complex interrelated problem, *Productivity, Education and Training: An international perspective* (Cambridge, 1995).
16. D. E. H. Edgerton, *Science, Technology and the British Industrial 'Decline', 1870–1970* (Cambridge, 1996), esp. ch. 5.

17. J. Clegg, 'The United Kingdom: a *par excellence* two-way direct investor', in J. H. Dunning and R. Narula, eds, *Foreign Direct Investment and Governments: Catalysts for economic restructuring* (1996), pp. 42–77.

18. Middleton, *Government versus the Market*, table 3.7; and ONS, *Public Finance Trends 97: A statistical background to public sector spending and revenues* (1997).

19. See S. N. Broadberry and N. F. R. Crafts, 'British economic policy and industrial performance in the early post-war period', *Business History*, 38 (October 1996), pp. 65–91; and the response to this article and the authors' reply, J. D. Tomlinson and N. Tiratsoo, '"An old story, freshly told"?: a comment on Broadberry and Crafts' approach to Britain's early post-war economic performance', *Business History*, 40 (April 1998), pp. 62–72, and S. N. Broadberry and N. F. R. Crafts, 'The post-war settlement: not such a good bargain after all', *Business History*, 40 (April 1998), pp. 73–9.

20. R. Landau et al., 'Introduction', pp. 1, 12, 15.

21. This evidence is reviewed in Middleton, *Government versus the Market*, p. 448.

22. Ibid., pp. 631–4.

23. See A. P. Thirlwall and H. D. Gibson, *Balance-of-Payments Theory and the United Kingdom Experience* (4th edn, 1992), ch. 9.

24. House of Lords select committee on overseas trade, vol. 1: *Report*, HL 238–1 (1984–5).

25. S. Bazen and A. P. Thirlwall, *Deindustrialization* (Oxford, 1989), p. 6.

26. B. W. E. Alford, 'De-industrialisation', *ReFRESH*, 25 (Autumn 1997), pp. 5–8.

27. P. Temple, 'Overview: growth, competitiveness and trade performance', in T. Buxton, P. Chapman and P. Temple, eds, *Britain's Economic Performance* (1998), table 4.5.

28. 'Services in the UK economy', *Bank of England Quarterly Bulletin*, 25 (1985), pp. 404–14.

29. M. Haq and P. Temple, 'Overview: economic policy and the changing international division of labour', in T. Buxton et al., *Britain's Economic Performance*, p. 467.

30. For example, Pollard, *The Wasting of the British Economy*, pp. 124–5.

31. See J. S. Foreman-Peck, 'Trade and the balance of payments', in N. F. R. Crafts and N. W. C. Woodward, eds, *The British Economy since 1945* (Oxford, 1991), pp. 145–50.

32. For example, R. P. Bootle, *The Death of Inflation: Surviving and thriving in the zero era* (1996).

33. See C. J. Wrigley, *British Trade Unions, 1945–1995* (Manchester, 1997).

34. For an accessible economic analysis of inflation, see J. Fender, *Inflation: A contemporary perspective* (Hemel Hempstead, 1990).

35. Wrigley, *British Trade Unions*, pp. 23, 26.

36. D. Metcalf and S. Milner, 'A century of UK strike activity: an alternative perspective', in D. Metcalf and S. Milner, eds, *New Perspectives on Industrial Disputes* (1993), p. 238.

37. See the survey of R. A. Church, *The Rise and Decline of the British Motor*

Industry (1994); and the more polemical, but very illuminating case study in K. Williams, J. Williams and D. Thomas, *Why are the British Bad at Manufacturing?* (1983), pp. 217–81.

38. H. W. Armstrong, 'Regional problems and policies', in Crafts and Woodward, eds, *The British Economy since 1945*, pp. 291–334.
39. For labour force, employment and unemployment trends, see S. N. Broadberry, 'Employment and unemployment', in R. C. Floud and D. N. McCloskey, eds, *The Economic History of Britain since 1700*, vol. 3: *1939–1992* (Cambridge, 2nd edn, 1994), pp. 195–220.
40. The current ONS definitions are used here with the workforce being 'workforce jobs', this being the sum of 'employee jobs' and the unemployment claimant count, with employee jobs measuring the sum of employees in employment, self-employment jobs from the Labour Force Survey, those in HM Forces and government-supported trainees.
41. Data from ONS, *Economic Trends, Annual Supplement*, 1998 edn (1999), table 3.7.
42. For a detailed breakdown, see A. K. Cairncross, *The British Economy since 1945: Economic policy and performance, 1945–1995* (Oxford, 2nd edn, 1995), table 8.6.
43. Middleton, *Government versus the Market*, p. 106.
44. ONS, *Economic Trends*, 1998 edn, table 3.4.
45. For historical perspective, see C. H. Feinstein and R. C. O. Matthews, 'The growth of output and productivity in the UK: the 1980s as a phase of the post-war period', *National Institute Economic Review*, 133 (1990), pp. 78–90; N. Oulton and M. O'Mahony, *Productivity and Growth: A study of British industry, 1954–1986* (Cambridge, 1994); and R. Millward, 'Industrial and commercial performance since 1950', in Floud and McCloskey, eds, *The Economic History of Britain since 1700*, vol. 3, pp. 123–67; for recent trends, see G. Cameron, J. Proudman and S. Redding, 'Deconstructing growth in UK manufacturing', *Bank of England Working Paper*, no. 73 (1997); and F. Livesey, 'The service industries', in B. Atkinson, F. Livesey and B. Milward, eds, *Applied Economics* (1998), pp. 273–87.
46. See D. Julius, 'Inflation and growth in a service economy', *Bank of England Quarterly Bulletin*, 38 (1998), pp. 338–46.
47. P. J. N. Sinclair, C. Ryan and M. Walker, 'Continuity, change and consumption: British economic trends, 1945–95', *Contemporary British History*, 10 (Winter 1996), pp. 35–59.
48. P. Warwick, 'Did Britain change?: an inquiry into the causes of national decline', *Journal of Contemporary History*, 20 (1985), p. 99.
49. For example, Pollard, *The Wasting of the British Economy*.
50. For example, B. Elbaum and W. H. Lazonick, eds, *The Decline of the British Economy* (Oxford, 1986); and Middleton, *Government versus the Market*.
51. Further detail is available in Middleton, *Government versus the Market*, pp. 29–39.
52. See Matthews et al., *British Economic Growth*, p. 326.
53. See B. Collins and K. Robbins, eds, *British Culture and Economic Decline* (1990); and W. D. Rubinstein, *Capitalism, Culture and Decline in Britain*,

1750–1990 (1993), for critical surveys; see also the illuminating comparative study by K. Brown, *Britain and Japan: A comparative economic and social history since 1900* (Manchester, 1998).

54. P. A. Hall, *Governing the Economy: The politics of state intervention in Britain and France* (Cambridge, 1986), p. 34.

55. P. Mottershead, 'Industrial policy', in F. T. Blackaby, ed., *British Economic Policy, 1960–74* (Cambridge, 1978), p. 483.

56. P. K. O'Brien, 'The costs and benefits of British imperialism, 1846–1914', *Past and Present*, 120 (1988), pp. 185–6.

57. Feinstein, 'Benefits of backwardness', p. 285.

58. G. C. Allen, *The British Disease: A short essay on the nature and causes of the nation's lagging wealth* (2nd edn, 1979).

59. S. N. Broadberry, 'How did the United States and Germany overtake Britain?: a sectoral analysis of comparative productivity levels, 1870–1990', *Journal of Economic History*, 58 (1998), pp. 375–407.

60. See, however, R. Millward, 'Productivity in the UK service sector: historical trends, 1856–1985, and comparisons with USA, 1950–85', *Oxford Bulletin of Economics and Statistics*, 52 (1990), pp. 423–36.

61. See the Department for Employment analysis of strikes between 1971 and 1973, which is cited by Wrigley, *British Trade Unions*, p. 27.

62. See C. F. Pratten, *Labour Productivity Differentials within International Companies* (Cambridge, 1976); and S. J. Prais, *Productivity and Industrial Structure: A statistical study of manufacturing industry in Britain, Germany and the United States* (Cambridge, 1981), esp. ch. 7.

63. The motor vehicle industry has been extensively studied from this viewpoint, see W. A. Lewchuk, *American Technology and the British Vehicle Industry* (Cambridge, 1987).

64. For a recent business history of Britain, see J. F. Wilson, *British Business History, 1720–1994* (Manchester, 1995).

65 F. H. Longstreth, 'The city, industry and the state', in C. Crouch, ed., *State and Economy in Contemporary Capitalism* (1979), pp. 157–90; and C. C. S. Newton and D. Porter, *Modernisation Frustrated: The politics of industrial decline in Britain since 1900* (1988)

66 For example, compare the basically pro-City account of F. H. Capie and M. Collins, *Have the Banks Failed British Industry?: An historical survey of bank/industry relations in Britain, 1870–1990* (1992), with the critical assessment of A. Cox, S. Lee and J. Sanderson, *The Political Economy of Modern Britain* (Cheltenham, 1997), ch. 6.

67. Elbaum and Lazonick, eds, *The Decline of the British Economy*; for a survey of this and later writings in this mould, see M. W. Kirby, 'Institutional rigidities and economic decline: reflections on the British experience', *Economic History Review*, 45 (1992), pp. 637–60.

68. B. Elbaum and W. H. Lazonick, 'An institutional perspective on British decline', in Elbaum and Lazonick, eds., *The Decline of the British Economy*, p. 2.

69. Hall, *Governing the Economy*, p. 35.

70. W. D. Rubinstein, 'Academics in the wasteland', *Times Literary Supplement*, 23 January 1998, p. 6, a review of P. F. Clarke and R. C. Trebilcock, eds,

Understanding Decline: Perceptions and realities of British economic performance (Cambridge, 1997).

71. For a forceful expression of this argument, see M. Kitson and J. Michie, 'Britain's industrial performance since 1960: underinvestment and relative economic decline', *Economic Journal*, 106 (1996), pp. 196–212.

3 Economic Policies since 1945

1. See, for example, the following discussion of macroeconomic policies in the context of international competitiveness: A. Boltho, 'The assessment: international competitiveness', *Oxford Review of Economic Policy*, 12 (Autumn 1996), pp. 1–16.
2. The political history of postwar Britain can be traced in K. O. Morgan, *The People's Peace: British history, 1945–1989* (Oxford, 1990); and P. F. Clarke, *The Penguin History of Britain*, vol. 9: *Hope and Glory: Britain, 1900–1990* (1996), chs 7–11.
3. A. M. Gamble and S. A. Walkland, *The British Party System and Economic Policy, 1945–1983: Studies in adversary politics* (Oxford, 1984), p. 20.
4. V. K. Borooah, 'The interaction between economic policy and political performance', in R. C. O. Matthews, ed., *Economy and Democracy* (1985), p. 20.
5. Borooah, 'The interaction', p. 21.
6. P. Mosley, *The Making of Economic Policy: Theory and evidence from Britain and the United States since 1945* (Brighton, 1984), ch. 7; and P. Whiteley, *Political Control of the Macro-Economy: The political economy of public policy making* (1986), ch. 3.
7. Mosley, *The Making of Economic Policy*, p. 38.
8. Middleton, *Government versus the Market*, p. 488.
9. For a broadly pro-consensus account from two political scientists, see D. Kavanagh and P. Morris, *Consensus Politics from Attlee to Major* (Oxford, 2nd edn, 1994), ch. 1; and for recent revisionist work by historians, see H. Jones and M. D. Kandiah, eds, *The Myth of Consensus: New views on British history, 1945–64* (1996).
10. Kavanagh and Morris, *Consensus Politics*, pp. 4–6.
11. Cited in Ibid., p. 2.
12. See K. Jefferys, *Retreat from New Jerusalem: British politics, 1951–64* (1997), esp. ch. 6.
13. See N. Rollings, 'Butskellism, the postwar consensus and the managed economy', in Jones and Kandiah, eds, *The Myth of Consensus*, pp. 97–119.
14. Cairncross, *The British Economy*, p. 95.
15. B. Pimlott, 'The myth of consensus', in L. M. Smith, ed., *The Making of Britain: Echoes of greatness* (1988), p. 136.
16. Initially quite optimistic about British politics, by the later 1970s S. H. Beer's diagnosis had become that of pluralistic stagnation in his *Britain against Itself: The political contradictions of collectivism* (1982); see also S. E.

Finer, ed., *Adversary Politics and Electoral Reform* (1975), esp. pp. 3–32, 99–116.

17. Gamble and Walkland, *The British Party System*, pp. 24–8.
18. R. Rose, *Do Parties make a Difference?* (2nd edn, 1984), p. 142.
19. Middleton, *Government versus the Market*, pp. 483–4, 528.
20. This section draws very heavily upon Middleton, *Government versus the Market*, ch. 3, with the terminal date of the public finance datasets extended to the 1990s where possible. See also J. E. Cronin, *The Politics of State Expansion: War, state and society in twentieth-century Britain* (1991).
21. R. A. Musgrave, *The Theory of Public Finance: A study in public economy* (1959).
22. M. Chalmers, *Paying for Defence: Military spending and British decline* (1985); Middleton, *Government versus the Market*, pp. 614–17.
23. K. Judge, 'State pensions and the growth of social welfare expenditure', *Journal of Social Policy*, 10 (1981), p. 505.
24. K. Judge, 'The growth and decline of social expenditure', in A. Walker, ed., *Public Expenditure and Social Policy: An examination of social spending and social priorities* (1982), p. 29.
25. As well as responsibility for the civil service until 1968.
26. R. A. Chapman, *The Treasury in Public Policy-Making* (1997), provides the best short history. See also, in addition to Pollard's *The Wasting of the British Economy*; A. Ham's polemic, *Treasury Rules: Recurrent themes in British economic policy* (1981); and C. Thain's balanced assessment, 'The Treasury and Britain's decline', *Political Studies*, 32 (1984), pp. 581–95.
27. C. Clifford, 'The rise and fall of the Department of Economic Affairs, 1964–69: British government and indicative planning', *Contemporary British History*, 11 (Summer 1997), pp. 94–116.
28. A. Ringe, 'Background to Neddy: economic planning in the 1960s', *Contemporary British History*, 12 (Spring 1998), pp. 82–98.
29. See the spirited account of their history and closure by a former Director General of NEDO, G. Chandler, 'The political framework: the political roller coaster', in Buxton et al., eds, *Britain's Economic Performance*, pp. 11–34.
30. On the latter, see R. Jones, *Wages and Employment Policy, 1936–1985* (1987); see also Middleton, *Government versus the Market*, table 12.2, for a complete listing of all incomes/price policies between 1945–79.
31. See P. A. Hall, 'Policy paradigms, social learning and the state: the case of economic policymaking in Britain', *Comparative Politics*, 25 (1993), pp. 275–96. For a review of this and other approaches, see Middleton, *Charlatans or Saviours?*, ch. 2.
32. For the evolution and effectiveness of policies during this phase, see J. C. R. Dow, *The Management of the British Economy, 1945–60* (Cambridge, 1964); A. K. Cairncross, *Years of Recovery: British Economic Policy, 1945–51* (1985); and J. D. Tomlinson, *Democratic Socialism and Economic Policy: The Attlee years, 1945–1951* (Cambridge, 1997).
33. See Dow, *The Management of the British Economy*; S. Brittan, *Steering the Economy: The role of the Treasury* (Harmondsworth, rev. edn, 1971); and for a recent assessment encompassing all areas of public policy, Jefferys,

Retreat from New Jerusalem.

34. J. D. Tomlinson, 'Inventing "decline": the falling behind of the British economy in the postwar years', *Economic History Review*, 49 (1996), pp. 735–9.
35. For literature for this phase, see Note 32 above; F. T. Blackaby, ed., *British Economic Policy, 1960–74* (Cambridge, 1978); R. Coopey, S. Fielding and N. Tiratsoo, eds, *The Wilson Governments, 1964–70* (1993), esp. chs 4–5; and A. K. Cairncross, *Managing the British Economy in the 1960s: A Treasury perspective* (1996).
36. M. Jarvis, 'The 1958 Treasury dispute', *Contemporary British History*, 12 (Summer 1998), pp. 22–50.
37. S. Brittan, *The Treasury under the Tories, 1951–1964* (Harmondsworth, 1964), ch. 7.
38. K. Steinnes, 'The European challenge: Britain's EEC application in 1961', *Contemporary European History*, 7 (1998), pp. 61–79.
39. Jones, *Wages and Employment Policy*, pp. 54–65.
40. R. Lowe, 'The core executive, modernization and the creation of PESC, 1960–64', *Public Administration*, 75 (1997), pp. 601–15.
41. See R. Coopey, 'Industrial policy in the white heat of the scientific revolution', in Coopey et al., eds, *The Wilson Governments*, pp. 102–22.
42. For literature for this phase, see Note 35 above; M. Holmes, *Political Pressure and Economic Policy: British government, 1970–1974* (1982); R. Coopey and N. W. C. Woodward, eds, *Britain in the 1970s: The troubled economy* (1996); and S. Ball and A. Seldon, eds, *The Heath Government, 1970–1974: A reappraisal* (1996).
43. R. Coopey, S. Fielding and N. Tiratsoo, 'Introduction: the Wilson years', in Coopey et al., eds, *The Wilson Governments*, p. 1.
44. See Cairncross and Eichengreen, *Sterling in Decline*, ch. 5.
45. R. Coopey and N. W. C. Woodward, 'The British economy in the 1970s: an overview', in Coopey and Woodward, eds, *Britain in the 1970s*, p. 10.
46. A. Seldon, 'Conservative century', in A. Seldon and S. Ball, eds, *Conservative Century: The Conservative Party since 1900* (Oxford, 1994), p. 56.
47. See G. Goodman et al., 'Symposium: the trade unions and the fall of the Heath government', *Contemporary Record*, 2 (Spring 1988), pp. 36–46.
48. Jones, *Wages and Employment Policy*, pp. 85–6.
49. For literature for this phase, see Note 42 above; and M. Holmes, *The Labour Government, 1974–79: Political aims and economic reality* (1985); M. J. Artis and D. Cobham, eds, *Labour's Economic Policies, 1974–1979* (Manchester, 1991); and A. J. C. Britton, *Macroeconomic Policy in Britain, 1974–87* (Cambridge, 1991).
50. D. E. Butler and D. Kavanagh, *The British General Election of February 1974* (1974), chs 2–3.
51. Speech to Labour Party Conference, 28 September, cited in F. T. Blackaby, 'The economics and politics of demand management', in S. T. Cook and P. M. Jackson, eds, *Current Issues in Fiscal Policy* (Oxford, 1979), p. 187. In fact, the highest rate of inflation this century was experienced between July 1919 and February 1920, equivalent on an annualised basis to 55.2 per cent. By contrast, the peak rate in 1975 had only been 26 per cent.

52. See K. Burk and A. K. Cairncross, *'Goodbye, Great Britain': The 1976 IMF crisis* (1992).

53. Holmes, *The Labour Government*, p. 92.

54. In his memoirs, Denis Healey, described himself as an 'eclectic pragmatist' who was deeply sceptical about *all* economic theories, and particularly monetarism (*The Time of My Life* (1989), pp. 382, 383, 434, 490–1).

55. W. Keegan and R. Pennant-Rea, *Who Runs the Economy?: Control and influence in British economic policy* (1979), pp. 132–3.

56. H. D. Harmon, *The British Labour Government and the 1976 IMF Crisis* (1997).

57. See Artis and Cobham, eds, *Labour's Economic Policies*; and Coopey and Woodward, eds, *Britain in the 1970s*.

58. For literature for this phase, see M. Holmes, *The first Thatcher Government, 1979–1983: Contemporary conservatism and economic change* (1985); Britton, *Macroeconomic Policy*; M. J. Oliver, *Whatever Happened to Monetarism?: Economic policy-making and social learning in the United Kingdom since 1979* (Aldershot, 1997); and S. R. M. Wilks, 'Conservative governments and the economy, 1979–97', *Political Studies*, 45 (1997), pp. 689–703.

59. Cited in W. Keegan, *Mrs Thatcher's Economic Experiment* (Harmondsworth, 1984), p. 183.

60. Middleton, *Charlatans or Saviours?*, p. 280.

61. Ibid., p. 339.

62. On the evolution of monetarism, see Oliver, *Whatever Happened to Monetarism?*, chs 5–6; on the problem of sterling, P. Stephens, *Politics and the Pound: The Conservative's struggle with sterling* (1996); and for overall assessments of policy and performance during this era, N. M. Healey, ed., *Britain's Economic Miracle: Myth or reality?* (1993); A. Boltho and A. W. M. Graham, 'Has Mrs Thatcher changed the British economy?', in M. Baldassarri, ed., *Keynes and the Economic Policies of the 1980s* (1992), pp. 259–89; and A. W. M. Graham, 'The UK, 1979–95: myths and realities of conservative capitalism', in C. Crouch and W. Streeck, eds, *Political Economy of Modern Capitalism: Mapping convergence and diversity* (1997), pp. 117–32.

63. N. Lawson, *The View from No. 11: Memoirs of a Tory radical* (1992), p. 9.

64. There is little academic literature for this final phase, but see the assessments of Buxton et al., eds, *Britain's Economic Performance*; M. J. Artis, ed., *The UK Economy: A manual of applied economics* (Oxford, 14th edn, 1996); and recent OECD reports on the UK economy.

65. Middleton, *Charlatans or Saviours?*, pp. 335, 338.

66. T. Burns, 'Managing the nation's economy: the conduct of monetary and fiscal policy', *Economic Trends*, 509 (1996), p. 21; *cf.* the earlier assessment of policy by another former Treasury Permanent Secretary: D. Wass, 'The changing problem of economic management', *Economic Trends*, 293 (1978), pp. 97–104.

4 Policy Effectiveness since 1945

1. Pollard, *The Wasting of the British Economy*, p. 165.
2. R. Rose and T. J. Karran, 'Inertia or incrementalism?: a long-term view of the growth of government', in A. J. Groth and L. L. Wade, eds, *Comparative Resource Allocation: Politics, performance and policy priorities* (1984), p. 44.
3. This relates to US policy, but is equally if not more applicable to the British case: M. S. Feldstein, 'The American economy in transition: introduction', in M. S. Feldstein, ed., *The American Economy in Transition* (Chicago, IL, 1980), p. 4.
4. Brittan, *Steering the Economy*, p. 455; see also Mosley, *The Making of Economic Policy*, pp. 116, 148. Mosley's description of the British and American economies at this time is particularly graphic: they 'presented the appearance of a cow wandering back and forth between two electric fences, one of them labelled "excessive unemployment" and the other labelled "excessive inflation" or alternatively "balance of payments crisis", but moving all the time towards the edge of a cliff labelled "stagnation and hyperinflation".'
5. See Broadberry, 'Employment and unemployment', in Floud and McCloskey, eds, *The Economic History of Britain since 1700*, vol. 3, pp. 219–21.
6. See the account by A. Budd, a future Chief Economic Adviser to the Treasury and Head of Government Economic Service, 'The future of demand management: reviewing the choices', in Cook and Jackson, eds, *Current Issues in Fiscal Policy*, esp. pp. 199–202.
7. See Middleton, *Government versus the Market*, pp. 577–8.
8. On the intellectual and political struggle to secure functional finance, see R. Middleton, *Towards the Managed Economy: Keynes, the Treasury and the fiscal policy debate of the 1930s* (1985).
9. The best short account of postwar fiscal policies is T. J. Hatton. and K. A. Chrystal, 'The budget and fiscal policy', in Crafts and Woodward, eds, *The British Economy since 1945*, pp. 52–88. See also C. J. Allsopp and D. G. Mayes, 'Demand management in practice', in Morris, ed., *The Economic System*, pp. 398–443; and B. Milward, 'Public expenditure' and 'Taxation', in B. Atkinson, F. Livesey and B. Milward, eds, *Applied Economics* (1998), pp. 322–34 and 335–48.
10. For the sceptics, see J. D. Tomlinson, *British Macroeconomic Policy since 1945* (1985); and for Keynesian triumphalism, M. Stewart, *Keynes and After* (Harmondsworth, 3rd edn, 1986).
11. R. C. O. Matthews, 'Why has Britain had full employment since the war?', *Economic Journal*, 78 (1968), pp. 555–69; and S. N. Broadberry, 'Why was unemployment in postwar Britain so low?', *Bulletin of Economic Research*, 46 (1994), pp. 241–61.
12. Maddison, *Dynamic Forces*, pp. 168–77.
13. Dow, *The Management of the British Economy*, p. 384.
14. See the two authoritative National Institute of Economic and Social Research studies: R. W. C. Price, 'Budgetary policy', in Blackaby, ed., *British Economic Policy*, pp. 135–217; and Britton, *Macroeconomic Policy*.

15. A. J. C. Britton, *The Trade Cycle in Britain, 1952–1982* (Cambridge, 1986), p. 84.
16. For a review of the extensive literature on this topic, see Middleton, *Government versus the Market*, pp. 578–82.
17. On the former episode, see R. Biswas, C. Johns and D. Savage, 'The measurement of fiscal stance', *National Institute Economic Review*, 113 (1985), pp. 50–64; and, on the latter, D. Cobham, 'The Lawson boom: excessive depreciation versus financial liberalisation', *Financial History Review*, 4 (1997), pp. 69–90.
18. See the influential article by two leading US monetarists which attracted much attention in the City of London and contributed towards monetarism taking root: K. Brunner and A. H. Meltzer, 'Government, the private sector and "crowding out"', *The Banker*, 126 (July 1976), pp. 765–9. For a balanced assessment of crowding-out in practice, see M. J. Artis, 'Fiscal policy and crowding out', in M. V. Posner, ed., *Demand Management* (1978), pp. 167–79.
19. R. W. Bacon and W. A. Eltis, *Britain's Economic Problem: Too few producers* (1976). This is now available in 3rd edition as *Britain's Economic Problem Revisited* (1996), with a new introduction and a preface by Robert Skidelsky charting the significance of the book.
20. Middleton, *Government versus the Market*, pp. 93–100, 103–6, 527–8.
21. The best short account of postwar monetary policies is N. H. Dimsdale, 'British monetary policy since 1945', in Crafts and Woodward, eds, *The British Economy since 1945*, pp. 89–140.
22. Committee on the working of the monetary system, *Report*, BPP 1958–9 (827), p. xvii.
23. Dimsdale, 'British monetary policy', p. 127.
24. S. K. Howson, 'Money and monetary policy in Britain, 1945–1990', in Floud and McCloskey, eds, *The Economic History of Britain since 1700*, vol. 3, p. 221.
25. Allsopp and Mayes, 'Demand management policy: theory and measurement' and 'Demand management in practice', in Morris, ed., *The Economic System*, pp. 384–5, 403.
26. M. J. Artis, 'Monetary policy, part II', in Blackaby, ed., *British Economic Policy*, p. 303.
27. N. M. Healey, 'The UK 1979–82 "monetarist experiment": why economists still disagree', *Banca Nazionale del Lavoro Quarterly Review*, 40 (1987), p. 196.
28. See, for example, the following, respectively from an influential City monetarist economist and a long-standing critic of monetarism: G. T. Pepper, *Inside Thatcher's Monetarist Revolution* (1998); and J. C. R. Dow, *Major Recessions: Britain and the world, 1920–1995* (1998), esp. ch. 9.
29. Cairncross, *Managing the British Economy*, p. 65.
30. Middleton, *Charlatans or Saviours?*, pp. 274–5.
31. See, for example, Britton, *Macroeconomic Policy*, pp. 13–15, 104.
32. C. Barnett, *The Audit of War: The illusion and reality of Britain as a great nation* (1986).
33. See Middleton, *Government versus the Market*, pp. 526–8, for a review of

these criticisms.

34. See, for example, A. P. L. Minford, 'Reconstruction and the UK postwar welfare state: false start and new beginning', in R. Dornbusch, W. Nölling and P. R. G. Layard, eds, *Postwar Economic Reconstruction and Lessons for the East Today* (Cambridge, MA, 1993), pp. 115–38.

35. M. W. Kirby's survey, 'Supply-side management', in Crafts and Woodward, eds, *The British Economy since 1945*, pp. 236–60, can be supplemented by the more recent: P. Robins, 'Government policy, taxation and supply-side economics', in Healey, ed., *Britain's Economic Miracle*, pp. 151–73; N. M. Healey and M. Cook, *Supply Side Economics* (3rd edn, 1996); and N. Oulton, 'Supply side reform and UK economic growth: what happened to the miracle?', *National Institute Economic Review*, 154 (1995), pp. 53–70.

36. R. J. Skidelsky, 'The political meaning of the Keynesian revolution', in R. J. Skidelsky, ed., *The End of the Keynesian Era: Essays on the disintegration of the Keynesian political economy* (1977), p. 39.

37. Healey and Cook, *Supply Side Economics*, p. 1.

38. Cited in N. Tiratsoo and J. D. Tomlinson, *Industrial Efficiency and State Intervention: Labour, 1939–1951* (1993), p. 19; see also Tomlinson, *Democratic Socialism*, esp. ch. 4.

39. Kirby, 'Supply-side management', p. 238.

40. Healey and Cook, *Supply Side Economics*, pp. 32–3.

41. J. Leruez, *Economic Planning and Politics in Britain*, trans. M. Harrison (Oxford, 1975).

42. But see the nuanced account of Edgerton, *Science, Technology and the British Industrial 'Decline'*.

43. Such arguments against government intervention are associated with what is known as public choice theory, a view of a political process and of its consequences which models choice using the economist's concept of rational utility maximisation and which, in Britain, was pressed by the influential, pro-market Institute of Economic Affairs (IEA) think-tank from the early 1970s onwards; see, for example, IEA, ed., *The Economics of Politics* (1978).

44. D. J. Morris. and D. K. Stout, 'Industrial policy', in Morris, ed., *The Economic System*, pp. 862, 866; see also W. P. Grant, *The Political Economy of Industrial Policy* (1982); and M. Chick, ed., *Governments, Industries and Markets: Aspects of government-industry relations in the UK, Japan, West Germany and the USA since 1945* (Aldershot, 1991).

45. Crafts, *Can De-industrialisation*, p. 47.

46. J. A. Kay and M. A. King, *The British Tax System* (Oxford, 5th edn, 1990), ch. 11.

47. S. R. Bond and T. J. Jenkinson, 'The assessment: investment performance and policy', *Oxford Review of Economic Policy*, 12 (Summer 1996), p. 18.

48. M. C. Fleming, 'Industrial policy', in P. Maunder, ed., *The British Economy in the 1970s* (1980), p. 149; and Z. A. Silberston, 'Industrial policies in Britain, 1960–80', in C. F. Carter, ed., *Industrial Policy and Innovation* (1981), p. 49.

49. Middleton, *Government versus the Market*, p. 613.

50. P. D. Henderson, 'Two British errors: their probable size and some possible lessons', *Oxford Economic Papers*, n.s. 29 (1977), pp. 159–205.
51. See, in particular, the widely cited G. Meeks, *Disappointing Marriage: A study of the gains from merger* (Cambridge, 1977).
52. M. A. Utton, *The Political Economy of Big Business* (Oxford, 1982), pp. 22–3.
53. J. G. Walshe, 'Industrial organization and competition policy', in Crafts and Woodward, eds, *The British Economy since 1945*, pp. 379–80.
54. Most recently, in Committee to review the functioning of financial institutions (Wilson committee), *Report*, BPP 1979-80 (7937).
55. This was an important element in W. Hutton's *The State We're In* (1995) which proved an influential analysis of the deficiencies of the Conservatives' economic record, 1979–97.
56. Middleton, *Government versus the Market*, pp. 569, 596.
57. For a broadly supportive appraisal, see N. F. R. Crafts, *The Conservative Government's Economic Record: An end of term report* (1998), pp. 22–36; and, for one much less so, Graham, 'The UK, 1979–95'.
58. Boltho and Graham, 'Has Mrs Thatcher changed the British economy', p. 286.
59. See J. F. Wright, 'Real wage resistance: eighty years of the British cost of living', *Oxford Economic Papers*, n.s. 36, Supplement (1984), pp. 152–67, for a balanced survey of the evidence.
60. P. R. G. Layard, S. J. Nickell and R. Jackman, *Unemployment: Macroeconomic performance and the labour market* (Oxford, 1991), pp. 129–38.
61. Middleton, *Government versus the Market*, pp. 595–6.
62. R. F. Elliott, 'Industrial relations and manpower policy', in Blackaby, ed., *British Economic Policy*, pp. 564–618.
63. D. H. Aldcroft, *Education, Training and Economic Performance, 1944 to 1990* (Manchester, 1992); and Prais, *Productivity, Education and Training*.
64. *Cf.* M. Sanderson, 'Education and economic decline, 1890–1980s', *Oxford Review of Economic Policy*, 4 (Spring 1988), pp. 38–50; and M. E. Porter, *The Competitive Advantage of Nations* (1990).
65. See R. Lowe, *Education in the Post-War Years: A social history* (1988).
66. Evidence reviewed in Middleton, *Government versus the Market*, p. 619.
67. F. Keep and K. Mayhew, 'Vocational education and training and economic performance', in Buxton et al., eds, *Britain's Economic Performance*, pp. 367–8.
68. W. A. Brown and S. Wadhwani, 'The economic effects of industrial relations legislation since 1979', *National Institute Economic Review*, 131 (1990), pp. 57–70.
69. Oulton, 'Supply side reform', p. 60; Bean and Crafts, 'British economic growth', pp. 153–8.
70. P. Johnson, 'The assessment: inequality', *Oxford Review of Economic Policy*, 12 (Spring 1996), pp. 1–14.
71. L. Simpson and I. Paterson, *The UK Labour Market* (2nd edn, 1998), p. 90.
72. OECD, *Economic Surveys, 1997–1998: United Kingdom* (1998), pp. 1–14.
73. R. Barrell, ed., *The UK Labour Market: Comparative aspects and*

international developments (Cambridge, 1994).
74. OECD, *Economic Surveys*, p. 10.
75. Crafts, *The Conservative Government's Economic Record*, p. 23; Graham, 'The UK, 1979–95', p. 130.
76. Graham, 'The UK, 1979–95', p. 125.
77. Oulton, 'Supply side reform', p. 66.
78. See A. Glyn and R. Miliband, eds, *Paying for Inequality: The economic costs of social injustice* (1994).

5 Conclusion

1. D. Coates, *The Question of UK Decline: The economy, state and society* (1994), p. 253.
2. The argument is developed much more fully in Middleton, *Government versus the Market*.
3. Warwick, 'Did Britain change?'.
4. B. W. E. Alford, *British Economic Performance, 1945–1975* (1988), p. 19.
5. B. E. Supple, 'Fear of failing: economic history and the decline of Britain', *Economic History Review*, 47 (1994), p. 457.
6. J. Obelkevich and P. Catterall, 'Understanding British society', in J. Obelkevich and P. Catterall, eds, *Understanding Post-War British Society* (1994), p. 1.

Appendix II

1. Mosley, *The Making of Economic Policy*, p. 243; see also Middleton, *Charlatans or Saviours?*, pp. 259–60.
2. Lord Croham, 'Were the instruments of control for domestic economic policy adequate?', in F. Cairncross and A. K. Cairncross, eds, *The Legacy of the Golden Age: The 1960s and their economic consequences* (1992), p. 92.

Appendix III

1. The following, whilst concerned with guiding the user through the perils and pitfalls of contemporary economic statistics, none the less contains much that is relevant to the whole postwar British economy – C. Johnson and S. Briscoe, *Measuring the Economy: A guide to understanding official statistics* (Harmondsworth, rev. edn, 1995), esp. ch. 1.
2. Cited in E. R. Tufte, *Data Analysis for Politics and Policy* (Englewood Cliffs, NJ, 1974), p. 1.
3. The data is taken from B. W. E. Alford, 'De-industrialisation', *ReFRESH*, 25 (Autumn 1997), table 4, and has been smoothed to heighten the

differences between version A and B.

4. *The Economist* magazine often runs articles on how to delude through graphical illusions (see, for example, the issue for 18 April 1998, p. 98 on 'the perils of percentages' and that for 16 May 1998, p. 103 on 'logged in'); see also the superb works of E. R. Tufte, especially *Visual Explanations: Images and quantities, evidence and narrative* (Cheshire, CT, 1997), the latest in a series on envisioning quantitative information.

5. M. Blaug, *The Methodology of Economics or How Economists Explain* (Cambridge, 2nd edn, 1992), p. 110.

GUIDE TO FURTHER READING

The total output, if not the average quality, of books and articles on the modern British economy certainly suggests that this is not an area in which British industry has failed. A comprehensive bibliography on both economic policy and performance can be found in my earlier study, *Government versus the Market: The growth of the public sector, economic management and British economic performance, c. 1890–1979* (Cheltenham, 1996); and on economic policy in my *Charlatans or Saviours?: Economists and the British economy from Marshall to Meade* (Cheltenham, 1998). In this guide to further reading we should stress first of all that there is no neat compartmentalisation of the literature between economic, social and political topics; indeed, it is the interconnectedness that is important for understanding British economic history since the Second World War.

In addition to my *Government versus the Market,* the issues of long-run decline are well introduced in M. Dintenfass, *The Decline of Industrial Britain, 1870–1980* (1992). Sidney Pollard's *The Development of the British Economy, 1914–1990* (4th edn, 1992) also provides a detailed and often provocative long-term perspective; while Jim Tomlinson's two volumes cover macro- and microeconomic policies respectively since the turn of the century: *Public Policy and the Economy since 1900* (Oxford, 1990) and *Government and the Enterprise since 1900: The changing problem of efficiency* (Oxford, 1994). This should be supplemented by a reading of Andrew Gamble's *Britain in Decline: Economic policy, political strategy and the British state* (4th edn, 1994), which gives a political scientist's view of long-term decline.

Until very recently there were very few documentary sourcebooks on twentieth-century British economic history, but we now have Alan Booth, ed., *British Economic Development since 1945* (Manchester, 1995); and Rex Pope's *The British Economy since 1914: A study in decline?*

189

(1998). In addition, David Coates and John Hillard have now edited three volumes on British decline: *The Economic Decline of Modern Britain: The debate between Left and Right* (Brighton, 1986); *The Economic Revival of Modern Britain: The debate between Left and Right* (Aldershot, 1987); and *UK Economic Decline: Key texts* (1995). Coates has also produced *The Question of UK Decline: The economy, state and society* (1994).

Chronologies of postwar economic history with a particular focus on policy are provided in A. K. Cairncross, *The British Economy since 1945: Economic policy and performance, 1945–1995* (Oxford, 2nd edn, 1995), app. I; and Booth's, *British Economic Development since 1945*, pp. ix–xiv. In addition, David Dutton's *British Politics since 1945* (Oxford, 2nd edn, 1997) provides not only an excellent short political history, one with a focus on the consensus debate, but a chronology of the major political events (pp. 163–75).

Those seeking studies of specifically postwar economic policy and/ or performance should begin with N. F. R. Crafts and N. W. C. Woodward, eds, *The British Economy since 1945* (Oxford, 1991); and Cairncross, *The British Economy since 1945*. In addition, but often much more technical, D. J. Morris, ed., *The Economic System in the UK* (Oxford, 3rd edn, 1985); and the third volume of R. C. Floud and D. N. McCloskey, eds, *The Economic History of Britain since 1700*, (Cambridge, 2nd edn, 1994) contains much of interest; as does B. W. E. Alford, *British Economic Performance, 1945–1975* (1988), for the early part of the period.

Some textbooks written by economists on the current British economy can also be recommended, namely R. M. Anderton et al., *The UK Economy*, (3rd edn, 1995) and other volumes in this series produced by the National Institute of Economic and Social Research; M. J. Artis, ed., *The UK Economy: A manual of applied economics* (Oxford, 14th edn., 1996), which was previously published as Prest and Coppock's *The UK Economy*, and with these earlier editions now containing much of historical interest; and T. Buxton, P. Chapman and P. Temple, eds, *Britain's Economic Performance* (2nd edn, 1998).

INDEX

Page numbers in heavy type refer
to definitions in the Glossary
(pp. 139–43).

A
adversary politics 71, 73–4, 119
AES 93, 115–16, 119
agriculture 32, 44, 46, 60
aircraft and aerospace sector 49,
55
Alford, B. W. E. 136, 189
Allen, G. C. 60
Anderton, R. M. 189
Artis, M. J. 111, 189
association and causation 167–70
averages, calculation of 159–60

B
Bacon, R. W. 109–10
balance of payments **139, 140**
capital account 139
competitiveness and 36, 46
current account 43, 139, **140**
devaluation and 49, 86, 89, 110
economic growth and 42, 67,
104
exchange rate and 91
government transactions and
45, 114
policies towards 18, 110
statistics, accuracy of 148
Stop-Go and 21, 42, 45, 87,
101, 105
trends 42–9, 93, 114
see also invisible trade balance;
visible trade balance
balance of trade 39, **139–40**
in manufactures 45

Bank of England 18, 83, 97
Barber boom 91, 107, 111, 115
Barro, R. J. 15
Beer, S. H. 73
Beveridge report 72
Blaug, M. 168–9
Boltho, A. 125
Booth, A. E. 188, 189
Bretton Woods 91, 98, **140**
British disease 39–40, 57–65
British historians
contemporary xvi, xvii, xviii, 71
and economics xvi
and quantitative analysis xvi–
xvii, 153–4, 161–2
and relative economic decline
xv, 65–6, 116, 138
Brittan, S. 88, 103
Broadberry, S. N. 39, 60–1, 107
Brown, Gordon 16
Brown, W. A. 129–30
business cycle(s) 23, 26, 27, 40–2,
44, 81, 88, 96, 108–9, 131
business history 63
Butskellism 72
Buxton, T. 189

C
Cairncross, A. K. 73, 114, 189
capital
markets 63, 124
productivity 29, 33, 122
catch-up and convergence 6–9,
15, 17–18, 35, 57–8, 108,
129–30, 135
ceteris paribus **140**
Chapman, P. 189
City of London 19, 44, 47, 59, 63,

114
coal and mining sector 53, 57, 90,
    91
Coates, D. 136, 189
comparative advantage 46, 47,
    49, 129, **140**
competition
    policies 19, 123–4, 131
    quality of 10, 13, 39, 123
competitiveness 35–40, 42, 46,
    49, 65, 96, 118, 129
consensus politics 71–3, 74
Conservative Party 68–9, 72, 73,
    79, 82, 86–7, 89, 90, 91, 103,
    111, 131
consumption 12, 14, 46, 57, 106
Cook, M. 120
Coppock, D. J. 189
corporatism 83, 91, 126
cost-control 12, 37, 39, 49
counterfactuals and
    counterfactual economic
    policies 22, 60, 64–5, 100,
    116, 132, 134
Crafts, N. F. R. 17–18, 23, 39,
    131, 189
crowding-out 81, 109, 110, **140**
cultural forces 58–9, 64, 127

D
DEA 83, 89
declinism xv, xvi, 22, 65, 137, 138
defence 55, 123
    and balance of payments 45, 59
    expenditure 78
    R&D 38, 121
deindustrialisation 26, 45–7, 55,
    125
demand 10, 14, 122, **140**
demand management 71, 72–3,
    86, 87, 89, 107–9, 110, 113,
    115, 118, 120, 126, 145
demand-side policies 10–11, 101,
    133
democracy 15
denominator 3, **140**, 155, 156

dependent variable **140**
deregulation 125
Dintenfass, M. 188
direct controls 19, 85–6, 86–7,
    110, 116
direct taxation 79
Dow, J. C. R. 108

E
EC see EEC
econometrics 7, 167
economic decline see relative
    economic decline
economic forecasting 109, 113,
    134
economic growth
    big government and 15, 20, 38,
        42, 59, 65, 107, 109–10, 169–
        70
    explaining 2, 15–18, 39, 40
    extent of British
        underperformance in 18, 27,
        57, 61–4, 65–6, 133–4, 137
    feasible rate of 2, 18, 133–4
    fundamental sources of 16, 118
    growth accounting and 26–35,
        55
    and inflation 41, 52
    investment and 8, 9, 16–17, 32,
        40, 42, 58, 59, 65, 106, 121–2
    league table approach towards
        37, 65
    as policy objective 18, 21, 70,
        87
    proximate sources of 16, 27,
        33, 188
    ultimate sources of 16, 33, 188
economic historians xvi–xvii, 6,
    13, 22–3, 57, 135
economic policy
    'back to basics' in 94
    conflicts in 67
    effectiveness of ch. 4 *passim*
    evolution of ch. 3 *passim*
    institutions of 82–5
    phases of 85–98, 103–4

politicisation of 65, 70, 73–4
social learning and 84–5
see also governments and
governmental policy; policy
instruments; policy objectives
economic statistics
quality of 3, 23–4, 109, 145,
161–2
using and interpreting xvi, xvii,
2, app. III *passim*
economics 2, 10–14, 16–17, 161
economies of scale 32, 61, 64,
123
economists xvi, 2, 16, 17, 21, 22–
3, 45
Edgerton, D. E. H. xv
education and training 8, 9, 15,
17, 27, 29, 30, 38, 59, 62, 84,
120, 126, 127–8, 131
EEC **140**
applications to join 88, 91
Britain's delayed membership
of 26, 39, 49, 98, 100
effects of membership 53
original six member states xviii
efficiency 12–13, 17, 123, 130
see also productivity
efficiency versus equity 14, 130
EFTA 98
Elbaum, B. 64
electronics sector 49, 55
Eltis, W. A. 109–10
empire xv, 47, 49, 58, 59, 72, 138
employers organisations 19, 72,
88, 118, 122
endogenous 16–17, **140**
ERM 95, 97, 134, 158
EU
labour markets in relation to
UK 131
public sectors in relation to UK
82, 117
and UK comparative
macroeconomic performance
35, 113–14
exchange rate 19, 39, 43, 45, 49,

59, 91, 92, 93, 95, 96, 106,
110, 111, **140**
exogenous 16–17, **140**
exports 11, 36, 39, 42, 43–4, 47,
95, 104, 139, 154–5, 156
externalities 13, 120, 121, **141**

F
factors of production 6, 11, 12,
16, 27, 118, **141**
Feinstein, C. H. 23
Finer, S. H. 73
fiscal policy 18, 71, 73, 90, 91,
92, 94, 96, 106–10
Floud, R. C. 189
Fordism 61, 66
foreign exchange
markets 92
reserves 19, 103, 105
Foreman-Peck, J. S. 49
France 3, 52, 120, 131
free-rider problem 120, 121
full employment 13, 18, 19, 25,
27, 36, 42, 70, 71, 74, 75, 81,
83, 85, 94, 105, 107, 108,
111, 113, 116, 118, 120, 126

G
G-7 economies xviii
Galbraith, J. K. 94
Gamble, A. M. 188
GATT **141**
GDP
composition of 11
deflator **141**, 161
headline growth rate of 1–2, 3,
26–7
general elections
(1945) 68, 86
(1950) 98
(1951) 86
(1959) 70, 88
(1964) xvii, 88
(1966) 70, 98
(February 1974) 91
(1979) 68, 90, 92

general elections *continued*
  (1983) 70
  (1997) 68
government popularity an
  probability of return at 19,
  70, 103
geopolitical power and posturing
  xv, 43, 45, 59, 72, 114, 134,
  137
Germany 3, 9, 33, 46, 60–1, 78,
  122, 128, 131, 135, 137
Gladstone, William E. 79
globalisation 20, 26, 96, 98, 132,
  141
golden age of capitalism 3, 18,
  25, 26, 27, 29, 32, 33, 35, 37,
  38, 41, 42, 45, 50, 53, 65,
  106, 107–8, 134, 135, 145,
  154–5
government and the market,
  changing roles of 9–10, 12,
  13, 14, 17, 19, 20, 21, 40, 55,
  59, 64–5, 66, 74, 75, 86, 94,
  96, 98–9, 109–10, 116, 117–
  18, 119–20, 121, 125, 132,
  135, 188
government failure 9–10, 13, 20,
  57, 59, 64–5, 72, 116, 120,
  121, 124, 125, 132, 136
governmental capacity 19–20,
  73–4, 75, 94, 98, 108, 118,
  120, 132
governments and governmental
  policy
  (1945–51) 80, 85–6, 110, 118,
    119, 120
  (1951–64) 50, 72–3, 83, 86–9,
    103, 108, 118, 120
  (1964–70) 50, 83, 88–90, 111,
    118, 120–1, 123
  (1970–4) 45, 89–91, 111, 115
  (1974–9) 26, 73, 81, 83, 90–3,
    118
  (1979–97) xviii, 45, 50, 72, 75,
    79, 81, 83, 93–8, 111–12,
    118, 130, 131–2, 134–5, 158

  (1997–) xviii, 37
Graham, A. W. H. 125, 131
growth rates, calculation of 155–6

H
Hall, P. A. 64
Healey, N. M. 120
Heath, Edward 89, 90
Hillard, J. 189
human capital **141**
  see investment

I
IMF 93, 110
imports 11, 36, 39, 42, 43, 44,
  45, 46, 47, 49, 93, 104, 139
income tax 11, 78–9, 82, 130, 134
incomes policies 52, 84, 88, 90,
  91, 93, 114
independent variable **141**
index numbers, calculation of
  156–9, 160–1
Indian restaurants 57
indirect taxation 79
industrial policies 59, 74, 90,
  119, 121–5, 131–2
industrial relations 40, 52–3, 58,
  59, 61–3, 64, 70, 75, 92, 116,
  126, 127, 129–30
Industrial Relations Act (1971)
  90, 91
inequality 25, 35, 59, 65, 134
inflation xv, 3, 40, 41, 50–2, 67,
  81, 88, 92, 94, 96, 101, 104,
  105, 108, 111–12, 113, 115,
  118, **141**, 160–1
innovation 16, 37, 58, 121
institutional rigidity school 63–5
interest rates 73, 85, 94, 95, 97,
  103, 111, 158
international trade
  Britain's share of 37, 39, 47
  and golden age growth 42, 107
  liberalisation of 32, 108
  as positive-sum game 37

investment
  efficiency of *see* capital
    productivity
  financing of 63, 124
  in human capital 7, 9, 15, 16,
    17, 38, 64, 66, 120, 128–9
  inward 38, 125
  overseas 32, 38, 124
  in physical capital 7, 16, 29, 32,
    42, 57, 58, 64, 66, 121–2
  public sector 80–1, 84
  and Stop-Go policies 106, 107
invisible hand 12, 120, **141**
invisible trade balance 43, **141**
iron and steel industry 53, 57
Italy 3, 52, 131

J
Japan 3, 6, 24, 33, 41, 46, 52, 53,
  58, 78, 135
Jay, P. 92
Judge, K. 78, 82

K
Keynes, J. M. 2, 106
Keynesianism 71, 72–3, 81, 85,
  86, 89, 91, 92, 93, 97, 101,
  105, 107–9, 110, 111, 115,
  118, 137
Korean War 82, 86
Krugman, P. R. 37

L
labour market
  flexibility 126, 130–1
  policies 119, 125–31
Labour Party xviii, 69–70, 74, 82,
  87, 88, 89, 90, 92, 93, 97–8,
  111, 132
labour process 61, 64
labour productivity 1, 6–7, 24,
  29, 30, 33, 55, 130, **142**
labour supply 11, 17, 27, 29, 30,
  54, 81, 126, 130
laissez-faire 6, 79, 90, 119
Lawson, N. 96

Lawson boom 96, 109, 132
Lazonick, W.H. 64

M
Maastricht Treaty 82
macroeconomic
  policy effectiveness 64, 84, 101,
    102–17
  stability 40–2, 106, 116, 126,
    132, 134
macroeconomics 10, 94, **142**
Maddison, A. 3, 23, 29–32, 108,
  116, 158–9
managed-mixed economy 11, 39,
  71–2, 85, 100, **142**
management 39–40, 52, 53, 58,
  65, 120
manufacturing 32, 44, 45, 46, 47,
  49, 53, 55–6, 60–1, 66, 95,
  122, 130
market
  failure 9–10, 12–13, 20, 58, 64,
    120, 121, 132, 136
  incentives and penalties 12, 16,
    40, 64, 94, 97, 102, 116, 121,
    124–5, 129, 132, 135
  triumphalism 17, 94, 98–9, 119,
    131
markets, efficiency of 11–13, 19,
  21, 64, 99, 120
Marshall Aid programme 32
Matthews, R. C. O. 27, 107
McCloskey, D. N. 22, 189
mergers 123
Metcalf, D. 53
microeconomics 10, 12, 94, **142**
Middleton, R. 188
Milner, S. 53
Ministry of Technology 123
modernisation xviii, 22, 64, 75,
  87, 116
monetarism 85, 88, 92, 93–5, 97,
  109, 110, 111–12, 113, 114,
  137, **142**
monetary policy 18–19, 71, 73,
  87, 90, 91, 92, 94–6, 108,

monetary policy *continued*
    110–12, 114–15
money
    markets 93
    supply 94, 95–6, 110, 111, 115
Morris, D. J. 189
Mosley, P. 71, 145
motor car and vehicle
    manufacturing sector 49, 53,
    120
Mottershead, P. 59
MTFS 94, 95, 96
multinational companies 38, 45,
    53, 141

N
NAIRU 95, 128–9, 131, **142**
National Enterprise Board 83–4,
    122–3
National Institute of Economic
    and Social Research 189
National Plan 83, 89, 120
nationalised industries 55, 76,
    80, 84, 118, 122–3
NEDC and NEDO 83, 88, 89
Nepal 7
Netherlands 7, 32
'new' growth economics 16–17
New Jerusalem critique 100, 116
New Right 42, 72, 75, 93
NHS 55, 134
nominal values xv, 141, **142**, 160–
    1
non-linear relationships 15, **142**
Northern Ireland xviii
North Sea oil and gas 32, 42, 45,
    105
numerator **142**, 155, 156

O
O'Brien, P. K. 60
OECD
    labour markets in relation to
    UK 131
    member states xviii
    public sectors in relation to UK

    75, 130
    and UK comparative
    macroeconomic performance
    27, 29, 35, 41, 42, 46, 47,
    106, 108, 113, 134, 137, 138
    and UK comparative political
    trends 70
Okun discomfort index 67
OPEC oil price shocks 25, 26, 32,
    38, 41, 44, 45, 50, 80, 91, 92,
    108, 113
openness of the economy 32, 47,
    155
opportunity cost 14, 24
opportunity state 72, 87
optimality 12, **142**
Oulton, N. 130

P
path-dependency 14, 102
percentages, calculation of 154–
    5, 157–8
pharmaceutical industry 23, 55
Phillips curve 14, 67–8, 103–5,
    165
Pimlott, B. 73
planning 11, 73, 93
policy
    instruments 18–19, 20–1, 60,
    84–5, 101, 103, 109, 134
    objectives 18–19, 35, 60, 67,
    74, 84–5, 94, 96, 101, 102–3,
    111, 113–14, 134
    space 9, 20–1, 98–9, 102, 106
political-business cycle 70–1
political competition 68–74, 87,
    121
political science and political
    scientists xviii, 73, 102, 135
Pollard, S. 40, 41, 100, 106, 116,
    188
Pope, R. 188–9
population 3, 17, 29
post-modernism xv, xvi
postwar
    reconstruction 26, 119

settlement 39, 71–2, 87, 116, 118
Prest, A. R. 189
price stability objective 18, 36, 85, 94, 113
  see also inflation
privatisation 55, 96, 97, 125
pro-cyclical **142–3**
production organisation 6, 12, 13, 39, 52, 53, 58, 61
productivity 2, 6–9, 12, 26, 28–9, 37, 39, 40, 45, 47, 49, 57, 61–3, 66, 86, 114, 135, 158–9, 167
  see also capital productivity; labour productivity
profits 12
PSBR 73, 95, 114, 115
public expenditure 18, 73, 75–8, 80–1, 82, 87, 93, 97, 110, 134, 170
public goods 13, **143**
public ownership 19, 82, 84, 93, 116
Public Record Office and official documents xvii, 72
public sector
  budget balance 81, 106, 109
  employment 55, 166–7
  growth of 74–82, 87, 106–7, 109–10

Q
quotients, calculation of 154–5

R
R&D 38, 58, 62, 63, 121, 132
R^2 statistic 7, 169
Radcliffe report on the working of the monetary system 110
rationality 11, 12–13, 64
real values xv, 141, **143**, 160–1
regional problems 53, 122, 126
relative economic decline
  benchmarks for assessing 1–2, 100–1

competitiveness and 21, 37
explained by catch-up
  elsewhere 6–9, 17–18, 46, 57–8, 108
government and 75, 100
market failure and 64, 136
misinterpretation of xv, 22, 25, 57, 63
quantitative evidence for 3–10, 26–7
and post–1979 abatement of 18, 23, 39, 133–4
service sector and 60–1
solutions to 23, 65, 137
Rose, R. 74
RPI 50–1, **143**, 156–7, 159

S
saving 14, 17
Second World War 20, 79, 82
self-employed and self-employment 54–5, 129
services and service sector 26, 32, 44, 46, 47, 55–7, 60–1, 66
short-termism 63
Skidelsky, R. J. 118
social capability 9, 17, 39
social contract 91
social learning 84–5, 86, 94–5, 101, 119
Soviet Union 11, 98
stagflation 71, 105, 109, **143**
standard of living xv, 1, 2, 3–6, 7, 25, 26, 35, 67, 137
sterling 19, 43, 83, 98, 103
  crises 45, 91, 93, 111
  floating of 49, 91, 93, 106
'Stop-Go' cycles and policies 21, 41–2, 44–5, 50, 87, 88, 100, 103, 104–6, 108–9, 114, 134
structural change 32, 43–4, 49, 55, 57, 122–3, 125
Supple, B. E. 137
supply 10, **143**
supply-side policies 10–11, 17, 37, 64, 83, 87, 89, 94, 96, 97,

supply-side policies *continued*
101, 106, 118–32, 133
Switzerland 7

T
taxation 18, 38, 52, 57, 78–9, 82,
87, 97, 106, 109–10, 116,
122, 125, 126, 129, 130, 170
technology and technological
progress 6, 9, 12, 13, 16–17,
29, 32, 39, 49, 52, 55, 58, 64,
88, 121, 123, 125
Temple, P. 189
terms of trade 15, **143**
Thatcherite project 18, 23, 25,
39, 42, 55, 60, 65–6, 74, 90,
94, 98, 100, 102, 116, 123,
124, 131–2, 133, 135
Tiratsoo, N. 119
Tomlinson, J. D. 119, 188
trade-offs 14, 19, 20, 21, 35, 40,
67, 84, 101, 103–4, 105
trade unions 19, 52–3, 57, 62, 65,
72, 88, 90, 91, 118, 125, 127,
128, 129–30
Treasury
1958 crisis 82, 87–8
as hybrid department 83, 84
mission statement of 97
and relative economic decline
40, 100
Tyneside 53

U
uncertainty 13, 120, 122
unemployment 25, 26, 29, 35, 40,
41, 45, 49–50, 51, 52, 53, 54,
65, 67, 71, 90, 91, 93, 94, 96,
103, 104, 105, 113, 114, 126,
128–9, 131, 134
unintended policy effects 39, 60,
102
United States 3, 6, 9, 26, 32, 33,
35, 38, 46, 60–1, 62, 86, 99,
117, 135, 158–9

V
visible trade balance 43, 104, **143**
visualising data 163–70

W
Wadhwani, S. 129–30
Warwick, P. 57
welfare expenditures 76, 78, 126
welfare state 57, 72, 82, 85, 100
Wilson, Harold 70, 88
Woodward, N. W. C. 189
women and employment 29, 30,
54–5, 56
working hours 24, 29, 30
working population 54–5
World Economic Forum 37